AMERICAN EPITAPHS
GRAVE AND HUMOROUS

by

Charles L. Wallis

Still from the grave their voice is heard.
SIR WALTER SCOTT

DOVER PUBLICATIONS, INC.
NEW YORK

Published in Canada by General Publishing Company, Ltd., 30 Lesmill Road, Don Mills, Toronto, Ontario.
Published in the United Kingdom by Constable and Company, Ltd., 10 Orange Street, London WC 2.

This Dover edition, first published in 1973, is an unabridged, corrected republication of the work originally published in 1954 by Oxford University Press, under the title *Stories on Stone*. This volume contains a new selection of illustrations.

International Standard Book Number: 0-486-20263-1
Library of Congress Catalog Card Number: 73-77790

Manufactured in the United States of America
Dover Publications, Inc.
180 Varick Street
New York, N. Y. 10014

To my wife
Betty Watson Wallis

Preface

This volume contains more than 750 epitaphs representing each decade
in American history and all sections of the country. The scope of the
collection, necessarily limited to the size of a portable edition, exceeds
that of all previous publications on this subject and the book offers the
first approach to a comprehensive collection of humorous, curious, and
historically significant American inscriptions. The specimens, arranged
according to subject and theme, afford many opportunities for com-
parison and contrast.

Every effort has been made to include only accurate copies of genuine inscriptions. The well-known spurious epitaphs and *jeu d'esprit*
have been omitted. Unless otherwise indicated within the text, all epitaphs have been verified from the grave markers in the course of the
preparation of this volume. This has been made possible through in-
vestigations in old graveyards and through extensive correspondence
with antiquarians, librarians, cemetery caretakers, morticians, clergymen, and genealogists associated with state and local historical groups,
and such historically minded societies as the Daughters of the American Revolution, Sons of the American Revolution, and Colonial Dames
of America. When time and the elements have in part obliterated
words from a gravestone, reliable local records have been used to complete a transcription.

In so far as it has been possible the epitaphs are reproduced in the
same way as they now appear on stone. Although an actual transcript
may include all manner of error in spelling, grammar, dates and facts,
the adverb *sic* has not been inserted. The transcriptions are usually
reprinted with the use of lower case letters, although many early stones
bear only Roman capitals. Certain elevated letters common to some
inscriptions, particularly *ye, nd,* and *th,* are here lowered to the level
of the other letters.

This volume is only incidentally concerned with graveyard sculpture, and it is not intended to represent a study of the epitaph as a literary form.

Names of cemeteries in larger communities have been indicated so that the interested reader may more easily locate the original stones. The editor, after having personally traced and photographed innumerable tombstones, is aware that a book cannot re-create adequately the quiet scene where amid tangled undergrowth a stone may have stood for a century or more. The reader is urged to find for himself strange word shadows of times now gone on tired old slabs in a crowded burying place.

C. L. W.

Keuka College
Keuka Park, New York

Contents

Preface, *vii*
Foreword, *xi*
American Stone Shadows, *3*
Farewell to Arms, *23*
Home Is the Sailor, *36*
O Pioneers!, *42*
Lo, the Poor Indian!, *49*
Out Where the West Begins, *58*
Freed from Bondage, *70*
Heaven's My Destination, *75*
Sermons in Stone, *84*
Ministers, *93*
The God Haters, *100*
Doctors and Patients, *105*
Victims of Chance and Circumstance, *116*
Crime and Punishment, *129*
Each by His Own Trade, *137*
The Course of True Love, *153*
A Word or Two for Mother, *173*
Brief Candles, *181*
Fraternal Sod, *190*
Written with an Iron Pen, *193*
The Unlettered Muse, *199*
Grave Figures, *207*
The Philosopher's Stone, *212*
Memento Mori, *220*
Requiescat in Pace, *226*
Here Lies, *223*
Man's Best Friend, *242*
Sources, *253*
Consultants, *255*
Index of Names, *259*
Index of Places, *267*

Foreword

The dictionary defines an epitaph as an inscription on or at a tomb in memory of one buried there, or a brief statement worded as if to be inscribed on a monument. The study of epitaphs, however, includes local and national history, biography, literature, religion, social behavior, and folklore. On old tombstones we can find stories of ancient loves and shattered dreams, bitter commentaries on life, speculations and affirmations of immortality, and noble tributes to the accomplishment of man. On these stone silhouettes of bygone days we may read the hopes and despairs, the joys and frustrations of Everyman. The manner of expression may be ribald and ridiculous, pompous and lugubrious, eloquent, or serenely simple.

The common grave slab probably originated as an effort to safeguard a new grave from wild beasts. Names and dates were inscribed for purposes of identification. An epitaph, representing pious sentiments consistent with a person's life, or words of advice or caution for the instruction of the living, later made one stone distinctive from another. Quotations from the Bible have long seemed singularly appropriate. Some scriptural verses show special wit and discernment of selection; while others, when removed from context, are curious and inept.

In Roman times inscriptions in the form of a curse were often used to warn intruders against a violation of a grave. Visitors to Holy Trinity Church, Stratford-on-Avon, are frequently surprised to find these inadequate lines marking the grave of William Shakespeare:

> Good frend for Iesvs sake forbeare,
> To digg the dvst enclosed heare!
> Bleste be ye man yt spares thes stones,
> And curst be he yt moves my bones.

The doggerel, probably adapted from another hand, did fulfill its purpose; although near-by graves were opened during succeeding generations for new burials, Shakespeare's grave remained unmolested.

Epitaphs, furthermore, have been an obvious device to perpetuate the name and reputation of both common citizens and rulers. The great Egyptian pyramids of ancient times and the tombs of Lincoln and Grant in more recent years indicate the desire to remember greatness beyond the season of an individual life. "Nature and reason have dictated to every nation that to preserve good actions from oblivion is both the interest and duty of mankind," wrote Dr. Samuel Johnson, adding, "No people acquainted with the use of letters [failed] to grace the tombs of their heroes and wise men with panegyrical inscriptions."

Inscriptions have been taken not only from the Bible but also from books of devotional verse. Some families had a domestic rhymster who accepted the chore of providing homespun verses as the occasion might demand. These often represent a genius for feeling rather than an excellence of skill. Many an aspiring poet, unable to secure a publisher, surely found a ready and continuing reading public among those whose sentiments or curiosity took them to the local graveyards. Clergymen not infrequently assumed the task of framing a poetic expression to match a personality or situation.

Originality in the composition of an epitaph has seldom been considered an essential virtue. The duplication of similar readings in a single graveyard suggests that much petty plagiarism was common. And a century or two ago ready-made verses were available in book form or might be purchased as a person today would select a greeting card.

Many books offered a wide selection to suit a particular mood or temperament. One such volume, published in England, has this generous title: *The Epitaph-Writer; Consisting of Upwards of Six Hundred Original Epitaphs, Moral, Admonitory, Humorous, and Satirical; Numbered, Classed, and Arranged, on a New Plan; Chiefly Designed for Those Who Write or Engrave Inscriptions on Tombstones* (Chester, 1791). John Bowden, the author, complains: "Travellers have been so long disgusted with Non-sense and Doggerel, that they will scarce condescend to peruse our Tombstones." To improve the situation he offers four rules for the writing of inscriptions: (1) "It is highly necessary that the Praise bestowed on the Dead should be restrained within the Bounds of Truth." (2) The epitaph should edify or admonish the reader, for "without this an Epitaph can be little more than a Piece of unpardonable Vanity; at best it can be but a dead, uninteresting narrative, if not a mere Land-mark." (3) "The serious reflections should be written in as lively and striking a manner as possible . . . so as to awaken and engage the Attention of the Thoughtless, and alarm the Fears of the Vicious and Guilty." (4) Brevity should be "consistent with the Design of the Writer and the necessary Information and Good of the Reader."

Among the sample inscriptions are offered these two-liners:

> God only knows who next must follow me;
> Reader, prepare, perhaps it may be thee.

> Be not high-minded, Friends, but fear;
> You're sure of Heaven—when you get there.

The preface to *The Churchyard Lyrist: consisting of Five Hundred Original Inscriptions to Commemorate the Dead, with a suitable selection of appropriate texts of scripture* (London, 1832) by George Mogride, says:

> The object of the present Volume is to offer to the Public a greater variety of original epitaphs than has hitherto appeared, the want of such variety having generally led to the repetition of common-place and inapplicable inscriptions.

The author then gives sample epitaphs "adapted to different degrees of intelligence." Seventy-four are "For Pious Characters," twenty-eight "For Affliction and Sudden Death," and so on.

Widely circulated was *The Silver Stole, being a collection of One Hundred Texts of Scripture and One Hundred Original Epitaphs, suitable for The Grave of a Child* by J. W. Cummings (New York, 1859), which offered inscriptions for infants' graves.

The mingling of gaiety and grief is not of recent origin. *The Greek Anthology* offers many specimens, dating back to classical origins, which show a complete abandon of that taste which is now considered proper for death. The motives for inscribing humorous sentiments on gravestones are numerous. Sometimes they represent a congenial defiance of the gloom of the usual stone. At other times the humor is designed to attract the attention of passers-by. This is often accomplished by strange and curious devices.

Many examples of humorous inscriptions are the result of an inadvertent wording or thought sequence. This type of epitaph may be the result of illiteracy or a stone cutter's error, or both. With the passing years alterations in the meaning and use of particular words tend to render ludicrous expressions that were formerly considered serious.

No less appealing than the humor of inscriptions is the value and significance of the historical associations of epitaphs. No history of Egypt is complete without reference to the pyramids. The monuments of Greece, the tombs of Persia, and the catacombs of Rome are an integral part of the story of these peoples and constitute fascinating archives for both the historian and the traveler. The murals within an English parish church and the tombstones in the churchyard may represent a permanent record of a community. In a New England township, where more persons rest below the ground than live above it, much local chronicle may be gleaned from gravestones. In recent years historical and patriotic groups have endeavored to copy old inscriptions so that local records may be preserved for later generations. In one way or another nearly every event of significance in a nation's history is described on the grave slabs of those who bore the burden of the day or suffered the consequences.

Epitaphs suggest a social pattern of a locality and of a generation. They reflect the temper and mood of a period. The stalwart individualism of the colonial years and the nationalism of the Revolutionary era have innumerable stone witnesses. The "ovens" of New Orleans and the wooden headboards of the boothill cemeteries of the West reflect their geographic and economic background.

More than any other literary form the epitaph mirrors intimately the thoughts and skills of the common man. Although many distinguished men of letters—Gray, Johnson, Garrick, Goldsmith, Burns, Coleridge, Wordsworth, and Pope, to name a few—have written epitaphs for themselves or others, the epitaph is most frequently thought of as "a literature of the masses." It is only on stone that the lines of many a domestic poet have been preserved; being on stone these rhymes have outlasted the efforts of more heralded contemporaries and have often been as widely read. On the tombstone are preserved names of persons whom the historian fails to notice. The personality, occupation, religious concept, achievement, opinions regarding the meaning of life, and anxieties and anticipations regarding death of the average individual are given in stark and pointed simplicity.

As the older monuments show more and more the signs of age and their inscriptions become less legible, interest in the study of epitaphs has increased. The following pages include many epitaphs from recent years, but the use of grave inscriptions has generally lost popularity, along with the widow's weeds, professional mourners, and protracted periods of grief. The "uncouth lines and shapeless sculpture" of which Thomas Gray once spoke are no longer in fashion. The present tendency toward uniformity and simplicity may add a sense of dignity to cemeteries, but graveyards lack somewhat the intriguing personality of an earlier day.

AMERICAN EPITAPHS
GRAVE AND HUMOROUS

American Stone Shadows

A small upright slab in Charter Street Cemetery, Salem, Massachusetts, which is purported to be the only original tombstone of a *Mayflower* passenger now extant, reads:

> Here
> Lyeth Buried
> Ye Body of Capt
> Richard More
> Aged 84 Years
> Died 1692
> A Mayflower
>   Pilgrim.

The Puritan tradition is remembered by several monuments on Burial Hill, Plymouth, Massachusetts. An inscription on a twenty-five-foot granite shaft records:

> Mary,
> widow of Elder Cushman
> and daughter of Isaac Allerton,
> Died XXVIII November, MDCXIX
> aged about XC years
> The last survivor of the first comers
> in the Mayflower.

The words on another monument, an eight-foot obelisk, erected in 1825, are:

> Under this stone rest the ashes of Willm
> Bradford a zealous puritan & sincere christian,
> Gov. of Ply. Col. from April 1621 to 1657,
> except 5 yrs. which he declined.

Beneath is a Latin sentence which reads when translated:

> What our father with so much difficulty
> secured, do not basely relinquish.

Near by the grave of Governor Bradford's son bears these lines:

> Here lies the body of ye honorable
> Major William Bradford, who expired Feb. ye
> 20th 1703-4, aged 79 yrs.
> He lived long but still was doing good,
> And in his countres service lost much blood;
> After a life well spent he's now at rest,
> His very name and memory is blest.

A tablet in Cooke Memorial Park, Fairhaven, Massachusetts, honors a person who made the *Mayflower* voyage as a cabin boy:

> Sacred to the Memory of
> John Cooke
> Who was buried here in 1695
> The last surviving male Pilgrim
> Of those who came over in the
> Mayflower
> The first white settler of this town
> And the pioneer in its religious
> Moral and business life
> A man
> Of character and integrity
> And the trusted agent for this
> Part of the Commonwealth

Of the Old Colonial
Civil Government
Of Plymouth.

One side of a monumental shaft in Old Burying Ground, Little Compton, Rhode Island, is inscribed:

Elisabeth Pabodie,
Daughter of
The Plymouth Pilgrims
John Alden &
Priscilla Mullin.
The First White Woman
Born in New England.

On the second side is a verse by a local citizen:

A bud from Plymouth mayflower sprung
Transplanted here to live and bloom.
Her memory ever fresh and young
The centuries guard within the tomb.

Set into the third side is the original gravestone reading:

Here lyeth the Body
of Elisabeth the wife
of William Pabodie
who dyed may ye 31st:
1717: and in the 94th
year of her age.

The epitaph to Lucy Eaton, died 1847, aged 96, in Middle Cemetery, Lancaster, Massachusetts, says:

Descended from the Pilgrims
She lov'd their doctrines
And practic'd their virtues.

A monument on the green in Hampton Falls, New Hampshire, to Meschech Weare, first president of New Hampshire, died 1784, aged 70, is inscribed:

> He was one of those good men
> who dare to love their country
> and be poor.

A miniature of this monument marks Weare's grave in the old burying place near by.

The Revolution is recalled by this epitaph from Fort Hill Cemetery, Winslow, Maine:

> Here lies the body of Richard Thomas
> An inglishman by birth,
> A Whig of '76.
> By occupation a cooper,
> Now food for worms.
>
> Like an old rumpuncheon, marked,
> numbered and shooked, he will be
> raised again and finished by his
> creator.
> He died Sept. 28, 1824, aged 75.
> America, my adopted country, my best
> advice to you is this, Take care
> of your liberties.

Patriotic fervor is contained in the following epitaph from Copp's Hill Burying Ground, Boston, Massachusetts:

> Here lies buried in a
> Stone Grave 10 feet deep
> Capt Daniel Malcom Marcht
> Who departed this Life
> october 23d 1769
> Aged 44 years.
> a true son of Liberty
> a Friend to the Publick
> an Enemy to oppression
> and one of the foremost
> in opposing the Revenue Acts
> on America.

Malcom led the first clash with the armed forces of England.

On a site which George Washington selected above the Potomac River at Mount Vernon, Virginia, is a brick tomb where the bodies of the first president and his wife lie. Before the completion of this structure in 1837, the old family tomb was used. Before his death, Washington stipulated that his body should lie in state at Mount Vernon for the usual three-day period and that the funeral at his home should be simple and private, "without parade or oration." When death came at 10:20 P.M. on 14 December 1799, the clock in his room was stopped. For many years the hands of dummy clocks produced as toys or for decorative purposes indicated this hour.

Martha Washington, who kept a vigil near an attic window overlooking the tomb until her death twenty-nine months later, asked that hinges be placed on the door of the tomb so that her burial might be more easily accomplished. The building of the new tomb was begun only after an intoxicated person, described as a disgruntled former employee on the estate, had sought one night to remove Washington's skull. The hinges that Martha had ordered made his entrance possible. He was detected after he had acquired the skull of the President's nephew but before he had obtained that of Washington. Although the complete story of this partially accomplished theft cannot be verified, it is supposed that as a precaution against further attempts the construction was begun on the tomb which now stands. After the burial of Jane Washington in 1855 the doors were locked and the key was thrown into the Potomac.

The architect of the new tomb inscribed at the foot of the marble sarcophagus:

Washington
By the permission of
Lawrence Lewis
The surviving executor of
George Washington,
this sarcophagus
was presented by
John Struthers,
of Philadelphia, Marble Mason,
A.D., 1837

This unfortunate inscription was later removed.

Before her death, Martha Washington, at the urging of Congressional leaders, agreed that her husband's body should be removed to the nation's capital when an appropriate crypt was constructed under the dome of the Capitol. Congress authorized the building of this crypt during the term of President Monroe, but those concerned finally agreed that removal from the simple and unimpressive tomb on the soil Washington loved should not be made.

Inscribed on a white marble slab, which is supported horizontally by four white marble posts, in Arlington National Cemetery, Virginia, is this citation:

Pierre Charles L'Enfant
Engineer Artist Soldier
Under the direction of George Washington
Designed the plan for the Federal City
Major U. S. Engineer Corps 1782
Charter Member of the Society of Cincinnati
Born in Paris August 2, 1755
Died June 14, 1825
While residing at Chilham Castle Manor
Prince George's County Maryland
and was interred there
Re-interred at Arlington April 28, 1909.

Above the inscription is a circle inclosing a plan of a part of the City of Washington as laid out by L'Enfant.

Three inscriptions associate Revolutionary soldiers with the name of their Commander-in-Chief. The first is a peculiar epitaph from Foxboro, Massachusetts:

This monument was erected by
Dr. N. Miller to the memory
of his friend Mr. Zadock Howe
who died 1819 Aet. 77 & who
fought under the great Washington
To those who view before you're gone
Be pleased to put this cover on.

Under an iron lid at the top of the monument may be read these words:

The
grave is waiting
for your body.
and Christ is waiting
for your soul:
O may this be your
cheerful study,
to be prepared when
death doth
call.

The epitaph to Samuel Cash, died 1847, aged 89, in Congregational Church Cemetery, Harwick, Massachusetts, suggests an individual responsibility:

I inlisted under Washington,
The battle fought the victory won.

Inscribed on the gravestone to John Gray, last surviving soldier of the Revolution, died 1868, aged 104, in McElroy Cemetery, Ava, Ohio, is this comment:

The last of Washington's
companions.
The hoary head is a crown of glory.

Perhaps the most maligned of the heroes of the Revolution was Tom Paine, yet few contributed as greatly to the achievement of independence as did Paine in his noble documents *Common Sense* and *The American Crisis*. When his life came to an end in 1809 he had been outlawed for treason by his native England, imprisoned in France, denied citizenship by the new republic he had valiantly served with gun and pen, and forbidden burial in a Quaker graveyard. He died, poor and sick, in a New York City lodging house after assassination had been attempted and after public condemnation by some members of the clergy. The only New York newspaper that mentioned his death concluded a brief obituary with the words: "He had lived long, done some good, and much harm." On the wagon which carried his coffin to his New Rochelle farm for burial were two Negro men, hired to dig the grave, a Quaker watchmaker, a French woman and her two small sons. Only these persons were present at his burial. American antagonism was occasioned by Paine's *The Age of Reason* (1795), a book setting forth his deistic views.

Only a fragment of the original Paine gravestone now exists and even this does not mark his mortal remains. Ten years after the burial of the man who is now called "the author-hero of the Revolution" and "America's godfather," his body was exhumed, taken to England by William Cobbett, inherited in 1835 by Cobbett's son, seized by the Lord Chancellor when the son became bankrupt, rejected as an asset, and finally lost to posterity.

A belated tribute was made in 1839 when a monument was erected in New Rochelle which bore these words:

"The world is my country;
To do good my religion."
Thomas Paine
Author of
Common Sense
Born in England, January 29, 1737
Died in New York City, June 8, 1809
"The palaces of kings are built upon
the ruins of the bowers of Paradise."
—Common Sense

In the early morning hours of 11 July 1804, two men faced each other on the banks of the Hudson River below Weehawken Heights, New Jersey. The American statesman, Alexander Hamilton, fell as the first shot was fired from the gun of his challenger, Aaron Burr, in one of the most tragic duels in American history. Hamilton had worked against Burr's campaign for the governorship of New York; he considered Burr to be an unworthy candidate. After Burr's defeat he sent the challenge which Hamilton, who despised dueling as an instrument of policy, had nevertheless accepted. He was buried in Trinity churchyard, New York City, where his monument is inscribed:

To the memory of
Alexander Hamilton
The Corporation of Trinity Church has erected this
Monument

In testimony of their Respect
For
The Patriot of incorruptible Integrity,
The Soldier of approved Valour,
The Statesman of consummate Wisdom;
Whose talents and Virtues will be admired
By
Grateful Posterity
Long after this Marble shall have moulded into Dust
He died July 2nd, 1804, Aged 47.

Burr is reported to have said: "He may thank me. I made him a great man." He fled to the South where the code of dueling was respected, but his life continued to be one of flight, suspicion, and frustrated ambition. When he died in 1836, aged 80, the former Vice President was buried, as he had requested, in the Princeton University graveyard at the feet of his father, Aaron Burr, Sr., and grandfather, Jonathan Edwards, both presidents of the school. The marker, which is in a dilapidated condition, records:

Aaron Burr
Born Feb. 6th 1756
Died Sept. 14th 1836
A Colonel in the Army of the
Revolution
Vice President of the United
States, from 1801 to 1805.

One of the remarkable coincidences in American history were the deaths of John Adams and Thomas Jefferson on 4 July 1826, the fiftieth anniversary of American independence. This fact is included on the tablet erected to the second President in the First Parish Church, Quincy, Massachusetts, which reads in part:

On the Fourth of July, 1776,
He pledged his Life, Fortune and Sacred Honour
To the Independence of His Country.
On the third of September, 1783,
He affixed his Seal to the definitive Treaty with Great Britain

Which acknowledges that Independence,
And consummated the Redemption of his Pledge.
On the Fourth of July, 1826,
He was summoned
To the Independence of Immortality
And to the Judgment of his God.

Shortly before his death, Adams said, "Thomas Jefferson still survives," but Jefferson, who had struggled to live to the anniversary day of American freedom, had actually died a few hours before Adams. Jefferson made specific plans for the erection of a simple monument in the family graveyard at Monticello, Virginia. By his direction the stone was inscribed:

Here was buried
Thomas Jefferson
Author of the
Declaration
of
American Independence
of the
Statute of Virginia
for
Religious Freedom
and Father of the
University of Virginia.
Born April 2, 1743 O.S.
Died July 4, 1826

Jefferson directed that his monumental obelisk be made from "the coarse stone of which my columns are made, that no one might be tempted hereafter to destroy it for the value of the materials." The original monument, after being chipped by many visitors, was removed to the campus of the University of Missouri. The present obelisk is twice the size of the first one.

The gravestone of Patrick Henry, Revolutionary statesman and orator, died 1799, aged 63, at his home, Red Hill, Virginia, reads:

His fame his best epitaph.

When Henry delivered his great "Give me liberty, or give me death" oration in St. John's Episcopal Church, Richmond, Virginia, on 23 March 1775, one of his listeners, Colonel Edward Carrington, soldier-statesman and jury foreman at the treason trial of Aaron Burr, leaped from the window sill on which he had been seated to the churchyard. He said that he hoped one day to be buried on the spot where he landed. Thirty-five years later this wish was granted.

A few weeks before his death in 1845, aged 78, President Andrew Jackson was offered for his own use an ancient sarcophagus, which had been found in Palestine and was believed to have once contained the remains of the Roman Emperor Alexander Severus. In a gracious letter addressed to the donor, Commodore J. D. Elliott, U. S. Navy, Jackson declined the offer, saying:

I cannot consent that my mortal body shall be laid in a repository prepared for an emperor or king. My republican feelings and principles forbid it; the simplicity of our system of government forbids it. Every monument erected to perpetuate the memory of our heroes and statesmen ought to bear evidence of the economy and simplicity of our republican institutions and of the plainness of our republican citizens, who are the sovereigns of our glorious union and whose virtue it is to perpetuate it.

In 1831, four years after the death of his wife Rachel, Jackson erected a simply designed tomb for his wife and himself on his property, The Hermitage, near Nashville, Tennessee. Jackson wrote the tender epitaph that appears on the vault of his wife who saw her husband elected but did not live to witness the inauguration:

> Here lie the remains of Mrs. Rachel Jackson,
> wife of President Jackson, who died the 22nd
> of December, 1828. Age, 61 years. Her face
> was fair, her person pleasing, her temper
> amiable, her heart kind; she delighted in re-
> lieving the wants of her fellow creatures, and
> cultivated that divine pleasure by the most
> liberal and unpretending methods; to the poor
> she was a benefactor; to the rich an example;
> to the wretched a comforter; to the prosperous
> an ornament; her piety went hand in hand with

her benevolence, and she thanked her Creator
for being permitted to do good. A being so
gentle and so virtuous slander might wound, but
could not dishonor. Even death, when he bore her
from the arms of her husband, could but transport
her to the bosom of her God.

The reference to slander suggests the bitter remarks which the Jacksons faced when they were inadvertently married before her divorce to her first husband was concluded.

Colonel Ezekiel Polk, grandfather of President James K. Polk and one of the first settlers in what later became Hardeman County, Tennessee, was apparently not wanting in the individualism typical of so many American pioneers, if we can judge his temperament by the inscription he wrote for his flat slab marker now in Polk Cemetery, Bolivar, Tennessee:

Sacred
to the Memory of
Col. Ezekiel Polk.
Born 7th. December 1747,
and died 31st. of August 1824,
aged 76 years 8 months
and 24 days.
Epitaph written by himself
in the 74th. year of his age.
Here lies the dust of old E. P.
One instance of mortality;
Pennsylvania born. Car'lina bred.
In Tennessee died on his bed.
His youthful days he spent in pleasure,
His latter days in gath'ring treasure;
From superstition liv'd quite free.
And practiced strict morality;
To holy cheats was never willing
To give one solitary shilling;
He can foresee, and for foreseeing
He equals most of men in being,

That Church and State will join their Pow'r
And Mis'ry on this country show'r;
And Methodists with their camp bawling,
Will be the cause of this down falling;
    An era not destined to see,
It waits for poor posterity.
First fruits and tithes are odious things.
And so are Bishops, Priests and Kings.

During James K. Polk's heated Presidential campaign opponents quoted the reference to Methodist camp meetings and these words were removed from the stone. They were, however, replaced in 1932.

Abraham Lincoln is buried in the impressive and costly memorial in Oak Ridge Cemetery, Springfield, Illinois. At the base of the spire, which rises to a height of 177 feet, is a ten-foot statue of the President. Within the tomb are eight four-foot statuettes representing significant periods in Lincoln's life. In the central chamber is a sarcophagus engraved with his name and dates. To the back are the American and Presidential flags and banners of the six states in which different generations of the Lincolns lived. The body of the President does not lie within the sarcophagus but some thirty inches north of the cenotaph and six feet below the surface of the ground.

Two years after the dedication of the tomb in 1874, the body was taken from the crypt by a group of Chicago counterfeiters headed by "Big Jim" Kenealy. Ben Body, their engraver, had been imprisoned at Joliet. The body, it was planned, would be removed to a secret spot in Indiana until the governor had released the engraver and paid a ransom of $200,000. The ghouls, however, unwittingly took a U. S. Secret Service agent, then working on the counterfeiting angle, into their confidence. On the night of 7 November 1876, when most Americans were preoccupied with the Hayes-Tilden election, the counterfeiters removed the casket from the grave. Secret Service men moved in before their designs were complete. The thieves escaped but were later apprehended and given the maximum sentence for grave robbery, one year in jail.

Some thirty miles from the Lincoln tomb is the grave of Ann Rutledge, whose name is linked by a few facts and much fancy to that of the President. Lincoln roomed in her father's house at New Salem and had she not died of malarial fever at the age of 22, we are sometimes told, she would have become his wife. Her monument, erected in 1922, in Oakland Cemetery, Petersburg, Illinois, is inscribed with Edgar Lee Masters' well-known lines:

> Out of me unworthy and unknown
> The vibrations of deathless music,
> "With malice toward none, with charity for all."
> Out of me forgiveness of millions toward millions,
> And the beneficent face of a nation
> Shining with justice and truth.
> I am Ann Rutledge who sleep beneath these weeds,
> Beloved of Abraham Lincoln,
> Wedded to him, not through union,
> But through separation.
> Bloom forever, O Republic,
> From the dust of my bosom.

January 7th, 1813   August 25th, 1835

A small slab in Mt. Olivet Cemetery, Washington, D. C., is inscribed simply:

Mrs
Surratt

The conspirators in the Lincoln assassination plot had met in her boarding house, and she was hanged as an accomplice. Her son, John, who was actively involved in the conspiracy, fled first to Canada, then to Italy, and from there to Egypt. He was brought back eighteen months after his mother's death, and eventually released when a jury disagreed and the statute of limitations prevented a second trial.

John Wilkes Booth, following the shooting of President Lincoln and stabbing of Major Henry Rathbone the night of 14 April 1865, had fled, accompanied by an immature young co-conspirator, David Herold. They fled into Virginia and were apprehended early in the morning of 26 April in a tobacco barn on the Garrett farm near Port Royal, Virginia.

Booth, dramatic and defiant to the end, was shot, it is presumed, by Sergeant Boston Corbett. Some biographers claim that Booth shot himself. The government paid a $100,000 reward and the body was given an obscure burial on government property. In February 1869, the body was restored to his family and, the remains having again been identified, the body was interred in the Booth plot in Green Mount Cemetery, Baltimore. No marker identifies the site, although his name is listed among the children of Junius and Mary Ann Booth on their monument. The cemetery records contain the following entry: "February 18th, 1869, Interment Permit No. 16821, John Wilkes Booth, removal Belle Plain (near Washington, D. C.) thence to Arsenal Grounds, Washington, D. C., John Weaver, Funeral Director."

Herold, who was hanged with other conspirators, was buried in Congressional Cemetery, Washington, D. C.

An interesting story, supported by reams of affidavits from a wide array of "authorities," says that Booth actually escaped from the Garrett barn. A person other than Booth was killed, for Booth, disguised from time to time by a formidable assortment of pseudonyms and costumes, was "seen" in cities in Europe and Asia. At the turn of the century, a self-styled Booth committed suicide at Enid, Oklahoma. An undertaker embalmed the body and waited for the War Department or the Booth family to make a claim. The body was unclaimed, however, and years later the mummified remains began a strange career as a roadshow attraction.

Although no monument marks the Baltimore grave of Booth, the actor did not go long without a monumental tribute, for a Confederate veteran put up a stone in front of his home on West Madison Street, Troy, Alabama, which read:

> Erected by Pink Parker
> In honor of John Wilks Booth
> for killing old Abe Lincoln.

Before his death in 1921, aged 82, Parker asked that this stone be placed on his grave. This was done but only after the inscription was replaced with a conventional identification.

On the monument to Henry Bacon, died 1924, aged 57, in Oakdale Cemetery, Wilmington, North Carolina, are these words:

> The Architect of the Lincoln
> Memorial at Washington.

Unlike the stately and impressive tombs of many of the Presidents, the grave of Calvin Coolidge is in the ill-kept hillside cemetery at Plymouth, Vermont, and is marked, as the President requested, with a simple upright slab. On the stone is a small reproduction of the Presidential arms and this inscription:

Calvin Coolidge
July 4, 1872
January 5, 1933

The original of Uncle Sam, the genial and dignified personification of the American government, was Samuel Wilson, a Troy, New York, meat packer, known to his friends as Uncle Sam. During the War of 1812, Elbert Anderson contracted for the purchase of beef for the armed forces. The shipments were stamped "EAUS" to designate the contractor and the purchaser. Soldiers from Troy identified the "US" with Uncle Sam, an associate of Anderson. What began as a jest in Troy soon became popular elsewhere. Wilson's monument in Oakwood Cemetery, Troy, New York, reads:

U. S.
In loving memory
of
"Uncle Sam"
The name
Originating with
Samuel Wilson
1766-1854
During the War of 1812
And since adopted by
The United States.

Persons living near Christian Chapel Cemetery, near Merriam, Indiana, are able to produce documentation proving that in this place and not in Troy is the grave of the actual prototype of Uncle Sam. An upright slab records:

Soldier of 1812
Samuel Wilson
Died
May 7, 1865
Aged
100 Years and 3 Days.

The traditions concerning both men have much in common.

Political differences with Ben Mead, a neighbor, led Elisha Bowman, died 1865, aged 33, to write this epitaph which is on his tombstone in Wilson's Cemetery, near Pekin, Indiana:

> He beleived that nothing but the sucksess of
> the Dmocratic Party would ever save this
> Union.

A different point of view is strongly expressed on the gravestone of N. Grigsby, died 1890, aged 78, in Attica District Cemetery, Attica, Kansas:

> Through this inscription I wish to enter
> my dying protest against what is called
> the Democratic Party. I have watched it
> closely since the days of Jackson and know
> that all the misfortunes of our Nation has
> come to it through the so called party.
> Therefore beware of this party of treason.

A tall, narrow marker to B. H. Norris, died 1900, aged 51, in Bethel Methodist Cemetery near Montgomery City, Missouri, advises:

> Kind friends I've
> Left behind
> Cast your vote for
> Jennings Bryan.

In Oakwood Cemetery, Statesville, North Carolina, is this inscription:

> Abner Columbus Sharpe
> Sept. 24, 1857   Mar. 25, 1927
> He was a Democrat

A Republican south of Mason and Dixon's line perpetuated his political affiliations on his gravestone in Dobson, North Carolina:

> In Memory of
> William Mitchel
> Born Oct. 11 1832
> Died Dec. 18 1889
> Politics Republican

The monument to the family of Robert R. Hallenbeck in a cemetery in Elgin, Minnesota, records:

> None of us ever voted for
> Roosevelt or Truman

In Blue Mountain Cemetery, Ryegate, Vermont, is this epitaph to Moses Buchanan:

> He died July 1st in the 83rd year of the
> American era. He was an active, honest
> and successful merchant and a firm Demo-
> cratic representative in the Legislature
> of Vermont. He died as he lived happy.
> > I lived on earth I died on earth
> > In earth I am interred
> > All that have life are sure of death
> > The rest may be inferred.

A tombstone in Wintergreen Cemetery, Port Gibson, Mississippi, reads:

> Sacred to the memory of Henry Devine
> a native of Ireland,
> who died in Port Gibson
> November 7th, 1844. Aged 32 years.
> During the protracted illness which preceded
> his death the deceased often expressed a wish
> only to live long enough to vote for Henry
> Clay for the Presidency. His wish was granted.
> The last act of his life was to vote the Whig
> ticket having done which he declared that he
> died satisfied.
> His remains were followed to the grave by his
> fellow members of the Port Gibson Clay Club and
> by them this stone is erected.

Different feelings toward Henry Clay were represented in the final request of John Randolph of Roanoke, died 1833, aged 60. He asked that he might be buried on Roanoke Plantation in a very deep grave at the foot of a tall pine tree. The grave was marked by a rude stone which Randolph had selected for the purpose. He was not buried, it was rumored, with his face toward the east as was generally the custom, but toward the west so that, as he wished, he might in death keep his eye on Henry Clay. He had once declared: "I would not die in Washington, be eulogized by men I despise and buried in the Congressional Burying Ground. The idea of lying by the side of _____! Ah, that adds a new horror to death." On 8 April 1826, Clay and Randolph, because of the harsh words the latter had hurled at his Senatorial colleague, fought an indecisive duel. In 1870, when Randolph's remains were removed to Hollywood Cemetery, Richmond, it was discovered that he had actually been buried as his neighbors had claimed.

When Clay died nineteen years later, aged 75, he was buried in Lexington, Kentucky, where an imposing monument is inscribed:

> I can with unshaken confidence appeal to
> the divine arbiter for the truth of the
> declaration that I have been influenced by
> no impure purpose, no personal motive, have
> sought no personal aggrandizement, but that
> in all my public acts, I have had a sole and
> single eye, and a warm and devoted heart, di-
> rected and dedicated to what in my best judgment,
> I believe to be the true interests of my
> country.

An inscription on a monument on the courthouse lawn in Platts-burg, Missouri, honors an American President whose name is not usually listed among the chief executives:

David Rice Atchison
President of the United States for one day.
1807-1886
Lawyer, Statesman and Jurist
United States Senate   1843-1855

This honor fell to Atchison, president pro tempore of the Senate, between the termination of the Presidency of Zachary Taylor and the inauguration of James K. Polk. Because the fourth of March fell on a Sunday, the inaugural ceremonies were delayed until Monday. By virtue of his Senate position, Atchison was President for a few hours. He delighted to tell friends that he slept through his moment of greatness. Some historians, however, question the legitimacy of Atchison's Presidency.

A twelve-foot granite cross, mounted on a trinity base, marks the grave of Wendell L. Willkie, died 1944, aged 52, in East Hill Cemetery, Rushville, Indiana. Near by is a recumbent book-shaped marker, measuring more than five feet in width, on which are inscribed fifteen quotations from his campaign speeches, *One World* (1943), and his creed:

> I believe in America because in it we are free—
> free to choose our government, to speak our minds,
> to observe our different religions.
> Because we are generous with our freedom, we share
> our rights with those who disagree with us.
> Because we hate no people and covet no people's lands.
> Because we are blessed with a natural and varied
> abundance.
> Because we have great dreams and because we have the
> opportunity to make those dreams come true.

Farewell to Arms

On 9 July 1755, Maj. Gen. Edward Braddock, captain general of all British soldiers in the American colonies, was hit by a musket ball in the Battle of Monongahela in the French and Indian War. He died four days later, having been borne by remnants of his defeated army to Fort Necessity. After he was buried in the middle of the Old Braddock Road, army wagons passed over the grave so that its location might not later be determined by Indians.

Thirty years later Washington, who had been a member of Braddock's staff, attempted unsuccessfully to locate the grave. About 1804, when repairs were being made on the road, workmen uncovered a skeleton which was identified by buttons and military insignia to be that of Braddock. The remains were reinterred near the road and within the present boundaries of Fort Necessity National Battlefield Site, Farmington, Pennsylvania. This inscription identifies the spot:

> Here lieth the remains of
> Major General Edward Braddock
> Who in command of the 44th and
> 48th Regiments of English regulars
> Was mortally wounded in an
> Engagement with the French and Indians
> Under the command of Captain M.
> De Beaujeau at the Battle of the
> Monongahela. Within ten miles of
> Fort Duquesne, now Pittsburgh,

July 9, 1755. He was borne back
With the retreating army to the
Old Orchard Camp, about one fourth
Mile west of this park, where he
Died July 13, 1755.
Lieutenant Colonel George Washington
Read the burial service at the grave.

Several unusual epitaphs commemorate the American struggle for independence. A tombstone in Westminster, Vermont, names one of the first Americans killed in the months preceding the Revolutionary War. On the night of 13 March 1775, when the King's troops fired indiscriminately upon a crowd of irate persons, William French was killed by a musket ball. His epitaph reads:

In memory of William French
Son to Mr. Nathaniel French. Who
Was Shot at Westminster March ye 13th
1775, by the hands of Cruel Ministerial tools
of Georg ye 3d, in the Corthouse at a 11 a Clock
at Night in the 22d year of his Age.
Here William French his Body lies
For Murder his Blood for Vengance cries
King Georg the third his Tory crew
tha with a bawl his head Shot threw.
For Liberty and his Countrys Good
he Lost his Life his Dearest blood.

The present stone is a duplicate of the original which was destroyed in a church fire years ago. The first stone is said to have had embedded in it a portion of the musket ball that entered French's body.

A hero of the pre-Revolution years is commemorated in Old Granary Burying Ground, Boston, Massachusetts, with the words:

Elisha Brown
of Boston
who in Octr 1769, during 17 days
inspired with
a generous Zeal for the LAWS

Tombstone of William French, Westminster, Vermont. See p. 24.

U. S.
IN LOVING MEMORY
OF
"UNCLE SAM"
THE NAME
ORIGINATING WITH
SAMUEL WILSON
1766 — 1854
DURING THE WAR OF 1812
AND SINCE ADOPTED BY
THE UNITED STATES.
★ ★ ★
ERECTED 1931
BY HIS GRANDDAUGHTER
MARION WILSON (SHELDON)

Tombstone of Samuel Wilson, Oakwood Cemetery, Troy, New York.
See p. 18.

bravely & successfully
opposed a whole British Regt
in their violent attempt
to FORCE him from his
legal habitation
Happy Citizen when call'd singley
to be a Barrier to the Liberties
of a Continent.

In Copp's Hill Burying Ground, Boston, is a tombstone reading:

Here Rests
Robert Newman
Born in Boston, Mch. 20, 1752,
Died in Boston, May 26, 1804
The Patriot who Hung the Signal Lanterns
In the Church Tower, April 18, 1775.

Tradition says that Lieutenant Ebenezer Munroe, a minuteman, fired in Lexington the first shot of the Revolution. What he shouted to his comrades on that occasion is inscribed on his gravestone in the graveyard on Meeting House Hill, Ashburnham, Massachusetts:

Lieut. Munroe
I'll give them the contents
of my gun.
Lexington, April 19, 1775
died May 25, 1825, age 73

This unusual story is preserved on a tablet in Christ Church, Boston:

Major John Pitcairn
Fatally wounded
while rallying the Royal Marines
at the Battle of Bunker Hill
was carried from the field to the boats
on the back of his son
who kissed him and returned to duty.
He died June 17, 1775 and his body
was interred beneath this church.

A wall tablet in the First Presbyterian Church, Elizabeth, New Jersey, honors the Reverend James Caldwell and his wife Hannah, "who fell Victims to their Country's cause in the Years 1780 & 1781." The lines to Hannah record:

Here also lies the remains of a Woman
who exhibited to the World
a bright Constellation of the female Virtues
On that memorable Day, never to be forgotten
when a british Foe invaded this fair Village
and fired even the Temple of the Deity.
This peaceful Daughter of Heaven
retired to her hallowed apartment
imploring Heaven for ye pardon of her Enemies
In that Sacred Moment She was
by the bloody Hand of a british Ruffian
despatch'd, like her divine Redeemer
through a Path of Blood
to her long wish'd for native Skies.

When the warfare had ceased, Lewis Boyer was given his horse, arms, and accouterments as a gratuity for his services. His gravestone in Wesley Chapel Cemetery, near Piqua, Ohio, reads:

Sacred to the meory of
Lewis Boyer,
who died Sept. 19 1843
aged 87 yrs.
He was a soldier of the American
revolution and by the side of the
great Washington fought many a
hard battle for his Country's independence, served as a life guard to
the Commander in Chief during the
war and was honorably Discharged
Dec. 19, 1783 by special certificate
signed by Gen. Washington.

Here Boyer lies who Britain's arms withstood,
Not for his own but for his Country's good.
Though victor oft on famed Columbia's fields
To death's repose at last the aged warrior yields.

This distinguished inscription is on a wall tablet near the grave of
General Charles Cotesworth Pinckney in Saint Michael's Church,
Charleston, South Carolina:

One of the founders of
the American Republic.
In war
he was the companion in arms
and the friend of Washington.
In peace
he enjoyed his unchanging confidence
and maintained with enlightened zeal
the principles of his administration
and of the Constitution.
As a Statesman
he bequeathed to his country the sentiment,
Millions for defence
Not a cent for tribute.
As a lawyer,
his learning was various and profound
his principles pure his practice liberal.
With all the accomplishments
of the gentleman
he combined the virtues of the patriot
and the piety of the Christian.
His name
is recorded in the history of his country
inscribed on the charter of her liberties
and cherished in the affections of her citizens.
Obeit xvi August MDCCCXXV.
Aetatis, LXXIX.

Near Old North Bridge, Concord, Massachusetts, where "the shot heard round the world" was fired, is a monument to two British soldiers who were killed there on 19 April 1775. The lines are by James Russell Lowell:

> Grave of the British Soldiers
> They came three thousand miles and died,
> To keep the past upon its throne;
> Unheard, beyond the ocean tide,
> Their English mother made her moan.

Foretelling the future good will between the English and Americans is this inscription on a stone built into the retaining wall of a garden on North Main Street, Ridgefield, Connecticut:

> In Defence of American Independence
> At the Battle of Ridgefield
> April 27, 1777
> Died
> Eight Patriots
> Who Were Laid In These Grounds
> Companioned By
> Sixteen British Soldiers
> Living Their Enemies, Dying Their Guests.
> "In Honor Of Service and Sacrifice
> This Memorial Is Placed
> For The Strengthening Of Hearts."

William Tyler Page, one-time clerk of the House of Representatives and author of *The American's Creed,* wrote this tribute for the Tomb of the Unknown Revolutionary Soldier in Presbyterian Meeting House churchyard, Alexandria, Virginia:

> Here lies a soldier of
> The Revolution whose identity
> Is known but to God.
> His was an idealism
> That recognized a Supreme
> Being, that planted
> Religious liberty on our

Shores, that overthrew
Despotism, that established
A people's government,
That wrote a Constitution
Setting metes and bounds
Of delegated authority,
That fixed a standard of
Value upon men above
Gold and lifted high the
Torch of civil liberty
Along the pathway of
Mankind.
In ourselves his soul
Exists as part of ours,
His memory's mansion.

Inscribed on a sixty-foot pylon cenotaph near the ruins of the Alamo in San Antonio, Texas, are the following tributes:

In memory of the heroes who sacrificed their lives
At the Alamo, March 6, 1836, in the defense of Texas.
They chose never to surrender nor retreat. These brave
hearts, with flag still proudly waving, perished in the flames
of immortality that their high sacrifice might lead to the
founding of this Texas.
From the fire that burned their bodies
rose the eternal spirit of the sublime, heroic
sacrifice which gave birth to an empire state.

This inscription to Captain William G. Williams, died 1846, aged 45, is found in Forest Lawn Cemetery, Buffalo, New York:

Conducting a Storming Party at
The Taking of Monterey, Mexico
Sept 21st 1846, He Fell and Died
In The Hands of The Enemy.
His Last Message to His Friends Was
"I Fell in the Front of the Column"

A silent reminder of what may have once been a bitter resentment is found in Mottville, Michigan:

> Ransom Beardsley
> Died Jan. 24 1850
> Aged 56 yr. 7 mo. 21 days
> A vol. in the war of 1812
> No pension

In Greensburg, Kansas, is a monument that recalls a hardship endured in the Civil War. When Joseph D. Mitchell was fighting under the command of General Sherman, he sent a hardtack biscuit to his family in Illinois. This memento was retained by the family even after they moved to Kansas. It was later embedded into the face of his gravestone. An identification reads:

> Joseph D. Mitchell, 1836-1916
> Serg. Co. A. 123 Ill. Vol.
> Wilders Brig. Mtd. Inf.

After numerous Union troops had been shot from ambush, Sherman announced that on the occasion of subsequent shootings, one Confederate prisoner would face the firing squad for each Union soldier killed. During Sherman's March in 1865, the body of a Federal soldier was found and General Francis P. Blair, commander of the 17th Army Corps, issued orders for certain Southern prisoners to draw lots. James Miller of Jefferson, South Carolina, drew the fatal lot. He was buried near Five Forks Methodist Church, South Carolina, where his tombstone records:

> Killed in Retaliation.

Abner Baker, who was hung as a spy in 1865, aged 22, is buried in First Presbyterian churchyard, Knoxville, Tennessee. His inscription, which includes a quotation adapted from Shakespeare's *Julius Caesar,* reads:

> A martyr for manliness and
> personal rights. His death was
> an honor to himself but an
> everlasting disgrace to his
> enemies.
> "Cowards die many times
> The brave but once!"

A patriotic episode which might otherwise have been lost to the annals of the Civil War is preserved on the tombstone to Rebecca Jones, died 1890, aged 78, in Pleasant Grove Cemetery, near Raleigh, North Carolina:

> Devoted Christian mother who whipped
> Sherman's bummers with scalding water
> while trying to take her dinner pot
> which contained a ham bone being
> cooked for her soldier boys.

These lines on the monument to John Decatur Barry, died 1867, aged 27, in Oakdale Cemetery, Wilmington, North Carolina, commemorate the fact that he enlisted in the Confederate Army as a private and rose to the rank of brigadier general:

> I found him a pigmy,
> And left him a giant.

Words for which he is best remembered are engraved on a memorial stone at Manassas National Battlefield Park, Virginia, to General Barnard Elliott Bee, killed in the first battle of Bull Run, 21 July 1861, aged 37:

> Just before his death,
> To rally his scattered troops,
> He gave the command:
> "Form, form, there stands Jackson
> Like a stone wall;
> Rally behind the Virginians."

Bee is buried in St. Paul's Episcopal churchyard, Pendleton, South Carolina.

One of the most dramatic exploits of the Civil War was an attempt by James J. Andrews and twenty-one other Union soldiers to slip into the heart of Georgia, capture a locomotive, and flee with it toward the Union lines. En route the men would destroy railroad bridges and make it difficult for Confederate troops to move. Disguised as Southerners, the men made their way to Marietta where they boarded a train. At Big Shanty, while passengers and crewmen were at breakfast, they took over the train and its engine, The General. They made a valiant though unsuccessful attempt to escape their pursuers. Many factors, including wet weather and irregular train scheduling along the line, contributed to their failure. Andrews and seven of his men were hung. A miniature bronze reproduction of the captured Western and Atlantic engine surmounts a marble pedestal in National Cemetery, Chattanooga, Tennessee. On the pedestal are inscribed the names of the eight who were executed, of eight others who made a successful escape from prison, and of six who were later exchanged. The monument to the Andrews' Raiders was erected in 1890, twenty-eight years after the exploit, by the state of Ohio.

A noble tribute, written by William Henry Trescot, to "South Carolina's Dead of the Confederate Army" is inscribed on a monument erected on the State House grounds, Columbia, South Carolina. On the north side are these words:

This Monument
Perpetuates the Memory,
Of Those Who
True to the Instincts of Their Birth,
Faithful to the Teachings of Their Fathers,
Constant in Their Love for the State,
Died in the Performance of Their Duty:
Who
Have Glorified a Fallen Cause
By the Simple Manhood of Their Lives,
The Patient Endurance of Suffering,
And the Heroism of Death,
And Who,
In the Dark Hours of Imprisonment,
In the Hopelessness of the Hospital,
In the Short, Sharp Agony of the Field,
Found Support and Consolation
In the Belief
That at Home They Would Not Be Forgotten.

On the south side are these words:

Let the Stranger,
Who May in Future Times
Read This Inscription,

Recognize That These Were Men
Whom Power Could Not Corrupt,
Whom Death Could Not Terrify,
Whom Defeat Could Not Dishonor,
And Let Their Virtues Plead
For Just Judgment
Of the Cause in Which They Perished.
Let the South Carolinian
Of Another Generation
Remember
That the State Taught Them
How to Live and How to Die,
And That from Her Broken Fortunes
She Has Preserved for Her Children
The Priceless Treasure of Their Memories,
Teaching All Who May Claim
The Same Birthright
That Truth, Courage and Patriotism
Endure Forever.

On the south side of the Confederate Memorial in Arlington National Cemetery, Virginia, are the words:

To our dead heroes by the United Daughters of the Confederacy.
Victrix causa diis placuit sed victa Catoni.

Inscribed on the opposite side is the following:

Not for fame or reward, not for place or
for rank, not lured by ambition or goaded
by necessity, but in simple obedience to duty
as they understood it, these men suffered all,
sacrificed all, dared all and died.

The Latin sentiment transcribes: "The victorious cause was pleasing to the gods, but the lost cause to Cato."

Among the most cherished of all commemorative words is the simply expressed inscription on the rear panel of the Tomb of the Unknown Soldier at Arlington:

HERE RESTS IN
HONORED GLORY
AN AMERICAN
SOLDIER
KNOWN BUT TO GOD

According to a custom of the family of President Theodore Roosevelt, sons killed in action were buried in the country where they were serving at the time of their deaths. The monument to Quentin Roosevelt marks the spot near Chaméry, France, where his plane fell. It was inscribed at his parents' request with a line from Shelley's *Adonais:*

He has out-soared the shadow of our night.

Kermit Roosevelt, died 1943, aged 54, is buried at Fort Richardson, Alaska, and Theodore Roosevelt, Jr., died 1944, aged 56, is buried at St. Laurent, Normandy.

A tombstone in Fort Gibson National Cemetery, Oklahoma, inscribed simply "Vivia," presents a mystery that has never been completely solved. Tradition says that Vivia was the sweetheart of a soldier stationed at Fort Gibson. To be near him, she disguised herself as a soldier. Her sex was not known until after her death. When the disturbed officials asked Washington for instructions concerning the disposition of the body, it is said they were instructed to bury her and say nothing.

After an unsuccessful lawsuit against the Tennessee Valley Authority, these words were inscribed on a monument in Pleasant View Cemetery, Maynardville, Tennessee:

Major Allen Hurst
Son of
John & Elizabeth Thompson
Hurst
March 4, 1810 Tazewell Co. Va.
May 26, 1873.
First Circuit Court Clerk
Of Union Co.
During Reconstruction
Days Robbed by the Carpet

Baggers of 4000 Acres
Of Land.
60 Odd Years Later T.V.A.
Confiscated Several
Thousand Acres of Mineral
Land Left to his Grand
Children
GONE WITH THE WIND.

In Oakwood Cemetery, Montgomery, Alabama, is this record from the gravestone of Pasqual Luciani, died 1853, aged 67:

A faithful soldier for nine years
under Napoleon, 1st.

An intriguing tall tale relates that the small Perrin Cemetery, located at the juncture of Big Barataria Bayou and Bayou des Oies, Jefferson Parish, Louisiana, is the burial place of Napoleon Bonaparte, John Paul Jones, and the pirate-smuggler Jean Lafitte. According to the popular legend, Lafitte, rescuing the ailing Napoleon from St. Helena, hoped to take him to New Orleans where he had a large following. During the voyage, however, Napoleon died, and he was buried, not on the banks of the Seine but in this isolated Louisiana graveyard. After his distinguished naval career, Jones, the story purports, became associated with Lafitte's smuggling activities and died valorously in that service. The pirate, who died about 1826, aged about 46, is buried between the emperor and the hero of the American Revolution. The enthusiasm of tourists is seldom lessened by the suggestion that Lafitte's birth preceded Jones' death by twelve years or so.

On the brick and cement tomb of Dominique You, Lafitte's lieutenant, in St. Louis Cemetery, New Orleans, Louisiana, is a Masonic emblem and an epitaph, which when translated from the original French reads:

This warrior bold on land and rolling sea
in hundred battles proved his bravery.
Nor had this pure and fearless Bayard known,
one tremor, though the world were overthrown.

Home Is the Sailor

If any one epitaph may be called an inscription particularly for a sailor, it is the one on the grave of Captain James Lacey, died 1796, aged 41, in St. Paul's churchyard, New York City:

Tho' Boreas Blasts and boist'rous waves have toss'd me to and fro
In Spight of both you plainly see I harbour here below
Where safe at Anchor though I ride with many of our Fleet
Yet once again I must set sail my Admiral Christ to meet.

Variations of these lines have been inscribed on the tombstones of seamen for more than two hundred years.

A similar epitaph appears on the grave of James Barnerd, died 1768, aged 48, in Sleepy Hollow Cemetery, Tarrytown, New York:

> Tho Boisterous Winds and Neptuns
> Waves have Tost me Too and Fro
> By Gods Decree you plainly see
> I am harboured here below.

In Young Street Cemetery, East Hampton, Connecticut, the grave of Harry Rockwell, died 1883, aged 89, is inscribed:

> Landsmen or sailors
> For a moment avast,
> Poor Jack's main topsail
> Is laid to the mast,

The worms gnaw his timbers,
His vessel a wreck,
When the last whistle sounds
He'll be up on deck.

An unusual monument at Sandy Point, Maine, memorializes the various experiences in the life of Captain Albert V. Partridge, died 1901, aged 58. The monument of polished granite represents the shape of the world. There is a map cut into the stone showing Boston, Liverpool, New Zealand, Valparaiso, and other places that Partridge visited in his travels.

A large stone globe of the world, with a bronze star at the North Pole, marks the grave in Arlington National Cemetery, Virginia, of Robert E. Peary, who on 6 April 1909, discovered the North Pole. Inscribed on the sides of the square granite base are the following:

Rear Admiral, USN, civil engineer, explorer, scientist
1856-1920
Inveniam Viam Avtfacium.
His beloved wife, Josephine Diebitsch 1863.

The monument was erected by the National Geographic Society.

On the top of the grave of Rear Admiral Samuel Livingston Breese, died 1870, aged 76, in Forest Hill Cemetery, Utica, New York, is an upright granite anchor which extends the full length of the vault.

After eighteen years in the U. S. Navy, James Anthony died in 1857, aged 73, and was buried in Common Burying Ground, Newport, Rhode Island, where his epitaph says:

He spent his life upon the sea,
Fighting for the Nation.
He doubled his enjoyment
By doubling all his rations.
Pomroy.

"Pomroy" was the name by which he was known to his shipmates.

In the same cemetery is the monument to Captain Augustus N. Littlefield, died 1878, aged 75, which records:

An experienced and careful master
mariner who never made a call upon
underwriters for any loss.

In Oak Grove Cemetery, Vineyard Haven, Massachusetts, is an epitaph to a sailor's wife:

Lydia the Wife of John Claghorn
She died in Child bed Decmr 30th 1776, in ye 23d Year of
her Age
John and Lydia, That lovely pair
A whale killed him, Her body lies here.
There souls we hope, With Christ now reign,
So our great Loss is there great gain.

A tombstone in Chesterfield, Connecticut, reads:

Daniel Chappell who was killed in the
act of taking a whale October 18, 1845,
age 25 years.
Blessed are the dead that die in the Lord.

Herman Melville's American classic *Moby-Dick* (1851) has made Seamen's Bethel famous, the original of the novel's Whaleman's Chapel, in New Bedford, Massachusetts. The epitaphs in the novel were devised by the author, although he perhaps was influenced by cenotaphs from the walls of the church. Among the inscriptions found in this whaling shrine are the following:

This Tablet was erected by
the Captain, Officers & crew of
the Ship Huntress
of New Bedford.
In memory of
William C. J. Kirkwood
of Boston, Mass., aged 25 y'rs.
who fell from aloft, off
Cape Horn, Feb. 10, 1850
and was drowned.
The Sea curls o'er him and the foaming billow,
As his head now rests upon a watery pillow;
But the spirit divine has ascended to rest,
To mingle with those who are ransomed and blest.

To Daniel Burns, died 1839, aged 26:

> We laid him in his watery bed,
> Beneath the mountain billow;
> No Mother, Sister placed his head
> Upon his foaming pillow;
> But here the sorrowing bosom finds
> The token of our kindred mind.

To Captain Wm. Swain, died 1844, aged 49:

> This worthy man
> after fastning to a whale
> was carried overboard by
> the line and drowned.

To Charles H. Petty, died 1863, aged 18:

> His death occured in nine hours
> after being bitten by a shark,
> while bathing near the ship.

To Captain George Fred Tilton, died 1932, aged 71:

> Whaleman
> who
> in 1897 walked 3380 miles
> through Alaskan winter to
> save the lives of 200 men
> on four whaleships caught
> in Arctic ice.

A monument in Mann Burying Ground, North Attleboro, Massachusetts, chronicles a story of seamen who were frozen to death and concludes with a particularly appealing line:

In memory of Doctor Herbert Mann, who with 119
sailors, with Capt. James Magee, master, went on
board the brig General Arnold, in Boston Harbor,
25th, Dec. 1778, hoisted sail, made for sea, and
were immediately overtaken by the most tremendous

snow storm with cold, that was ever known in the
memory of man, and, unhappily, parted their cable
in Plymouth harbor, in a place called the Cow-yards,
and he, with about 100 others, was frozen to death;
sixty-six of whom were buried in one grave. He was
in the 21st year of his age.

And now Lord God Almighty, just and true are all
thy ways, but who can stand before thy cold.

A white marble obelisk on Burial Hill, Plymouth, Massachusetts,
bears this commemoration:

In memory of Seventy two Seamen who perished in Plymouth harbour on the 26, and 27,
days of December 1778, on board the private
armed Brig. Gen. Arnold, of twenty guns,
James Magee of Boston, Commander, sixty of
whom are buried on this spot.

Oh! falsely flattering were yon billows smooth
When forth, elated, sailed in evil hour,
That vessel whose disastrous fate, when told,
Fill'd every breast with sorrow and each eye
With piteous tears.

The monument was erected by Stephen Gale of Portland, Maine, a
stranger to the victims.

In Evergreen Cemetery, Eastham, Massachusetts, is an inscription to
Captain Freeman Hatch, died 1889, aged 69, which boasts a record that
seems less significant to our age of speed:

In 1852 he became famous making the
astonishing passage in Clipper Ship
Northern Light from San Francisco
to Boston in 76 days 6 hours an
achievement won by no mortal
before or since.

An ironical story is offered by this epitaph in Center Cemetery,
Harvard, Massachusetts:

Erected
In memory of
Capt. Thomas Stetson
who was killed by the fall
of a tree November 28, 1820
aet. 68
Nearly 30 years he was master
of a vessel and left that
employment at the age
of 48 for the less hazardous
one of cultivating his farm.

O Pioneers!

The body of Christopher Columbus, who pioneered strange seas, seems to have traveled as widely in death as the explorer did in life. When the Admiral of the Ocean Sea died in 1506, aged 70, he was buried in the crypt of the Franciscan monastery at Valladolid, Spain. The irons in which he had been returned as a prisoner to Spain from the West Indies were interred, as he had requested, with him. In 1509, at the insistence of his son Diego, the body was moved to the Carthusian monastery of Santa Maria de la Cuevas near Seville. His royal master, Ferdinand V of Castile and Leon, erected a monument which bore these words:

A Castilla y a Leon
nuevo mundo dio Colon.

"To Castile and Leon Columbus gave a new world."

In 1541 the remains of Columbus were moved again. Diego's widow, knowing her father-in-law's wish to be buried in Hispaniola, successfully appealed to Emperor Charles V, and the body was removed across the sea to the Cathedral of San Domingo. In 1655, whatever inscription may have marked the grave was removed when an English force led by Admiral Penn threatened to capture the city. When in 1795 the island was ceded to France, the Duke of Veragua received permission to disinter what were assumed to be the remains of Columbus and move them to Havana, Cuba. Following the Spanish-American War, Cuba passed from the control of Spain and the bones were taken to Spain once more. The relics were received with wild enthusiasm. Seville struck a medal for the occasion: "Spain receives the remains of Columbus," the inscription said. A mausoleum was constructed and the earthly fragments of Columbus were presumably laid to rest forever.

In 1877, however, a leaden box was discovered in the Cathedral of San Domingo. On the box was a plate reading:

> Illustrious and renowned man, Christoval Colon.
> Discoverer of America

The remains transferred by the Duke of Veragua to Havana and thence back to Spain had not been those of Columbus but of his son, Don Diego, who had been buried beside the Discoverer in 1541. Thus the mausoleum in Seville dedicated to Columbus contained the remains of Don Diego.

Columbus was buried once again in the San Domingo Cathedral and a new monument was raised to his memory.

Although Captain John Smith is one of the heroes of American lore, he actually devoted only a short portion of his adventurous life to the Jamestown settlement and is buried in St. Sepulchre Church, London. Near his grave a memorial tablet reads:

> To the living memory of his deceased friend
> Captain John Smith,
> sometime Governour of Virginia,
> and Admiral of New England,
> who departed this life the 21st of June 1631.
> Accordiamus, Vincere est Vivere.[1]

Here lyes one conquered that hath conquered Kings,
Subdu'd large territories, and done things
Which to the World impossible would seem,
But that the Truth is held in more esteem
Shall I report his former Service done
In honour of his God and Christendom?
How he divide from Pagans three
Their Heads and Lives, Types of his Chivalry,
For which great Service in that Climate done,
Brave Sigismundus, King of Hungarion,

---

[1] Let us agree, to conquer is to live.

Did give him as a Coat of Armes to wear,
These Conquered Heads got by his Sword and Spear,
Or shall I tell of his Adventures since
Done in Virginia, that large Continent?
How that he subdu'd Kings unto his Yoke,
And made those Heathen flee, as Wind Doth Smoke;
And made their land, bring of so large a Station,
An Habitation for our Christian Nation,
Where God is glorify'd, their Wants supply'd;
Which else for Necessaries must have dy'd.
But what avails his Conquests, now he lyes
Interr'd in Earth, a Prey to Worms and Flyes?
O! May His Soul in sweet Elysium sleep,
Until the Keeper that all Souls doth keep,
Return to Judgment: and that after thence,
With Angels he may have his Recompence.

Less distinguished pioneers cleared the land and built homes. Inscribed on a monument to the Reverend John Starman, died 1854, aged 72, in the old German Cemetery, Waldoboro, Maine, is this commentary:

This town was settled in 1748 by Germans who
emigrated to this place with the promise and
expectation of finding a prosperous city,
instead of which they found nothing but wilderness.

A monument to the Reverend Frederick Ritz, died 1811, aged 59, is similarly inscribed.

A marker to the Reverend Samuel Hidden, died 1837, aged 77, in Town Cemetery, Tamworth, New Hampshire, relates:

He came into the Wilderness
And left it a fruitful field.

In East Cemetery, near Marlboro, New Hampshire, is the tombstone of Daniel Emerson, an early settler, died 1829, aged 82, which records:

The land I cleared is now my grave
Think well my friends how you behave.

The footstone on the grave of Mrs. Martha Hale, died 1723, aged 47, in Old Cemetery, Groveland, Massachusetts, says:

> If you will look
> It may aper
> She was ye forst
> That is buried here.

An old superstition says that the spirit of the first person buried in a graveyard is the "official" ghost.

Strange Creek, West Virginia, was named for William Strange, who was lost from his companions during a surveying trip in 1795. His bones were found several years later near a tree against which his gun still rested. On the bark Strange had carved this epitaph before he perished of hunger and exposure:

> Strange is my name and I'm on strange ground
> And Strange it is I can't be found.

When John Patterson, "the first white child born in Arkansas," died in 1880, aged 90, he was buried with his six wives and twenty children behind his cabin home near Marianna, Arkansas. Words that he frequently recited are inscribed on his grave:

> I was born in a kingdom
> Reared in an empire
> Attained manhood in a territory
> And now a citizen of a state
> And have never been 100 miles from
>   where I now live.

The kingdom was Spain; the empire, France; the territory, the Louisiana Purchase; and the state, Arkansas.

An old stone in Bethesda churchyard, near Aberdeen, North Carolina, reads:

> In Memory of Colin Bethune (an honest man),
> A native of Scotland by accident, but a
> citizen of the U. S. from choice who died
> Mar. 29, 1820. Aged 64 years.

A cement log cabin, five feet long, three feet wide, and five feet high, marks the grave of Moses Sailor, first settler in Faribault County, died 1896. This cabin, in Riverside Cemetery, Blue Earth, Minnesota, has a chimney, a window, and a door on which his name appears.

A colored, bas-relief reproduction of a sod house is found on the monument to a pioneer couple in Beulah Cemetery, Colby, Kansas. Beneath are the words:

The Sod Home of James and Melissa Wallace Built
in 1887. James Wallace Came to Thomas Co. March 1885.
Melissa Alger April 1885 Were Married Oct. 20, 1886.
"The Soddy Will Always Be a Symbol
of the Western Kansas Pioneer Spirit."

During the past century the forces of nature have obliterated most of the grave sites along the wagon trails that led westward to California and Oregon. At the sides of these trails are thousands of unknown and unmarked graves. Between 1840 and 1870 more than 34,000 pioneers are said to have died of heat, exposure, and various sicknesses, particularly Asiatic cholera. The graves were usually unadorned, although occasionally a wooden headboard, a roughly carved boulder, or a wagon wheel designated a burial place. Many of the wooden crosses were used as firewood by subsequent travelers.

Inscribed on a bronze tablet attached to a granite boulder near Emmett, Idaho, is this tribute:

Freeze Out Hill
Look to the East. The first hogsback
is the original Freeze Out road. This
monument was erected July 1928 by the
Payette River Pioneer Society in memory of the Pioneers of 1862 to 1868
who traveled said original road and
stood the hardships in the early devel-
opment of the Valley.

A monument at Guernsey, Wyoming, reads:

To all Pioneers who passed this
way to win and hold the west.

Guns, swords, oxen shoes, wagon irons, and other relics found along the Oregon Trail have been set into the sides of this concrete structure.

When a railroad survey was being made near Gering, Nebraska, a half-sunken wagon wheel, inscribed "Rebecca Winters, Aged 50 Years," was found. The proposed railroad bed was altered so that the grave might remain undisturbed. Descendants who heard of the discovery raised a monument near by which reads:

> Our Beloved Mother
> Rebecca Burdick
> Wife of Hiram Winters. She died a
> faithful Latter Day Saint. Aug. 15,
> 1852. Aged 50 years.
> While making the memorable journey
> across the plains with her people to
> find a new home in the far distant
> Salt Lake Valley she gave her life
> for her faith. Her reward will be
> according to her works.

A career, typical of many of those who blazed western trails, is recorded on a gravestone in Alhambra Cemetery, Martinez, California:

> Capt. Joseph R. Walker
> Born in Roan Co. Tenn.
> Dec. 13, 1798
> Emigrated to Mo. 1819
> To New Mexico 1820
> Rocky Mountains 1832
> California 1833
> Camped at Yosemite Nov. 13, 1833
> Died Oct. 27, 1876
> AE 77 ys 10 ms & 14 ds

Several years before his death in 1887, Hugh Whittell erected an eight-foot pyramid monument in the old Masonic Cemetery, San Francisco, California. Inscribed on the marker, now removed to Cypress Lawn Cemetery, Colma, California, is the following account:

All you who chance this grave to see,
If you can read English, may learn by me.
I traveled, read and studied mankind to know;
And what most interested them here below.
The present, or the future state, and love of power,
Envy, fear, love, or hate, occupied each wakeful hour.
All would teach, but few would understand,
The greater part, know little of either God, or man.
Love one another, a very good maxim, all agreed,
Learn, labor, and wait, if you would succeed.
In the five divisions of the world I have been,
The cities of Peking and Constantinople I have seen,
On the first railway I rode, before others were made,
Saw the first telegraph operate so useful to trade;
In the first steamship, the Atlantic, I crossed,
Suffered six ship-wrecks where lives were lost,
In the first steamer to California I did sail,
And went to China by the first Pacific Mail.
After many endeavours my affairs to fix,
A short time I will occupy less than two by six.

The story of a refugee is recorded on a monument in Cedar Park Cemetery, Emerson, New Jersey:

Charlotte Stern
Born Nov. 19, 1869 in Germany
Died Feb. 23, 1939 on board ship
bringing her to the Land of Liberty
and buried in these United States
March 5, 1939.

Lo, the Poor Indian!

A dramatic episode of debatable historicity which John Smith included in his *The General Historie of Virginia, New-England, and the Summer Isles* (1624) has made Pocahontas one of the popular figures in American folklore. After fifty-one-year-old John Rolfe, a Jamestown settler, married the eighteen-year-old princess, she became a Christian and later with her husband and small son visited England where she was received as a royal visitor. The change of climate killed her, however, before she could return to her native shores, and she was buried in the chancel of the Gravesend Church, Kent. In the church register is this entry:

> 1616, May 2j, Rebecca Wrothe, wyff of
> Thomas Wroth, gent., a Virginia lady borne,
> here buried in ye chauncell.

After the original church burned in the eighteenth century, her remains and those of others are believed to have been deposited in a common grave. Her son returned to Virginia, where many descendants now reside.

Nearly two and a half centuries after his burial, the bones of Iyanough, an Indian chief who showed good will to the Pilgrim Fathers, were unearthed by a plow in Cummaquid, Massachusetts. He had been buried, Indian fashion, in a sitting position with a kettle over his head. Near him were interred various relics. These are now on exhibit at Pilgrim Hall, Plymouth. The Cape Cod Historical Society in 1894 erected a marker on the site of his original grave:

On this spot was buried the
Sachem Iyanough, the friend
and entertainer of the Pilgrims, July 1621.

A monument in Friends Meeting House graveyard, Burlington, New Jersey, reads:

His   Mark
Near this spot lies the body of the Indian
Chief Ockanickon, friend of White Man, whose
last words were: Be plain and fair to all,
both Indians and Christians, as I have been.
1681

On a tombstone in the old Moravian Cemetery, Bethlehem, Pennsylvania, is an epitaph to an Indian who is claimed to be "the last of the Mohicans":

In memory of Tachoop, a Mohican Indian,
who in holy baptism April 16, 1742, received the name of John, one of the
first fruits of the Mission at Shekomeko
and a remarkable instance of the power
of divine grace whereby he became a distinguished teacher among his nation. He
departed this life in full assurance of
faith at Bethlehem, August 27th, 1746.

Before his death, Red Jacket, the Senecan orator, said to his wife: "When I am dead, it will be noised through all the world, they will hear of it across the great waters, and say, Red Jacket the great orator is dead. And white men will come and ask you for my body. They will wish to bury me. But do not let them take me. Clothe me in my simplest dress, put on my leggins and my moccasins, and hang the cross I have worn so long around my neck, and let it lie upon my bosom. Then bury me among my people . . . I do not wish to rise among pale faces." Red Jacket, whose nickname was given to him because of a British uniform he wore, was buried among white people in the Old Mission Cemetery, East Buffalo, New York. In 1852, white men, concerned by the dilapidated condition of the graveyard, removed the bones. Red Jacket's family secured the remains and they were kept for a long time, it is alleged, by his favorite stepdaughter, Ruth Stevenson, in a bag under her bed.

In 1884, the Buffalo Historical Society secured a permanent burial spot for Red Jacket and a group of Senecan chieftains in Forest Lawn Cemetery, Buffalo. Near the site stands an imposing statue of the orator which bears this inscription:

Red Jacket
Sa-Go-Ye-Wat-Ha
(He-Keeps-Them-Awake)
Died at Buffalo Creek
Jan. 20 1830
Aged 78 Years
"When I am gone and my warnings are no longer
heeded, the craft and avarice of the white
man will prevail. My heart fails me when I
think of my people, so soon to be scattered
and forgotten."

Inscribed on a fifty-six-foot obelisk, erected to the memory of Tah-gah-jute, or Logan, chief of the Cayugas, in Fort Hill Cemetery, Auburn, New York, are these words:

Who Is There To Mourn For Logan.

The monument of the chief, whose entire family was murdered by white men, surmounts a mound which is said to be an ancient Indian altar.

Many years before his death, Sarasen, a friendly Indian, rescued two white children who had been kidnapped by members of an unfriendly tribe. This event is commemorated on his gravestone in Roman Catholic Cemetery, Pine Bluff, Arkansas:

Sarasen
Chief of the Quapaws
Died 1832
Age 97 Years
Friend of the Missionaries
Rescuer of Captive Children.

At Suquamish, Washington, is a grave monument that records:

Seattle
Chief of the Suquampsh
and Allied Tribes
Died June 7, 1866
The firm friend of the whites
and for him the
City of Seattle
was named by its
Founders.
Sealth.

A monument in National Cemetery, Fort Gibson, Oklahoma, commemorates the wife of Sam Houston and ancestress of Will Rogers:

Sacred to the Memory of
Tahlihina
Cherokee Wife of
Gov. Sam Houston
Liberator of Texas
Died at Wilson's Rock, C. N.
In the Year 1838
Removed to Fort Gibson
May 30, 1905.

An unusual headstone in National Cemetery, San Francisco, California, gives only a name and date:

Two Bits
October 5, 1873

Cemetery records show that Two Bits was an Indian scout who was attached to the U. S. Army during the Indian campaigns in the Pacific Northwest. He died at Fort Klamath, Oregon.

A gravestone in Tishomingo, Oklahoma, records:

Douglas H.
Johnston
Governor of the
Chickasaw Nation
1898-1939

> Born Oct. 16, 1856
> Died June 28, 1939
> Served his people with
> Distinction for 40 years.
> He was loyal, honest and a
> Statesman of great ability.
> He fought many battles in
> The courts for the preser-
> vation of the rights and pro-
> perty of his people. His two
> Greatest achievements were
> Saving $20,000,000.00 by
> Defeating the enrollment
> of 4000 fraudulent claim-
> ants and exempting tax on
> all allotments for 21 years.

The monument to Henry Chee Dodge, Navajo tribal leader and interpreter for the padres, died 1947, aged 86, in Navajo Memorial Cemetery, Fort Defiance, Arizona, reads:

> Xast^{x}i·n 'adi·'ca'iyê·
> K^{w}l^e Te ·Sit^{x}i̧

This is translated as "Mr. Interpreter rests here."

Over the Indian mound at Fernleigh-over, near Cooperstown, New York, is a modern marker that reads:

> White Man, Greeting!
> We, near whose bones you stand,
> Were Iroquois. The wide land
> Which now is yours was ours.
> Friendly hands have given back
> To us enough for a tomb.

An old legend says that anyone who removes a stone from a certain six-foot cairn near Cherokee Forest Reserve, Lumpkin County, Georgia, will be cursed. The grave is that of a beautiful Indian princess, Trahlyta, who found a secret spring whose waters offered perennial youth. With the passing years she failed to show signs of advancing age. Although many young warriors loved her, she refused to leave her treasured spot. Finally Wahsega, disappointed by her rejection of marriage, sent braves to take her by force. She was removed from the secret haunt, but soon thereafter died. She was then buried, as she had asked, near the waters she loved. To this day campers at near-by resorts add stones to the cairn.

One of the best-known Scottish epitaphs is said to have been found in Elgin Cathedral churchyard:

> Here lie I, Martin Elginbrodde:
> Hae mercy o' my soul, Lord God;
> As I wad so, were I Lord God,
> And ye were Martin Elginbrodde.

The inscription was printed in George Macdonald's *David Elginbrod* (1863). A variation of these lines formerly marked the grave of John Konkapot, one time chief of the Housatonic Indians, died about 1751, in Stockbridge Center, Massachusetts. The original headstone read:

> Here lies Captain John Konkapot.
> God, be as good to him as he would be
> If he were God and You were John Konkapot.

These lines were removed about 1900 by the church fathers who considered the sentiment irreverent. The present marker gives a simple identification.

An epitaph from Copp's Hill Burying Ground, Boston, tells of a victim of Indian treachery:

> Capt.
> Thomas Lake
> Aged 61 Yeeres
> An EmineNet Faithfull
> ServaN of God & One
> Of a Publick Spirit Was
> Perfidously Slain by
> Ye Indians at Kennibeck
> August ye 14th 1676
> Here Interred He 13
> Of March Following.

A later gravestone in North Cemetery, Vernon, Vermont, records:

> Mrs. Jemima Tute
> Successively Relict of Messrs.
> William Phipps, Caleb Howe & Amos Tute.
> The two first were killed by the Indians
> > Phipps July 5 1743
> > Howe June 27 1755
> When Howe was killed she & her children
> Then seven in number
> Were carried into captivity
> The Oldest Daughter went to France
> > And was Married to a French Gentleman
> > The Youngest was torn from her breast
> > And perished with hunger
> > By the aid of some benevolent Gentlemen
> > And her own personal heroism
> She recovered the Rest.
> She had two by her last Husband
> Outlived both him and them
> And died March 7th 1805 aged 82
> Having past through more vicissitudes
> And endured more hardships
> Than any of her Contemporaries.
> > No more can Savage Foes annoy
> > Nor aught her widespread fame Destroy.

Two ancient tombstones, now set into a large modern monument, near Felchville, Vermont, record:

> On the 31st of
> August 1754
> Capt. James
> Johnson had
> a Daughter born
> on this spot of
> Ground, being
> Captivated with

his whole Family
by the Indians.

this is near the spot
that the Indians Encamped the
Night after they took Mr Johnson &
Family Mr Laberee & Farnsworth
August 30th 1754. And Mrs
Johnson was Delivered of her Child
Half a mile up this Brook.

The following inscription is from the grave in Santa Fe National Cemetery of Charles Bent, first American territorial governor of New Mexico, who was killed by the Indians in the Massacre of Taos, 19 January 1847:

He was a man of kind and gentle manners,
of true benevolence of heart, of untarnished
probity and lofty carriage. He laid down
his life to save those dearer to him than
life itself.

Another grave in the same cemetery is inscribed:

A la Memoire de
Christian Velton,
blesse Mortellement
par les Navajoes
Le ler aout 1860;
decede 2 jours apres
a lage de 35 ans.

A memorial tablet near Cascade, Idaho, records:

Long Valley Massacre
These martyrs of Idaho's early settlement were killed
from ambush by a band of Sheepeater Indians, August 20, 1878.
William Monday
John Healy
Jake Grosclose

Three Fingered Smith, fourth member of the party, was seriously wounded but escaped. The original inscription was chiseled on this rock by the scout Calvin R. White and a detachment of C. Company, Second U. S. Inf., who buried the bodies 150 feet south of this rock.

Inscribed on the grave of Joseph Williams, died 1724, aged 80, son of Roger Williams, in Roger Williams Park, Providence, Rhode Island, is the following:

In King Philip's War he courageously went through
And the Native Indians bravely did subdue
And now he's gone down to the grave and will be no more
Until it please Almighty God his body to restore
Into some proper shape as He thinks fit to be
"Perhaps as a grain of wheat—as Paul sets forth you see."

The last line alludes to 1 Corinthians 15:37.

Out Where the West Begins

The old West had a tradition and lore that were distinctive. The graveyard stories and inscriptional matter, no less than the songs, the dress, the tales of Indians, cowboys, Spanish missions, and the quest for gold, were unique. Unfortunately many of the wooden head-boards and rough hewn crosses weathered poorly the sun's rays and the desert sands. Many of the improvised graveyards are lost among the ruins of ghost towns. A number of the most unusual epitaphs, characterizing the idiom and life of range and mining camp, can no longer be verified.

Among those most frequently quoted is the following:

> To Lem S. Frame, who during his life shot 89
> Indians, whom the Lord delivered into his hands,
> and who was looking forward to making up his
> hundred before the end of the year, when he fell
> asleep in Jesus at his house at Hawk's Ferry,
> March 27, 1843.

During the nineteenth century a San Diego newspaper published this unlocated epitaph:

> Here lies the body of Jeems Humbrick
> who was accidentally shot
> on the bank of the pacus river
> by a young man

He was accidentally shot with one of the large colt's
revolvers with no stopper for the cock to rest on it
was one of the old fashion kind brass mounted and of
such is the kingdom of heaven.

The following couplet was published as early as 1880, although no
further identification is available:

Here lies a man whose crown was won
By blowing in an empty gun.

Two others read:

Here lays Butch,
We planted him raw
He was quick on the trigger
But slow on the draw.

He had sand in his craw
But was slow on the draw
They buried him in '72.

Bret Harte in his short story "The Outcasts of Poker Flat" includes
this epitaph which is suggestive of the spirit of many Western inscriptions:

Beneath this tree
Lies the body
of
John Oakhurst,
Who struck a streak of bad luck
On the 23d of November 1850,
and
Handed in his checks
On the 7th December, 1850.

In the memoirs of Richard E. Sloan, one-time territorial governor
of Arizona, is the following epitaph which formerly marked the desert
grave of John Coil, a laborer on the Arizona canal north of Phoenix
who died in 1884:

> Here lies John Coil,
> A son of toil,
> Who died on Arizona soil.
> He was a man of considerable vim
> But this here air was too hot for him.

An inscription, regarded by old timers as genuine, and carved on a boulder near Mount Pisgah Cemetery, Cripple Creek, Colorado, reads:

> He Called
> Bill Smith
> A Liar.

Buried in Carson City, Nevada, is the pioneer stage driver Hank Monk, died 1883, aged 50, who was immortalized when Mark Twain included in *Roughing It* the story of the wild ride Monk gave to Horace Greeley. The name of Monk, who was christened Henry James Monk, was a household word in mining camps throughout the West where he was both revered and feared by outlaws. His original tombstone recorded:

> Sacred to the memory of Hank Monk,
> the whitest, biggest hearted and
> best stage driver of the West, who
> was kind to all, thought ill of none.
> He lived in a strange era, and was a hero.
> The wheels of his coach are now ringing
> on golden streets.

A conventional monument now marks the grave.

Western bravado is found on a gravestone, dating back to 1905, in Douglas Park Cemetery, Douglas, Wyoming:

> Underneath this stone in eternal rest
> Sleeps the wildest one of the wayward west
> He was gambler and sport and cowboy too
> And he led the pace in an outlaw crew
> He was sure on the trigger and staid to the end
> But he was never known to quit on a friend
> In the relations of death all mankind is alike
> But in life there was only one George W. Pike.

On the monument of John Allen Morrow, rancher, died 1944, aged 68, in Canyon City, Oregon, is carved an image of a horse with bowed head, an empty saddle, and reins resting on the ground. Beneath are these lines:

> When my soul haunts range and
> rest beyond the great divide—
> Just plant me on some strip of
> West that's sunny lone and wide.
> Let cattle rub my headstone
> round and coyote wail their kin.
> Let horses come and paw the mound
> But do not fence me in.

Boothill cemeteries, the burial places of those who died with their boots on, were once a common feature throughout the West. The overgrown or wind-swept remains of these graveyards may occasionally be found near the ruins of a ghost town.

One of the best-known boothill graveyards is at Tombstone, Arizona. The history of the town dates back to the time when Ed Schieffelin, after being told that he would find no silver but only a tombstone, discovered the Lucky Cuss Mine. In 1880, when Tombstone was one of the largest communities in the southwest, the local newspaper, appropriately named *The Epitaph*, began publication.

In Boothill Cemetery are the graves of 260 persons, most of whom died unnatural deaths. The graves of Tom McLowery, Frank McLowery, and Billie Clanton are marked with a common identification:

> Murdered on the streets of Tombstone.

The six-shooter of Ormsby did not miss its mark on two occasions:

> Bronco Charlie
> Shot by Ormsby
>
> Red River Tom
> Shot by Ormsby

Two other graves are marked with iron crosses and the words:

> Margarita
> Stabbed by Gold Dollar

Six-Shooter Jim—1885
Shot by Burt Alvord

John Heath was hanged from a telegraph pole by an angry mob for his part in the cold-blooded Bisbee massacre. His large headboard reads:

John Heath
Taken from
County Jail &
Lynched
By Bisbee Mob
In Tombstone
Feb. 22nd 1884.

Near by is a headboard that tells of five persons who apparently received an honest trial:

Dan Dowd
Red Sample
Tex Howard
Bill DeLaney
Dan Kelly
Legally
Hanged
Mar. 8 1884

One inscription records:

George Johnson
Hanged by mistake

Another explains:

M. E. Kellogg—1882
Died Natural Death

Inscribed on the four sides of a ten-foot commemorative shaft in Boothill Cemetery near Billings, Montana, are these lines:

The stream flows on, but it matters not
To the sleepers here by the world forgot.
The heroes of many a tale unsung,
They lived and died when the West was young.

This monument marks a historic spot,
Where thirty-five lie buried.
They played the drama called life
For fortune and fame;
Lost their lives, lost their game.

Upon this rugged hill
The long trail past,
These men of restless will
Find rest at last.

In memory of those who
Blazed the trail
And showed to us our west.
In boots and spurs they lie
And on this hill find rest.

Few communities in the West have had a history as colorful in action and personality as Deadwood, South Dakota. In the local boot-hill cemetery, named Mt. Moriah, lie the remains of such romantic figures of Western lore as Wild Bill Hickok and Calamity Jane. Near by Seth Bullock and Preacher Smith are buried.

James Butler Hickok, trapper, stage driver, Union scout, and marshal, was known as "the prince of pistoleers" at a time when law enforcement was a perilous occupation. When he settled in Deadwood, those engaged in lawless pursuits plotted his assassination and engaged Jack "Crooked Nose" McCall, a notorious gambler of dubious mental capacity, to kill him. On a hot summer day in 1876, while Wild Bill was playing cards in Saloon No. 10 on Deadwood's main street, McCall accomplished the feat. When he was shot fatally in the back of the head, Wild Bill held a fist of black aces and eights, a hand known as "dead man's hand" since that time. His original headboard was inscribed:

Wild Bill
J. B. Hickok,
killed by the assassin
Jack M'Call,
in Deadwood, Black Hills,
Aug. 2d, 1876.

> Pard, we will meet
> again in the happy
> Hunting Ground
> to part no more.
> Good Bye
> Colorado
> Charlie
> C. H. Utter

Two monuments previously erected over Wild Bill's grave have fallen prey to over-zealous souvenir hunters. What still remains of a headless statue, formerly protected in the cemetery by a large wire cage, has been removed to Deadwood's Adams Memorial Museum. A replica of the original headboard now identifies the grave.

Twenty-seven years after Hickok's death, Martha Jane Burke, known as Calamity Jane and famous for her buckskin attire, proficient vocabulary, and intemperance, was buried, as she requested, next to Wild Bill. After her funeral, the largest in Deadwood's history, a mail-order monument—a cement urn surmounting a cement pedestal—was erected. On the pedestal was the image of the mask of comedy and the words:

> Calamity Jane
> Mrs. M. E. Burke
> Died Aug. 1, 1903
> Aged 53 yrs.

The name plate was later stolen and the monument, badly chipped and scarred, is now in the museum.

Near by Seth Bullock is buried, a cowboy who organized the Rough Riders and later served as U. S. Marshal in South Dakota. He asked to be buried within sight of the thirty-five-foot monument to his hero, Theodore Roosevelt, which was raised through his efforts at the summit of Mt. Roosevelt.

Eighteen days after the slaying of Wild Bill, Preacher Smith, famous frontier parson, was buried in Boothill Cemetery, Ingleside, and later removed to Mt. Moriah. Over his grave was placed a life-size statue of questionable artistic merit. Smith was shown heavily bearded and wearing a Prince Albert coat. His left hand was on his heart and his right hand lay on an open Bible which was atop a tree stump pulpit.

Memorial markers near Felchville, Vermont. See p. 55.

Tombstone of Horace and Elizabeth Tabor, Mt. Olivet Cemetery, Denver, Colorado. See p. 65.

Most of the statue has been chipped away by visitors, although this epitaph can still be read:

Conn. 1827   Dak. 1876
In Memory of
Rev. Henry Weston Smith
A Minister of the
M. E. Church, the
Pioneer Preacher
in the
Black Hills,
Killed by Indians, Aug. 20, 1876
while on His Way from Deadwood to
Crook City to Preach.
Faithful Unto Death.

General John A. Sutter, died 1880, aged 77, is buried in Moravian Cemetery, Lititz, Pennsylvania, with the inscription: "Requiescat in pacem." He was nationally heralded as the discoverer of gold in California. An employee of Sutter, James W. Marshall, according to the state of California, actually spotted gold specimens in Sutter's millrace. A fellow worker, Captain Charles Bennett, is, however, given this distinction on his gravestone in I.O.O.F. Cemetery, Salem, Oregon:

Capt. Bennett
Died Dec. 7, 1855
Age 44 yrs. 3 ms. 30 ds.
Erected by his wife.
Capt. Chas. Bennett was the discoverer
of gold in Cal. and fell in the defense
of his country at Walla Walla.

Some historians suggest that neither Marshall nor Bennett were first to see gold, but an eight-year-old boy, John Elijah Ezekiel Wimmer, whose father was a partner of Marshall.

An unusual monument in Mt. Olivet Cemetery, Denver, Colorado, commemorates the career of Horace A. W. Tabor, bonanza king, died 1899, aged 68. Bordering the inscription are sketches symbolizing a rising sun, a rocky road leading to wealth through silver mine holdings, the United States Capitol which represents Tabor's appointment to the Senate, and a steep decline to poverty and a setting sun. The inscription reads:

Unknown to fame until approaching the age of fifty, chance suddenly brought him considerable wealth and reputation. A few years later another throw of the dice as quickly returned him to his former obscurity but left in the wake a colorful character in the annals of Colorado history.

Just north of Bennett's Well in Death Valley National Monument, California, is an eight-foot monument with a bronze tablet bearing these words:

Bury me beside Jim Dayton in the
Valley we loved. Above me write:
"Here lies Shorty Harris, a single-
blanket jackass prospector." Epitaph
requested by Shorty (Frank) Harris
Beloved Gold Hunter. 1859-1934.
Here Jas. Dayton, Pioneer, Perished, 1898.
To these trailmakers whose courage matched
the dangers of the land, this bit of earth
is dedicated forever.

The tablet is located at the foot of two graves, the names "Dayton" and "Harris" being inscribed on rocks placed at the head of each. When Dayton died in 1898, aged 62, he was the only white resident in the valley. Returning from a supply trip to Daggett, 160 miles away, he became sick near Bennett's Well. His body was found near his wagon and the carcasses of his four horses were still held by their harnesses. His faithful dog, who was free to search for food and water, survived, and fought off coyotes from his master's body. Those who found his body buried him at that spot and committed him to his grave with the words: "Well, Jimmy, you lived in the heat and you died in the heat, and now you've gone to hell." Three decades later the body of Shorty Harris was laid near by.

Few stories of the blighted hopes of accumulating fortunes in the California gold rush equal that of five persons, buried in a common grave in City Cemetery, Grass Valley, California. The inscription reads:

Michael	Dorinda	Ellen	Robert	Dorinda	Brennan
Aged 38	32	7	5	2	Years

Died Feb. 21, 1858. Natives of Ireland.

Brennan, one-time newspaperman in New York City, was sent to California to be superintendent of the Massachusetts Hill Mine. Investing heavily in the Brennan shaft, he worked the stringer down to a depth of 260 feet, but the venture was unproductive. Disillusioned and in debt he put to death his family and himself with prussic acid. Ironically, his claim covered what later became the famous North Star Mine.

Under a large oak tree in Fort Tejon State Historical Monument, Lebec, California, is a marker that recalls the tragic death of a prospector in furs:

Peter Lebec
Shot a bear under this tree and
supposing it dead, went up to it.
It caught and killed him. His companions buried him under this tree
upon which they cut his epitaph
Peter Lebec was killed here
Oct. 17 1837. The bark with the
epitaph was cut out and can be seen
at library in Bakersfield.

The story of Lebec, long a part of the folklore of the vicinity, was substantiated in 1890 when the body was exhumed at the foot of "Lebec Oak." The bark which had grown over most of the epitaph was removed and the portion of the tree was removed. The epitaph has long intrigued readers:

I H S
Peter
Lebec
Killed
by
a X bear
Octr. 17
1837

⸝e 1877, horse thieves held up a vehicle on the Black ⸝ine. Three thieves were apprehended within a week and ⸝iled in Rapid City, South Dakota. Unknown persons broke into ⸝⸝ ail on the night of 21 June, took out the criminals and hanged them. Over their triple grave a pine headboard, no longer extant, was put up, which warned:

| A. J. Allen | Louis Curry | Jas. Hall |
| Age 35 years | Age 29 years | Age 19 years |

HORSE THIEVES BEWARE

Here lie the bodies of Allen, Curry and Hall.
Like other thieves they have their rise, decline
and fall.
On yon pine tree they hung till dead,
And here they found a lonely bed.
Then be a little cautious how you gobble horses up,
For every horse you pick up here, adds sorrow to your cup;
We're bound to stop this business, or hang you to a man,
For we've hemp and hands enough in town to swing the
whole damn clan.

The grave of another horse thief is said to have been marked:

He found a rope and picked it up,
And with it walked away.
It happened that to the other end
A horse was hitched, they say.
They took the rope and tied it up
Unto a hickory limb.
It happened that the other end
Was somehow hitched to him.

Two victims of Vigilante justice are buried in the graveyard of Mission Dolores, San Francisco. The tombstone to James P. Casey, died 1856, aged 27, was erected by members of Engine Company No. 10 and bears a fireman's insignia:

May God forgive my
Persecutors.
Requiescat in pace.

The second hanged himself before the Vigilance Committee could bring him to trial. His epitaph reads:

> Sacred to the memory of the late deceased
> James Sullivan Who died by the hands of the V. C.
> May 31, 1856, aged 45 years, a Native of Bandon
> Ireland.
>> Remember not, O Lord, our
>> Offences, nor those of our parents
>> Neither take thou vengeance of our sins.
>> Thou shalt bring my soul out of
>> Tribulation, and in thy mercy thou
>> Shalt destroy mine enemies.
>> A native of Bandon, Ireland.
>> Erected by James Mulloy Jan. 26, 1858.

James "Yankee" Sullivan was a champion pugilist.

Freed from Bondage

An inscription in Hill Burying Ground, Concord, Massachusetts, commemorates a slave whose industry gained him his freedom:

God wills us free, man wills us slaves.
I will as God wills Gods will be done.
Here lies the body of
John Jack
A native of Africa who died
March 1773, aged about sixty years.
Tho' born in a land of slavery,
He was born free.
Tho' he lived in a land of liberty,
He lived a slave,
Till by his honest, tho' stolen, labors,
He acquired the source of slavery,
Which gave him his freedom;
Tho' not long before,
Death the grand tyrant,
Gave him his final emancipation,
And set him on a footing with kings.

> Tho' a slave to vice,
> He practiced these virtues
> Without which kings are but slaves.

A remarkable slave whose autobiography publicized widely the varied experiences of his life is buried in the First Church Cemetery, East Haddam, Connecticut, where his epitaph records:

> Sacred to the Memory
> of Venture Smith an
> African tho the son of a
> King he was kidnapped
> & sold as a slave but by
> his industry he acquired
> Money to purchase his
> Freedom who Died Sept 19th
> 1805 in ye 77th Year of his
> Age.

The tombstones of Amos Fortune and his wife near the Meeting House in Jaffery, New Hampshire, read:

> Sacred to the memory of Amos Fortune,
> who was born free in Africa, a slave
> in America, he purchased liberty, pro-
> fessed Christianity, lived reputably,
> and died hopefully, Nov. 17, 1801, Aet. 91.

> Sacred to the memory of Violate, by
> sale the slave of Amos Fortune, by
> marriage his wife, by her fidelity
> his friend and solace, she died his
> widow Sept. 13, 1802, Aet. 73.

In Aspen Grove Cemetery, Burlington, Iowa, two inscriptions say:

> In Memory of Benj. Sandridge, Commonly
> Known as Uncle Ben, Born a Slave in
> Virginia, Held in Bondage for 49 Years,
> Died a Free Man by the Law of His Country

and the Grace of His God, in Iowa Nov. 7,
1853, Being About 53 Years of Age. Erected by His Wife, Kitty.

In Memory of Catherine Sandridge, Commonly
Known as "Aunt Kitty", Born a Slave. The
Wife of Uncle Ben and with Him Made Free
by the Payment of $1,000 to their Master.
Both Became Members of the First Baptist
Church of Burlington, Iowa, at its Organi-
zation in 1849 and Were Faithful As Such to
the End. Died Sept. 10, 1863, Being about
60 Years of Age. To Depart and Be With
Christ Is Far Better.

A miracle is described on a tombstone in Old North Burying
Ground, North Attleboro, Massachusetts:

Here lies the best of slaves
Now turning into dust
Caesar the Ethiopian craves
A place among the just.
His faithful soul has fled
To realms of heavenly light,
And by the blood that Jesus shed
Is changed from Black to White.
Jany. 15 he quitted the stage
in the 77th year of his age.
1780

This epitaph comes from Pioneer Cemetery, Canandaigua, New
York:

Jacob Hodges
An African Negro
Born in Poverty and Ignorance,
Early Tempted to Sin
By Designing and Wicked Men,
Once Condemned as a Felon,

Converted by the Grace of God
in Prison,
Lived many years, a Converted
and useful Christian,
died Feb. 2, 1842,
in the Faith of the Gospel,
About 80 years of age.

In 1835, Capt. Jonathan Walker, engaged in transporting fugitive slaves to Mexico and the West Indies, was run down off Florida, stood in a pillory, and branded on his right palm with the letters "SS" for slave stealer. This is believed to be the only record of a federal court ordering branding. After a year's imprisonment, during which time his name was heralded by John Greenleaf Whittier's poem, "The Branded Hand," Walker settled on a farm near Muskegon, Michigan, where he died in 1878, aged 79. A granite shaft that marks his grave in Evergreen Cemetery is inscribed:

This Monument is Erected
To the
Memory of
Capt. Jonathan Walker
By his
Anti-slavery Friend,
Photius Fisk,
Chaplain in the
United States Navy.

On another side is the image of Walker's palm showing the branded letters and giving the words:

Capt.
Walker's
Branded
Hand

When the aggressive abolitionist Thaddeus Stevens, majority leader in the House of Representatives during the Civil War, died in 1868, aged 76, he was buried in Schreiners Cemetery, Lancaster, Pennsylvania, where his epitaph explains:

I repose in this quiet and secluded spot,
Not from any natural preference for solitude,
But finding other cemeteries limited as to race,
By charter rules,
I have chosen this that I might illustrate
In my death
The principles which I advocated
Through a long life:
Equality of man before his Creator.

Heaven's My Destination

Going, but know not where.

This is in the inscription on the monument in Grove Street Cemetery, Putnam, Connecticut, to Phineas Gardner Wright, died 1918, aged 89. Also on the stone is a reproduction of the head and shoulders of Wright, who is shown with a long beard and his eyes gazing toward heaven. He is still remembered locally as the village atheist.

Inscribed on a narrow stone in Wellsboro, Pennsylvania, are these words:

Daniel E. Cole
Born Feb. 2, 1844
Went Away
Mar. 22, 1921
I Wonder
Where He
Went.

A similar indefiniteness concerning the future is expressed on a large monument to Charles A. Miller, died 1905, aged 65, in Siloam Cemetery, Vineland, New Jersey:

I came I know not whence,
I go I know not whither.

A hesitancy to claim heaven as an eternal home is found on the tombstone to Emma Luther, died 1880, in Harmony, Rhode Island:

> If there is another world
> I live in bliss
> If not another
> I have made the most of this.

An undated monument to Potie Choate, died 1912, aged 68, in Forest Hill Cemetery, Bridgton, Maine, is inscribed:

> Her task in life, divinely planned,
> Was finished with the fading light;
> She took her ready lamp in hand
> And softly said, "Good-night."

There was little question concerning the heavenly reward of Mrs. Adelaide Savage, died 1827, aged 20, as suggested on her grave marker in West Parish Burying Ground, Barnstable, Massachusetts:

> If heaven is the reward for a life
> passed in innocence and usefulness
> then she was a favored candidate.

From Vienna, Louisiana, comes this unusual story of salvation:

> James H. Mays
> Born in Lincoln County Georgia
> November 17, 1821
> Died in Ruston, La. August 9, 1911
> Born spiritually, October 18, 1839, under
> no eyes save the Lords and my
> horses.
> Joined the Methodist Church on
> September 4, 1839 and feel that I
> have been an unworthy member
> since, but hope to join the
> redeemed above in the first
> resurrection.
> (Dictated by Deceased)

The epitaph to Elezer Holmes, died 1798, aged 84, on Burial Hill, Plymouth, Massachusetts, says frankly:

> Thro' a long life in devious paths I trod
> And liv'd alas! forgetful of my God:
> But oh! the triumph of redeeming Power
> A Sinner ransomed at the Eleventh hour
> Repairs to Christ the Lord his Righteousness
> And dies proclaiming free and sovereign Grace.

Salvation found at the last moment is described in an epitaph recorded in William Camden's *Remains Concerning Britain* (1636):

> My friend judge not me,
> Thou seest I judge not thee:
> Betwixt the stirrup and the ground,
> Mercy I ask'd, mercy I found.

The lines are evidently dependent on St. Augustine's phrase: "The Lord's mercy between the bridge and stream."

Having sown his wild oats, Seth Newcomb, died 1811, aged 25, found the eternal hope just in time. His epitaph in Greenlawn Cemetery, Keene, New Hampshire, says that his

> life though short was
> active, too much devoted however to the
> world, and too little to his maker and not
> till the chastening Hand of Providence was in
> mercy extended to him, did he duly
> estimate the evidence of Christianity,
> but a severe and long continued sickness induced
> reflection and inquiry, and the result was re
> gret that his conduct had been so long influ
> enced by worldly views, and full conviction
> of the truth of our holy religion, and he
> died as he believed, a humble and pen
> itent sinner, resting his hopes of
> pardon and salvation on the
> merits of his
> redeemer.

On the grave of Henry Hudson Godfrey, died 1868, aged 11, in Aspetuck Cemetery, Easton, Connecticut, is the following:

Gone to a better land.

A similar device is carved on the stone of Rodney Webber, died 1872, aged 61, in Rural Cemetery, Virgil, New York:

He's gone home.

In Friends' Church Cemetery, Orchard Park, New York, is the simple epitaph to Erastus B. Hambleton, died 1876, aged 40:

I See Daybreak.

A one-word inscription on the monument to Lorenzo Sabine, died 1877, aged 74, in Hillside Cemetery, Eastport, Maine, reads:

Transplanted.

The widow of Maleleel W. Carter, died 1849, aged 50, planned one day to tell her husband of the grief she experienced. His stone in Old Masonic Burying Ground, Fredericksburg, Virginia, records:

Farewell, but not a long farewell
In heaven may I appear
The trials of my faith to tell
In thy transported ear
And sing with thee the eternal strain
Worthy the lamb that once was slain.

The lines in the following epitaph may have been selected because of the first name of Mrs. Silence Glazier, died 1851, aged 66, in Adams Cemetery, Barre Plains, Massachusetts:

Husband farewell, a long farewell
And children all adieu
And when we meet no tongue can tell
How I shall welcome you.

At Knowles' Corner in Aroostook County, Maine, is the gravestone of Ruth Cooper, died 1886, aged 40, which records:

> She is waiting for us in the glorious Eden-land
> Which lies beyond the sunset of life.

A weather-beaten marble slab in Mount Albion Cemetery, Albion, New York, to Timothy Bailey, died 1841, aged 80, says:

> Our aged father is now conveyed
> To his long home in silence laid
> Hast burst his cage and winged his way
> To realms of bliss in endless day.

In Old North Cemetery, Nantucket, Massachusetts, was transcribed fifty years ago this epitaph from a small slate stone:

> Under the sod
> Under these trees
> Lies the body of Jonathan Pease
> He is not here
> But only his pod
> He has shelled out his peas
> And gone to his God.

The origin of this peculiar epitaph, which seems to have been frequently copied in one fashion or another, is not known. *Extracts from the Letters of Theo. Brown* (1879) contains this passage:

We tried our hands at making epitaphs at Chamberlin's the other evening. The name of Solomon Pease was suggested. I was so much absorbed in mine that I do not remember any of the others. So here it is:

> *Under this sod, beneath these trees*
> *Lieth the pod of Solomon Pease.*

Closely related to the Pease inscription is this one quoted by Sir Walter Scott in his novel *The Antiquary* (1816):

> Heir lyeth John o' ye Girnell,
> Erth has ye nit and heuen ye kirnell.

The following inscription is found in First Parish Burying Ground, Newbury, Massachusetts:

Here lies
In a state of perfect oblivion
John Adams
who died Sept 2 1811
AE 79
Death has decomposed him
And at the great resurrection Christ
will recompose him.

This epitaph, no longer readable, was formerly copied in Pleasant Grove Cemetery, Ithaca, New York:

While on earth my knee was lame,
I had to nurse and heed it.
But now I've gone to a better place
Where I do not even need it.

An inscription, long familiar to English and American graveyards, is found on the small marble slab to Lucy Swarbreck, died 1821, aged 4, in Old Colonial Cemetery, Savannah, Georgia:

Rest here, blest daughter,
Wait thy Maker's will,
Then rise unchanged,
And be an angel still.

The heavenward journey is described on the gravestone to Mrs. Anne Buckingham, died 1766, aged 19, in Milford, Connecticut:

Mature from Heaven the fateful mandate came
With it a chariot of AEtherial Flame
In which Elijahlike she passed the spheres
Brought joy to Heaven, but left the world in tears.

In the old Baptist Cemetery, Pittsford, Vermont, is found this epitaph to Nathan Jenner, died 1824, aged 43:

This hallowed spot hath proved the home
Of him who bright in science shone.

> I saw him on that fatal night:
> With visage clothed in purer light:
> When life had fled I saw him rise
> To brighter worlds beyond the skies.

An interestingly worded epitaph in Grace Parish churchyard, Jamaica, New York, marks the grave of Mrs. Alletta Willett, died 1780, aged 76:

> At length ye Christian's Race is Run
> A Glorious prize She now has won.
> With ye Angelle Host She's fixt,
> In Joys celestial & unmix'd.

The grave of her daughter, Joannah, who died thirty years earlier, aged 21, bears similar lines:

> Unto Thy courts, O Lord, she fled,
> Through the dark mansions of the dead.
> Within Thy palace now she's fixt,
> In joys celestial and unmixt.

Beneath the motto, "My glass is run," is this inscription to Mrs. Mary Humphrey, died 1792, aged 36, in Old Pleasant Street Cemetery, Athol, Massachusetts:

> With graceful & engaging Mein
> She trod the carpet & the green
> With such refulgent virtues deck't
> As gained her wide & warm respect.
> Prim health sat blooming on her cheeks
> Till Fortune play'd her cruel freaks
> Her limbs in tort'ing pains confin'd
> That wrecked her joints tho not her Mind
> By faith and patience fortified
> The rudest tempest to abide
> Bove which she soard to realms of bliss
> When Jesus haild her with a kiss.

The archaic language of the epitaph to Mrs. Elizabeth Sheldon, died 1809, aged 24, in Old Burying Ground, New Marlborough, Massachusetts, is appealing:

Oh may you scorn these
cloths of flesh
These fetters and this load
And long for evening to undress
That you may rest with God.

A comparable figure of speech is found on the gravestone to Lieutenant William Kittredge, died 1789, aged 92, in Old Centre Burying Ground, Tewksbury, Massachusetts:

He's gone at length, how many grieve
Whom he did gen'rously relieve
But O how shocking he expire
Amidst the flames of raging fire!
Yet all who sleep in Christ are bless'd
Whatever way they are undress'd.

In Lewis Cemetery, Bemus Point, New York, is the inscription to Belvera Annis, died 1841, aged 36:

Tho' greedy worms devour my skin
And knaw my wasting flesh
When God shall build my bones again
He'll clothe them all afresh.

More judicious is the inscription to Richard Tomlinson, died 1886, aged 59, in Gunnings' Cemetery, near Blountville, Tennessee:

Jesus can make a dying bed feel
soft as down pillows are
While on His breast I lean
my head and breathe my life
out sweetly there.

Abraham Simons, a veteran of the Revolution, died 1824, buried near Washington, Georgia, evidently planned one day to ruin the devil. On a hill near his home, where he trained fine race horses, he built his grave and enclosed it with a rock wall. He requested that after his burial the heavy iron gate be closed and the key thrown away. He further requested that he be buried in his army uniform and in a standing position. At his side was to be placed his musket, for he intended one day in the future *to shoot the devil*. Simon's widow, after a respectable period of mourning, married the Rev. Jesse Mercer and used Simon's fortune to found Mercer University in Macon, Georgia.

Sermons in Stone

Sermons in stone can be found on many a monument in an old grave-yard near a family home, at the side of a church, or next to a village green. Frequently these didactic old epitaphs were copied from a volume of pious sentiments or were written by a local clergyman for the moral instruction of the passer-by.

For example:

> The grave hath eloquence and doth teach
> lectures in silence louder than devines
> can preach.

This is said on the stone erected in memory of Sarah B. Claypool, who died in 1886 at the age of 78 years, in Claypool Cemetery, Liberty, Ohio.

The sentiment was old then. The gravestone of Edward Cary, who died in 1812 at the age of 74 years and was buried in Old North Cemetery, Nantucket, Massachusetts, advised:

> Learn then, ye living! by these mouths be taught
> Of all these sepulchres, instruction true,
> That, soon or late, dath also is your lot;
> And the next opening grave may yawn for you!

The most ubiquitous of all epitaphs is the familiar admonition:

> Behold my friends as you pass by
> As you are now so once was I
> As I am now, so you must be
> Prepare for death and follow me.

Variations of these lines have been used on tombstones throughout the English-speaking world for more than three centuries and may possibly date back to the following lines, translated from the original French, which appear on the tomb to Edward, the Black Prince, died 1376, in Canterbury Cathedral, Canterbury, England:

> Such as thou art, sometime was I,
> Such as I am, such shalt thou be.

The moralizing sentiment disturbed Charles Lamb, who in his *Essays of Elia* (1823) commented: "More than all I abhor those impertinent familiarities inscribed upon your ordinary tombstones. Every dead man must take upon himself to be lecturing me with his odious truism that such as he is, I must shortly be."

Nearly as common is the epitaph:

> Death is a debt
> By nature due
> I've paid my debt
> And so must you.

Inventiveness or error may account for the version on the grave of Lucina Willcox, died 1800 aged 20, in Surry, New Hampshire:

> Death is a debt
> By nature due
> I've paid my shot
> And so must you.

In the same family lot is an epitaph to Eunice Wilcox, died 1803, aged 30:

> For sudden death
> Prepared be
> Resign your breath
> And follow me.

Discovered during excavations near the Old State House, Boston, in 1830, was the tombstone of William Paddy, one-time representative of Plymouth in the General Court of Deputies for Plymouth Colony, died 1658, aged 58. The stone, now set in King's Chapel Burying Ground, reads:

Hear·sleaps·that
Blesed·one·whoes·lief
God·help·vs·all·to·live
That·so·when·tiem·shall·be
That·we·this·world·must·liue
We·ever·may·be·happy
With·blesed·William·Paddy.

In Old Cemetery, Boylston, Massachusetts, is this verse to Isaac Temple, died 1791, aged 88:

Behold my friends, in me you all may see
An Emblem of what you e'er must be,
Remember you like me was form'd of dust,
And with the earth unite again you must.

The epitaph to Tomkins Brush, died 1809, aged 87, who gave land for Central Cemetery, Brookfield, Connecticut, reads:

My friends, ime here the first that come,
And in this place for you there's room.

A gravestone to a Revolutionary officer, Major Francis Turpin, died 1829, aged 70, buried near Cambridge, Maryland, adds a new note to the familiar idea:

Passenger stop as you pass by
As you are now, so once was I
I had my share of worldly care
As I was living as you are
But God from all has set me free
Prepare for Death and follow me.

Lines to Hannah Crane, died 1852, aged 45, in First Presbyterian churchyard, Elizabeth, New Jersey, beckon:

Tombstone of Solomon Field, Providence, Rhode Island. Epitaph reads:

My glass is run my life is done,
Death will to you my parents come,
With brothers seven and sisters six,
For all the day of doom is fix'd.

Stop my friend! O take another view!
The dust that moulders here
Was once belov'd like you!
No longer then on future time rely
Improve the present
And prepare to die!

The macabre wording on the grave of Dr. Isaac Bartholomew, died 1710, in Hillside Cemetery, Cheshire, Connecticut, comments:

He that was sweet to my repose
Now is become a stink under my nose
This is said of me
So it will be said of thee.

Emily Merritt, died 1857, aged 18, is remembered by her tombstone inscription in Ludingtonville, New York:

Now she is dead and cannot stir
Her cheeks are like a faded rose.
Which one of us must follow her
The Lord Almighty only knows.

This quotation from the gravestone of Timothy Noyes, died 1718, aged 63, in First Parish Burying Ground, Newbury, Massachusetts, is addressed to members of the Noyes family:

Good Timothy In
His Youthfull Days
He Lived Much
Unto Gods Prays
When Age Came On
He & His Wife
They Lived A Holy
& A Pious Life
Therefor You Children
Whose Name Is Noyes
Make Jesus Christ
Your Ondly Choyes.

Another call to religious devotion is on the tombstone of Prudence
Shattuck, died 1819, aged 49, in Groton, Massachusetts:

> With grace and piety her days were crown'd
> With lustre bright her virtue shine around
> Reader could ashes speak they'd loudly cry
> Make God your friend and so prepare to die.

A whole array of admonitory epitaphs are given on stones to members of the Temple family, Hill Burying Ground, Concord, Massachusetts: To Mrs. Louis Temple, died 1816, aged 69:

> Lord I commit my soul to thee
> Accept the sacred trust
> Receive this nobler part of me
> And watch my sleeping dust.

To James Temple, died 1806, aged 14:

> No help for me was found
> Death me o'er took, here I'm inshrin'd
> Till the last trump shall sound.

To John Temple, died 1806, aged 26:

> Death is a debt to nature due
> Which I have paid & so must you.

To Peter Temple, died 1806, aged 22:

> Whilst oe'r my grave you stand and see
> Remember you must follow me.

To Anna Temple, died 1783, aged 30:

> Hark from the tomb a dolful sound
> Mine Eare attend the cry
> Ye living men come view ye ground
> Where you must shortly lie.

To Mrs. Abigail Temple, died 1780, aged 63:

> Retire my friends, dry up Your Tears
> Here I must lie till Christ appears.

Advice based on experience is carved onto a common field boulder, four feet in diameter and showing many plow scratches, marking the grave of Richard C. S. Pond, died 1904, aged 35, in Milford, Connecticut:

> Who among you plow boys ever
> associated the blow of the plow point
> on the hidden stone as one of happin-
> ess? Not one of you until you have tast-
> ed the disappointments, sorrows
> and rottenness of yonder city.

On a footstone is inscribed one of the most beautiful of all memorial sentiments:

> R. C. S. P.
> To live in hearts
> We leave behind
> Is not to die.

The identity of "yonder city" cannot be determined.

On the marble slab to Solomon Hornbeck, died 1819, aged 18, in Milford, Pennsylvania, the warning is given:

> Come all ye mourners to the tomb
> See here a youth cut off in bloom,
> Although he's hurried to his last
> We hope the Lord hath found him rest.
>
> This be a warning to ye all
> Should at your house a sick youth call,
> It's not a secret for to keep,
> But let his parents know of it.

The suggestion that all men are equal in death is made on the tombstone of John Kerr, died 1835, aged 46, in Grace Church Cemetery, Providence, Rhode Island:

> I dreamt that buried in my fellow clay,
> Close by a common beggar's side I lay;
> Such a mean companion hurt my pride!
> And, like a corse of consequence, I cried,

Scoundrel begone; and henceforth touch me not,
More manners learn, and at a distance rot.
"Scoundrel" in still haughtier tones cried he,
Proud lump of earth, I scorn thy words and thee;
All here are equal, thy place now is mine,
This is my rotting place, and that is thine.

The monument to Aaron J. Beattie, Sr., died 1950, aged 50, in Elm Lawn Cemetery, Bay City, Michigan, is inscribed:

For the other fellow.

The effort of one man to cleanse the English language of profane words is told on a tombstone in Old North Cemetery, Portsmouth, New Hampshire. His purpose was to substitute harmless, though effective, curse words for references to deity.

Benjamin M. Burnham
Originator of the Trite Swearing
Departed this life at
Boston, Mar. 14, 1855 aged 58 years.
Dead but yet speakets
Swear not at all
To change to praise the swearer's wicked prayer
And show the love of God seemed all his care
To keep away from human eye, the lights we see
God's glory by.

Inscribed on an impressive memorial canopy to Benjamin Saxon Story, died 1901, aged 67, in Metairie Cemetery, New Orleans, Louisiana, are the words:

He did acts of kindness
and charity, as stealthily as
some men commit crimes.

The wife of William H. Duggan, died 1874, aged 71, devised a sermon in stone for his grave in the cemetery of St. Charles Borromeo Church, St. Charles, Missouri. She warned him about his intemperance and predicted his final tragedy. This event is described by a carving on his gravestone which shows a man lying prostrate near a mule that has just kicked him. Chickens are shown fleeing from the scene. On the top of the marker is a stone whiskey jug. When the children objected to the memorial, Mrs. Duggan refused to remove the stone she had designed and the children then erected a conventional marker to stand near by.

In the Clayton, Alabama, cemetery is a peculiar monument raised by a woman whose husband, a drunkard, died of delirium tremens. A large headstone, half the height of a man, is shaped like a whiskey flask. The footstone is in the shape of a bottle. The sideboards suggest serpentine figures which may represent the mental sickness apparent at the time of the man's death. A strange inscription on the headstone reads:

> In memory of W. T. Mullen,
> Son of J. and N. Mullen.
> Born in Talbotton, Georgia,
> June 18, 1834,
> Died July 18, 1863.
> The happy sinle to slumber and forget:
> The weary find from toil, repose and rest.

At the grave of W. H. Frush, an early saloon keeper, died 1865, aged 54, in Lone Fir Cemetery, Portland, Oregon, is the large bowl in which Frush annually mixed his Tom and Jerry drinks.

Inscribed on a handsome monument to Carry A. Nation, died 1911, aged 65, in Belton, Missouri, are the last words spoken in her final temperance address:

> Faithful to the cause of prohibition
> "She hath done what she could"

In Riverside Cemetery, Oneco, Connecticut, is a monument to Alonzo P. Love, died 1908, aged 62, which reads:

> Vote No License

His wife, a prohibitionist, attributed his death to his intemperance, and was mindful of the annual town meetings when the citizens determined whether the saloons should be licensed or not.

Judge Samuel Nelson wrote this epitaph for Jenny York, a cook in his home who was occasionally too generous in distributing the judge's possessions among her friends:

She had her faults
But
She was kind to the Poor.
Jenny York
Died Feb. 22, 1837
Aet. 50

This tombstone is in Christ churchyard, Cooperstown, New York.
The epitaph on the grave of Judge James W. Remick, died 1943,
aged 83, in Parish Burial Ground, Kittery Point, Maine, records:

I have chosen to have my ashes placed here
because I revere this ancient cemetery and
the historic church across the way by which
it is governed. And I have selected the
rough boulder which marks this spot because
it was found imbedded in the trail leading
through the woods on my own Sunshine Hill, where
I have passed so many happy years, and because
my dog Teddy and I have walked it so often.

Ministers

A clergyman who particularly recommended himself to his parishioners was Thomas Bailey, died 1688, aged 35, whose slab in Old Burying Ground, Watertown, Massachusetts, is inscribed:

Here lies ye Precious Dust of
Thomas Bailey

A painfull Preacher	A most desirable neighbor
An Exemplary liver	A pleasant companion
A Tender Husband	A common good
A careful Father	A cheerful doer
A brother for Adversity	A patient Sufferer
A faithful Friend	Lived much in a little time

A good copy for all Survivors.

The monument to another minister, David Little, died 1801, in Hope Cemetery, Kennebunk, Maine, employs a Latin motto common to many old stones:

Memento mori! preach'd his ardent youth,
Memento mori! spoke maturer years,
Memento mori! sigh'd his latest breath,
Memento mori! now this stone declares.

From his tombstone in Old Burying Ground, Norwichtown, Connecticut, the Reverend Benjamin Lord, died 1784, aged 90, preaches his last sermon:

> Tho' now unconscious in Death may the living
> hear (or seem to hear) from him the following
> address
> Think, Christian, think!
> You stand on vast Eternity's dread brink
> "Faith and Repentance, Piety and Pray'r!"
> Despite "this" World, the "next" by all "your" care
> Thus while my Tomb the solemn silence breaks
> And to the eye this cold dumb marble speaks
> Tho' dead I preach, if e're with ill success
> "Living" I strove the important truths to press
> Your "precious, your immortal souls" to save
> Hear me, at least O hear me from my "Grave."

A conscientious sermonizer was John Wilson, pastor of the Presbyterian Church, Chester, New Hampshire, from 1734 to 1779. His stone in Congregational Cemetery, Chester, reads:

> Here Lies the Body of
> Mrs. Jean Wilson
> Spous of the Revd. John Wilson
> who departed this Life April 1st AD
> 1752 Aged 36 years.
> She was a Gentlewoman of Piety
> A good Oeconamist
> Likewise the Revd. John Wilson
> who departed this Life Feby ye 1st AD
> 1779 Aged 69 years.
> He was a Servant of Christ in the most
> Peculiar & Sacred Relation, both in Doctrine &
> Life. It was his great Delight to Prich a Crucefied
> Christ as our wisdom, Righteousness, Sanctification &
> Redemption. He did not Entertain his hear-
> ers with Curiosities, but Real Spiritual

good. His Sermons were Clear, Solid,
affictionate. A Spirit of Vital Christianity
Ran through them. His Life was Sutable to
his holy Profession, he was a Steady friend a
Loving husband and tender Parent. His Inward
Grace was visable in a convercation
become the gospel.

In the Old Cemetery, Milford, Connecticut, is this ministerial
achievement of the Reverend Bezaleel Pinneo, died 1849, aged 80,
pastor of the Congregational Church for fifty-three years:

> During his ministry
> He enjoyed 7 revivals
> Admitted 716 members
> Baptized 1117 and
> Buried 1126 of his flock.

Another ministerial record is found on the tombstone of the Reverend
Matthew Ellison, died 1889, aged 84, in Old Greenbrier Baptist churchyard, Alderson, West Virginia:

> Baptized at 16
> Preached 65 years
> 7000 sermons
> Baptized 2000
> Organized 25 churches.

An upright stone on Burroughs Hill, Hebron, Connecticut, marks
the grave of a wife of an early Methodist circuit rider:

> Peggy Dow
> Shared the
> Vicissitudes of
> Lorenzo
> 15 years &
> Died
> Jan. 6, 1820
> Aged 39 years.

On a white marble shaft in Christian Church Cemetery, Johnsonburg, New Jersey, is this inscription:

Joseph Thomas
Minister of the Gospel in the
Christian Church
Known as the White Pilgrim
by reason of wearing
white raiment
Died April 9, 1835
Aged 44 yrs. 1 mo. & 2 d's.

Thomas, an itinerant preacher, wore white clothing and boots and rode a white horse with white trappings. He entered Johnsonburg on a preaching mission in 1835, but after his first service he was stricken with smallpox and died. Some of the parishioners, thinking that Thomas represented a strange new gospel, thought that his burial in the churchyard might contaminate the sacred soil. He was, therefore, interred in a local potter's field. Later the conscience of a synod meeting prevailed and Thomas' body was laid with the orthodox.

The gravestone to Martin Harris, died 1875, aged 92, in Clarkston, Utah, records:

One of the Three Witnesses to the Divine
Authenticity of the Book of Mormon.

An interesting bit of Southern folklore is chronicled on the gravestone to the Reverend George Pope in Flat Creek Baptist churchyard, Jefferson, South Carolina:

To the Memory of Rev. George Pope
A Baptist preacher who lived in the lower part of
Virginia or the upper part of North Carolina who
had a dream to go to Lynch's Creek to preach, as
it was only a dream he did not heed it, later he
had the same dream, but he paid little attention
to it, as it was only a dream. Soon his stock began to die. He still did not go. One morning
he went to his wheat field and found the frost
had killed all his wheat, and in despair he cried

"Lord what shall I do?" A voice or deep impress-
ion replied "Go to Lynch's Creek and preach." He
went home, saddled his horse and started, not knowing which way to go, but knew he was right by see-
ing objects that he had seen in the dream.
Arriving at the place next day he and some friends
went to the log school house where services were
being held. At the conclusion he arose and said
he was going to preach, just so, describing a
cross with his fingers. The effect of his preaching was such as had never been seen in all the
country before. The theme of his whole preaching
was that it was dangerous to lie down to sleep a
sinner. The people followed him and extended him
a call to preach and he erected and organized Flat
Creek Church July 4, 1776. He moved his family
here and preached until he died, being the first
person buried here. Some years after the death of
Rev. Pope, Joseph Copeland, a Baptist preacher,
dreamed that he must go and cut down the saplings
which had grown up in the field cleared by Mr. Pope.

A monument shaped to suggest the lines of traditional church archi-
tecture and inset with a bas-relief of his church identifies the grave
in Hillcrest Memorial Park, Dallas, Texas, of the Rev. Dr. George W.
Truett, one-time president of the Baptist World Alliance and for forty-
seven years pastor of the First Baptist Church of Dallas, died 1944,
aged 77. Inscribed are the words:

My greatest desire
is to help the people
and to magnify the
matchless name of Christ.

An epitaph in Old Burying Ground, Groton, Massachusetts, to
James Park, died 1741, aged 36, offers a glimpse of the strong religious
persuasions of colonial America:

He died no Libertine, there is two extremes,
the world has always run into, since ye fall of Adam.

1st Papists here have exceded in boundlesse domination & tyranny over ye consciences of men: & what ever is contrary to ye lawlesse decrees of there Councells & Popes, is an unexpiable heresie, & cannot be purged but by fire & fagot. 2. Whoever refuse subjection of conscience to that Enemy of Christ, & to that woman-mistress of witchcraft, on whose skirts is found ye Blood of ye martyres of Jesus, is Presently an heretick, & his arguments answered with burning-quicke, this tyranny over conscience we disclaime; yet for that ought not ye other extremity of wild toleration to be imbraced.

A marble slab, known locally as the "Cutter Stone," in Elm Street Cemetery, Milford, New Hampshire, includes a bitter last word:

Caroline H., wife of Calvin Cutter, M.D.
Murdered by the Baptist Ministry and Churches,
as follows: Sept. 28, 1838, Aet. 33, she was
accused of lying in Church Meeting by the Rev.
D. D. Pratt and Deacon Albert Adams—was condemned by the church unheard. She was reduced
to poverty by Deacon William Wallace. When an
exparte council was asked of the Milford Baptist
Church, by the advice of their committee, George
Raymond, Calvin Averill and Andrew Hutchinson, they
'voted not to receive any communication upon the
subject.' The Rev. Mark Carpenter said he thought
as the good old Deacon Pearson said, "we have got
Cutter down and it is best to keep him down." The
intentional and malicious destruction of her character and happiness, as above described, destroyed
her life. Her last words upon the subject were
"tell the truth and this iniquity will come out."

All clergymen are criticized in a peculiar inscription in Green Ridge Cemetery, Kenosha, Wisconsin. A tall shaft is inscribed:

Farewell
Susan Perrigo Foster
wife of
Lewis Knapp
Emigrated to the land of
Paradise June 26, 1871.
AE 54 yrs.

To the side of the shaft are two identical stones. The first reads:

My dear and loving wife: Meet me with our
spirit friends at the gate of the Elysian
Fields of Paradise where I am coming by
natures fast express until there we meet
a loving adieu. P. S. Our friends W. and A.
will soon join us there.

Lew
Happy Happy day Hallelujah Amen

The second stone reads:

Old Broad Gauge Lewis Knapp Aged _____ Years
Emigrated _____
To join his wife and other friends in the
Celestial Fields of Paradise: thanking God for
sense enough to die as he had lived for
thirty years thoroughly infidel to all ancient
and modern Theological humbug myths as taught
for fine clothes and place at others cost by
an indolent egotistic self-elected Priestly
crew.
The fear of the Right Reverend Doctors of
Divinity, Theological scarescrow of Hell-
fire and damnation to all who refuse to pay
tithes to their support had no force or effect
on Lewis Knapp.

Knapp erected the markers before his death. No one added the age
and date to his stone. When a local citizen sunk Knapp's marker into
Lake Michigan, he promptly erected another.

The God Haters

A number of the following epitaphs, representing a wide range of anti-religious and anti-clerical sentiments, date back to the latter half of the nineteenth century when a choice between science and religion seemed necessary to some people.

A two-word inscription on a monument to Arthur Haine, died 1907, in City Cemetery, Vancouver, Washington, recalls to old timers a bonafide and zealous atheist who wore his Sunday best on weekdays but, donning old work clothes on Sunday, fussed at his pious neighbors as they went to church. Two years before his death he wrote in his will, now on file in the Vancouver Court House: "Know everybody by these present that I, Arthur Haine, knowing what I am about, make this my last will and testament . . . My funeral is to be of the cheapest kind and I don't want my body to be transported but buried in the vicinity where I may die. As I have lived as an Infidel, I must be buried as such without any monkey business."

His wishes were carried out. His coffin was taken to the cemetery in a beer truck while a band played popular tunes and kegs of beer were made available to friends and spectators. His monument reads briefly:

Haine Haint

Joseph Coveney, before his death in 1897, aged 92, erected a spectacular monument in Oak Ridge Cemetery, Buchanan, Michigan, at a cost of $3000. It was made in England because local stonecutters refused to cut the sentiments Coveney requested. Many of the sentences are no longer legible, but among those which may still be read are the following:

> The more peace, the more plenty.
> The more Saints, the more Hypocrits.
> The more Priests, the more poverty.
> The Christian religion begins with a dream and
> ends with a murder.
> The Constitution is the end of liberty because
> you unite Church and State Catholics will burn
> Hereticks and Protistants will hang Quakers and
> Witches.

Before Coveney's death, the defacement of the monument had begun. Coveney wrote bitterly:

I was raised in a Catholic country, but it remained for a Protestant Christian to try to refuse me the right to maintain this monument in a public cemetery. I had inscribed thereon some of my sentiments on the religious fallacies of the day. These inscriptions, not coinciding with the view of the orthodox element, a minister's son, urged on by Christian hate, marred and defaced the monument in a barbarous manner. His act received the commendation of some of the strictly orthodox, though it is fair to say that all of the most prominent citizens of Buchanan condemned the act, and used every effort to prevent its repetition.

After his death, members of his family had portions of the inscriptions sandblasted from the stone. Other townspeople took to chiseling.

Quotations from the rational gospel of George F. Spencer, died 1808, aged 83, are inscribed on the sides of his rectangular granite monument in Lyndon Center, Vermont:

> Beyond the universe there is nothing and within the
> universe the supernatural does not and cannot exist.
> Of all deceivers who have plagued mankind, none are so
> deeply ruinous to human happiness as those imposters who
> pretend to lead by a light above nature.

> Science has never killed or persecuted a single
> person for doubting or denying its teachings, and
> most of these teachings have been true; but religion
> has murdered millions for doubting or denying her
> dogmas, and most of these dogmas have been false.

In Siloam Cemetery, Vineland, New Jersey, is a tombstone to Jeremiah Hacker, an ardent exponent of agnosticism, died 1895, aged 94:

> Teacher, lecturer and 15 years Editor
> and Publisher of the Pleasure Boat.
> The angry, wrathful Bible, God is a Myth.

These words mark the grave of his wife who died four years later:

> Where Is God?

Another editor, William Cowper Brann, is buried in Oakwood Cemetery, Waco, Texas, where a six-foot monument, surmounted by a large image of the classical Lamp of Truth, was erected. At the foot of the lamp is a pen and scroll upon which is the word "Truth." On one side of the pedestal are the initials "WCB" and on the opposite side is a profile of Mr. Brann. A noticeable nick on the temple is supposed to have been made by a pistol bullet fired by an unknown enemy. Brann edited the *Iconoclast,* a periodical that attacked conventional ideas and institutions, especially Baylor University. He was killed in 1898 at the age of 43 years in a pistol duel on the streets of Waco.

In East Thompson, Connecticut, is an upright slab to Jonathan Richardson, died 1872, aged 82, which gives an interesting revision of an Old Testament story which particularly disturbed nineteenth-century theological rebels:

> Who never sacrificed his reason
> at the alter of superstitions God
> who never believed that Jonah
> swallowed the whale.

Cy Deeter of Woodington, Ohio, became an atheist, it is said, because of the excessive attentions given by a minister to his wife. Before his death early in the present century, he erected a tombstone at the grave of his wife Hattie, died 1876, aged 20, in the old Teagarden Cemetery near Greenville, Ohio. These caustic words in Deeter's own spelling and grammar were carved onto the stone:

> There is no God. Man has no soul
> Life ends forever at death. The human
> race has advanced, not on account of
> the Church, but in spite of it. Civili-
> zation is due to science and not to Christ-
> ianity. Does a Catholic priest or a preach-
> er realize how unnecessary they are on earth?
> I hope there is a hell for all those hell
> fire preachers.

There are persons still living in Darke County who remember when someone pasted to the stone a paper bearing this comment:

> He who wrote this did it well
> The devil is waiting for him in hell.

Before Deeter's death, curious people began to visit the cemetery and to carry away chips as mementos. Nothing of the stone now remains.

Alvin Lusk faced death fearlessly, if his self-written inscription in West Berkshire, Vermont, may be taken literally. The opening lines are in the form of an acrostic, a device rarely found on nineteenth-century monuments.

> Name and Sentiments
> A-ll Nature, self existent, powers innate
> L-ife gives & takes, forms, solves, as adaptate
> V-irtue obeys, vice disobeys her laws;
> I-n THAT all good, THIS only evil draws;
> N-o good nor ill by supernatural cause.
>
> L-et not imagination take its flight
> U-pward to fancied regions for delight;
> S-cience & virtue lend to happiness;
> K-nown truth not fantom faith gives real bliss.
>
> Aged 75 years Sept. 14, 1858

I have no fears because I've got
No faith nor hope in juggernaut,
Nor Foh, Grand Lama, Boud nor Zend,
Nor Bible systems without end;
Nor Alcoron nor Mormon views,
Nor any creeds that priest-dupes use;
Enlightened minds the whole detest,
In strongest faith no virtue lies;
And unbelief no vice implies:
A Bare opinion hurts no man,
Then prove it hurts a God who can,
To others do to others give,
As you'd have done or would receive.

These belligerent words mark the grave of John L. Jones, died 1875, aged 64, in West Ripley, Maine:

I came without my own consent
Liv'd a few years much discontent
At human errors grieving.
I ruled myself by reason's laws
But got contempt and not applause
Because of disbelieving.
For nothing e'er could me convert
To faith some people did assert
But now the grave does me inclose
The superstitious will suppose
I'm doomed to hell's damnation.
But as to that they do not know
Opinions oft from ignorance flow
Devoid of sure foundation.
Tis easy men should be deceived
When anything by them's believed
Without a demonstration.

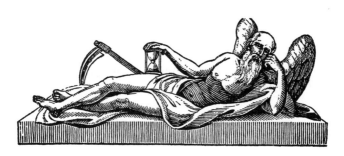

Doctors and Patients

In many old graveyards are found inscriptions and other reminders of the sicknesses that caused untimely deaths.

After suffering many years with tuberculosis, Leslie Hansell asked that she be buried in the sunlight. Her husband erected a tomb in Oakdale Cemetery, Hendersonville, North Carolina, designed to fulfill the request. The top of the tomb was covered with glass lenses and when Mrs. Hansell's body was interred in 1915 the tomb was hermetically sealed. Some years ago, when weathering had caused cracks in the tomb's walls, workmen were asked to seal the bricks with tar. Inadvertently they covered the entire surface.

The inscription to a victim of heart disease, Artemas Howe, died 1840, in North Cemetery, Princeton, Massachusetts, says:

> His languishing head is at rest
> Its thinking and aching are ore
> His quiet immoveable breast
> Is heav'd by affliction no more.
> His heart is no longer the seat
> Of trouble and torturing pain
> It ceases to flutter and beat
> It never will flutter again.

Medical statistics are offered in the epitaph to Benjamin Rowe, in Old Cemetery, Kensington, New Hampshire:

> In memory of Benjamin Rowe
> Esq. who after a life of great

usefullness & Patiently enduring 4
Years Illness with a Dropsy, underwent
the operation of Tapping 67 times, from
his Body was drawn 2385 pounds
of Water quietly Departed this Life
the 28 Day of March, Anno Domini
1790 In the 71st. Year of His Age.

This inscription comes from Milford, Connecticut:

Entombed is here desposited the
Dear remains of
Mrs Margaret DeWitt
who closed her eyes upon a
vain world Feby 11 1794 age 54.
Her exemplary conduct in Life
her unparralled patience
when wrecked with pains
the most excruciating & her
perfect resignation in her last
illness disarmed the King of
Terrors of his Sting & softened
him to a Prince of Peace.

Hannah Harlow, died 1836, aged 48, "after a distressing illness of 6 months, which she bore with unexampled fortitude untill exhausted nature compelled her to say I must give up," is buried on Burial Hill, Plymouth, Massachusetts.

The following sentiments are found on the four sides of a tombstone in West Barnstable, Massachusetts:

Beneath this consecrated vase lies entombed the remains of the lovely and beloved Maria Otis Colby who was consort to Rev. Philip Colby of Middleboro, and died at their residence on the 20th of May 1821 in the 34th year of her age.

Her bed of Death, what pen can portray! In the distress of excruciating miseries, she firmly recommended God and heaven to a crowd of weeping parishioners and poured out her soul in the most devout Universal Prayer, to God and her

Savior, while her Spirit seem'd wafted in that upward path to a "Better world that is an Heavenly, wherein dwelleth Righteousness." Write "Blessed are the dead that die in the Lord."

In whose short day was comprized the most sweet, engaging, useful and meritorious transactions, progressing day by day until maturer age had prepared her for the life of the most eminent Christian, administering consolation and support to many. Her thirst for knowledge led her into the walks of literature and through a vast variety of the best writers yearly.

The Sacred Oracle were the manna of her Soul. Her Bible, marked throughout by her pen, gave evidence that she embraced truth, in the love and the purity of it. Filial, fraternal and conjugal love, glowed throughout her life, not expired but in death.

In Pleasant Hill Cemetery, Blountville, Tennessee, is the following:

> Fannie Ben, Left by Dr. J. J. Ensor,
> March 10, 1857, with Ben & Katie Wine,
> Weight 4 lbs. No finger nor toe nails.
> With a gold eye tooth. Nursed on a pillow
> for nine weeks. Afflicted with St. Vitus Dance
> four years. Knee out of joint three times. Broken
> leg, mad dog bite. A scholar, talented musician.
> Studied medicine, a nurse for fifty years.
> Married twice, no children. A member of the
> Quaker Church since 1876. An intelligent,
> accomplished woman, admired by all.

The tombstone of her sister, Maggie Cate Wine, reads:

> A truthful child, mild tempered, quiet
> disposition, near sighted, strong mind. She
> grew a great favorite, speaking evil of no one.
> Fine in art and penmanship, a sweet singer,
> enjoyed work, never idle in house or on farm.

A lover of Church and Sunday School, believed in
the Bible, lived the life of a Christian. Afflicted 18
months, never complaining, died of dropsy, talking in
her right mind sitting in a chair.

In Village Cemetery, Warsaw, New York, is the inscription to Clarrisa Knapp, died 1819, aged 6, who was poisoned:

> A poisoned plant among the rest
> In nature's order stood
> I eat and was distressed
> It poisoned all my blood
> So sudden was the stroke
> By which I was snatched away
> That in one hour life's thread
>   was broke
> And I moldered to the clay.

No warning of impending death was given to an early Hartford,
Connecticut, resident, according to his stone in Ancient Burying
Ground:

> Here lyeth the body of Mr. David Gardiner
> of Gardiner's Island deceased July 10th, 1689
> in the fifty-fourth year of his age.
> Well-sick-dead in one hour's space.
> Engrave the remembrance of Death on thine heart
> When as thow dost see how swiftly hours depart.
> Born at Saybrook April 29, 1636
> The first white child born in Connecticut.

This epitaph in St. Thomas Episcopal Church, Bath, North Carolina, was given prominence when Edna Ferber included it, with only
a change of name and place, in her novel *Show Boat* (1926):

Here lyes the body of Mrs: Margaret Palmer, wife of
Robert Palmer, Esqr: one of His Majestys Council & Surveyor
General of the Lands of this Province, who departed this
life Octr 19t 1765. Aged 44 Years. After labouring ten of
them under the severest Bodily Afflictions brought on by

Change of Climate and tho' She went to her Native Land
receiv'd no relief but returnd & bore them with
uncommon Resolution and Resignation to the last.

Having gone South for the benefit of his health, Robert Mitchell,
died 1808, aged 32, was buried in St. Paul's churchyard, Augusta,
Georgia, with this comment on his tombstone:

> He left his home in search
> Of health, but sunk under his
> Disease at Augusta.

An epitaph in Steele Creek Presbyterian churchyard, near Charlotte,
North Carolina, reads:

> Sacred
> to the Memory of
> John Lees,
> who after a painful illness of five
> days, died on the 22nd of Dec.
> 1817, Aged 19 years.
> He died on his way to Charleston
> 5 miles above Monks Corner.
> His tender and affectionate Father
> had his corpse put in a coffin and
> brought home, and buried here, on
> the 8th day after he died. He had
> left his Mother, Brothers, and Sisters
> with a wish to see the City of
> Charleston. But was stopped short
> of his expectations, and brought
> home a corpse to his Mother.
> "Diseases are thy servants, Lord,
> They come at thy command.
> I'll not attempt a murmuring word
> Against thy chastening hand."

The following lines are inscribed to George Augustus Clough, died
"suddenly of Stranger's fever," in 1843, aged 22, in St. Michael's churchyard, Charleston, South Carolina:

Of all thy kindred at thy dying day
Were none to speed thee on thy solemn way;
Yet ever lives distinct and deeply dear
Their sight with them of this thy corner here;
Each heart so oft hath come and sought and seen
That ocean space hath shrunk to naught between,
And more their own seems now the stranger's shore
Than when with thee they dwelt on it before.

Since God doth early break the golden bowl,
And loose the silver cord that links the soul
To earth, His will be done. Oh, may he rise
A chosen vessel to a heavenly prize.

The first eight lines were written by a brother, Arthur Hugh Clough, the English poet, and the last four by another brother, Charles.

Precaution against infection is suggested on a board marker in Boothill Graveyard, Tombstone, Arizona:

John Blair
Died of Smallpox
Cowboy Throwed Rope
over Feet and dragged him
To his Grave.

Cut into the rock bluff on Rainsford's Island, Boston Harbor, is a reminder of the epidemic of 1832 when victims were isolated at that place:

Nearby these gray rocks
Enclos'd in a box
Lies Hatter Cox
Who died of smallpox.

Inoculation brought death to Jonathan Tute, died 1763, aged 14, whose inscription in North Cemetery, Vernon, Vermont, reads in part:

But tho' His Spirits fled on high
His body mould'ring here must lie
Behold the amazing alteration
Effected by Inoculation

The means Employed his Life to save
Hurried Him Headlong to the Grave.

An implied slur at the medical profession is found in many old graveyards:

Affliction sore long time I bore
Physicians were in vain
Till death gave ease and God did please
To ease my grief and pain.

Charles Dickens in *David Copperfield* (1849) describes the young and restless hero in Blunderstone, Suffolk, during a church service. During his wayward musings, the boy thinks of this epitaph on a near-by monument: "I look up at the monumental tablets on the wall, and try to think of Mr. Bodgers late of this parish, and what the feelings of Mrs. Bodgers must have been, when affliction sore, long time Mr. Bodgers bore, and physicians were in vain. I wonder whether they called in Mr. Chillip, and he was in vain; and if so, how he likes to be reminded of it once a week."

A bitter denunciation of the medical profession is found on the tombstone of Ruth Sprague, died 1816, aged 9, in Maple Grove Cemetery, Hoosick Falls, New York. After the girl's burial, Roderick R. Clow, a student, exhumed the grave and removed the body to a local doctor's laboratory for study. When the remains were recovered the following words were inscribed on the stone:

She was stolen from the grave
by Roderick R. Clow & dissected at Dr. P. M. Armstrong's office
in Hoosick, N. Y. from which place
her mutilated remains were
obtained & deposited here.
Her body dissected by fiendish **Men**
Her bones anatomised,
Her soul we trust has risen to **God**
Where few Physicians rise.

On Wednesday, 29 May 1878, the body of former Congressman John Scott Harrison, son of President William Henry Harrison and father of President Benjamin Harrison, was interred in Congress Green Cemetery, North Bend, Ohio. As the mourners paid their final tribute, it was noticed that a newly closed grave close by had been opened and was empty. The Harrison family then placed a huge stone on the Congressman's grave and posted a guard at the spot. The following morning the mourners went to the old Medical College on Sixth Street, Cincinnati, to secure the body taken from the grave next to their plot. The laws prohibited the securing of bodies in a legitimate fashion, so "resurrectionists" throughout the Midwest undertook to supply the medical schools in any way they might devise. At the Medical College the Harrisons did not find the body they sought but found, instead, that of the Congressman.

On the grave of Frances Cerny, died 1902, aged 6, in St. Mary's Cemetery, Winona, Minnesota, is this indignant comment:

Killed by unskilled Dr.

The following blunt epitaph is found in Oasis Cemetery near West Branch, Iowa:

Ralph A	John R
Died	Died
Feb 15 1861	Mar 30 1871
Aged	Aged
2 yr 6 m	2 months
& 30 ds	& 27 ds

Children of
R. & T. Akers
Let Medical Science loom up
High as it will
The Order of Quacks
Will stick to it still.

In the old graveyard near the Unitarian Church, Barnstable, Massachusetts, are stones to a doctor and his wife. The front of the doctor's monument indicates the pride of ancestry:

Dr. Thomas Wd Fossett
Born 1813
9th son of Obil

and
Grandson of John Fossett
and
Great, great, great grandson
of Patrick of Ireland
John's mother was Scotch
I am over 80 years of age.

On the reverse side is his record in medicine:

I have practiced on the eclectic system
in Mass., Ohio and Mich., for over 50 years
and have never lost that number of patients.

The inscription on the stone to Emily Fossett, died 1885, aged 72, reads:

Here lies my body
Mouldering to clay
But the spirit has
Flown to the realms of day,
Where all can dwell
in peace and love
In the beautiful city
The fair courts above.
I conversed with the spirits of the dead for
forty years, as with the living.

This noteworthy tribute on the monument in Margaretville, New York, to Dr. Gordon Bostwick Maurer, accidentally shot while hunting in 1938, aged 39, was originally an editorial in the *Catskill Mountain News:*

Thirteen years ago there came here a city
chap, trained in one of the great universities.
The other members of his class went to
"Big Towns."
He, with the best records of them all, wanted
to begin the practice of medicine in a country
village.

He had compiled a list of prospective
communities. He looked over several and
chose us.

An untried city college boy with magic hands,
a keen vision, and uncanny knowledge of both
the human body and the soul which activates it.

Soon after arrival he was called upon to
care for a life given up as lost. He saved it.

He began to save others. He worked day and
night. When he did not have proper apparatus
or appliances he built some. When the snows kept
him from patients he constructed a snowmobile.

Neither storm nor night nor mud nor snow
kept him from the sick. He took people into his
home. It became a veritable hospital.

The fame of the boy spread throughout the
section. Men and women from all walks of life
asked for his attention.

The community built a hospital that he and
others might the better care for those who
needed care, medication and operation.

He continued. When a tired body all but
gave up, he took a year out and returned to
Yale for special work that he might come
home and serve better.

He had tired of city pastimes. The lure of the
country had been breathed into his soul.
Camp, rod and gun, open fires, life in the great
outdoors gave zest, relief, happiness.

He loved our hills, our mode of life. He knew
our ambitions. He smiled at our shortcomings.

He gave freely. Much of the work he did was
without charge. Few knew the extent of his
help to those who needed help. He served as
few had ever served here before.

He was physician, parson, priest, confessor. We
told him both our physical and mental
troubles. And he put us back on the road
to reason and living.

Thirteen years he served. It was a life work
worth while.

Today our hearts are numb at his loss. Our
senses befogged to know how to live
without him. May we turn from the tragedy
of the golden Indian Summer morning that
knew his death.

And in the bleak days of the approaching
Thanksgiving season thank God for those
thirteen years.

The epitaph to Clara Barton, "Angel of the Battlefield" and founder
of the American Red Cross, died 1912, aged 90, in Burial Knoll, North
Oxford, Massachusetts, is a quotation from one of her letters:

Nature has provided cure and final rest
for all the heartache that mortals are
called to endure.

A congenial doctor of Pawtucket, Rhode Island, long in the habit of
accepting the meal check at a local drugstore where he and his cronies
congregated, inscribed a large boulder, now marking his grave in Oak
Grove Cemetery, with these words:

William P. Rothwell M.D.
1866-1939
This is on me ℞

The laconic epitaph to Dr. Fred Roberts, died 1931, aged 56, in
Pine Log Cemetery, Brookland, Arkansas, reads:

Office up stairs.

Briefly stated is the sentiment on the gravestone of Dr. J. J. Subers,
died 1916, aged 78, in Rosehill Cemetery, Macon, Georgia:

Been Here
and Gone
Had a Good Time.

Victims of Chance and Circumstance

In the Old School Baptist churchyard, near Roxbury, New York, is a stone listing the children of Timothy and Eleanor Corbin. The death of David, died 1839, aged 1, is explained in this manner:

> His death was produced by being spured in
> the head by a rooster.

Transcribed in the old Ross Park Cemetery, Williamsport, Pennsylvania, before the site was cleared for the city hall, is an epitaph to Henry Harris, died 1837, aged 15, which says that he was killed

> by the kick of a colt
> in his bowels.
> Peaceable and quiet, a friend to
> his father and mother, and respected
> by all who knew him, and went
> to the world where horses
> don't kick, where sorrows and weeping
> is no more.

An earlier tragedy is described on a monument in the Old South Cemetery, Montague, Massachusetts:

> In Memory of Mr. Elijah Bardwell
> who died Janry 26th 1786 in ye 27th

Year of his Age having but a few days
surviv'd ye fatal Night when he was
flung from his Horse & drawn by ye Stirrup
26 rods along ye path as appear'd by ye place
where his hat was found & where he had
Spent ye whole following severe cold night
treading ye Snow in a Small Circle.

The top of the monument is in the shape of a clock, with the hands
set at twelve-thirty.

A memorial stone in Center, North Dakota, commemorates the heroism of Hazel Miner, died 1920, aged 15, who during a prairie blizzard
froze to death even as she saved the lives of a younger brother and
sister by protecting them with her own body:

To the dead a tribute
To the living a memory
To posterity an inspiration
The Story
Of
Her Life
And Of
Her Heroic
Tragic Death
Is Recorded
In The
Archives Of
Oliver County
On Pages 130-131
Book-H
Misc. Records
Stranger Read It.

The dangers of carriage riding are chronicled on the tombstone of
Mary Blue, died 1825, aged 33, in Gravesville, New York:

Sudden and awful was the sight
To see the horses take a flight

Thrown from the caraige to the ground
Breathing her last when she was found.

The commentary on the stone to Timothy Ryan, died 1814, in Greenwood Cemetery, near Manchester, New York, is ironical:

A thousand ways cut short our days; none are exempt
from death.
A honey bee, by stinging me, did stop my mortal breath.
This grave contains the last remains of my frail house
of clay;
My soul is gone, not to return, to our eternal day.

In Elmwood Cemetery, Holyoke, Massachusetts, is this epitaph:

In Memory of
Mr. Nath. Parks,
AEt 19, who on
21st March 1794
Being out a hunt-
ing and conceal'd
in a Ditch was
Casually shot by
Mr. Luther
Frink.

A gravestone to Jotham W. Curtiss, died 1842, aged 22, at Fitchville, Ohio, reads:

Mr. Curtis was accidently
Shot by a rifle in the hands
of Mr. Chester Mais his
brother in law on the 30 of
Nov. 1842, while they were
in Company hunting deer.

The tragedy which brought to a close the life of Elihu Fowler, died 1784, aged 3, is permanently recorded on a tombstone in Milford, Connecticut:

His Life a Span—the Mournful toll
Declares the exit of his Soul

Grim death is come
His life is called
To take its flight
The means a scald.

The death of a four-year-old member of the Cubberly family in 1843 is explained on a gravestone in Baptist churchyard, Hamilton Square, New Jersey:

The boiling coffee did on me fall,
And by it I was slain,
But Christ has bought my liberty,
And in Him I'll rise again.

In the same place is a stone to another child, Lockhart Tindall, died 1799, who fell head first into the hopper of a cider mill:

The apple wheel did roll on me
And by it I was slain,
But Christ has bought my liberty,
In Him I'll rise again.

The tombstone of Peter Baker, died 1887, aged 24, in Deer Park Methodist churchyard, Smallwood, Maryland, reads:

Here lieth our Son dead
Someone struck him on the
head.

Inscribed on a marble shaft in Mount Pleasant Cemetery, Newark, New Jersey, is the following:

Andrew C. Hand
Born March 12th, 1842
that Cherry Tree of luscious fruit
beguiled him too high a branch did break
and down he fell and broke his neck and
died July 13th, 1862.

The following identifies the grave of Marvin Westbrook, died 1824, aged 7, in a private burial ground in Aroostook County, Maine:

Here I lie and no wonder I'm dead,
I fell from a tree,
Roll'd over dead.

An epitaph in Girard, Pennsylvania, comments:

In memory of
Ellen Shannon
Aged 26 Years
Who was fatally burned
March 21st 1870
by the explosion of a lamp
filled with "R. E. Danforth's
Non Explosive
Burning Fluid"

Nathaniel Ledyard and four other youths were killed in June 1766 when a schoolhouse full of fireworks and powder collected for a celebration of the repeal of the Stamp Act blew up. His inscription in Ancient Burying Ground, Hartford, Connecticut, reads:

Just when delivered from her brooding fears
My cheerful country wiped away her tears
Materials wrought the public joy to aid
With dire explosion snapped my vital thread
And life's rich zest, the bliss of being free
Proved the sad cause of bitter death to me.

The stone to Captain Joseph Talcott in Silver Street Cemetery, Coventry, Connecticut, records that he was

Casually Drowned in the Proud Waters of
Scungamug river on the 10 day of June
1789 in ye 62nd year of his age.

Divine intervention brought to a close the life of Henry Cooke, "whose death was caused by bathing being taken in a fit & immediately expired," 1789, aged 15, according to his marker in Edgartown, Massachusetts:

> Just as this youth began to tower
> And tender branches spread
> Almighty God to show his power
> Did strike the prospect dead.

The parents of Abel McMahon, died 1844, aged 2, described on his tombstone in Center Cemetery, New Milford, Connecticut, their tragic experience:

> In a moment he fled
> He ran to the cistern, and raised the lid
> His father looked in, then did behold
> His child lay dead and cold.

When Abial Perkins, died 1826, aged 13, was drowned, his gravestone in Center Cemetery near Plainfield, Vermont, was inscribed:

> This Blooming Youth in Health Most Fair
> To His Uncle's Mill-pond did repair
> Undressed himself and so plunged in
> But never did come out again.

Parish Burial Grounds, Kittery Point, Maine, has a stone to Margaret Hills, died 1803, aged 28, which records:

> I lost my life in the raging seas
> A sovereign God does as he please
> The Kittery friends they did appear
> And my remains they buried here.

Caution is the counsel of this epitaph from Oakwood Cemetery, Montgomery, Alabama:

> Stop as you pass my grave.
> Here I,
> John Schockler, R . . . EY
> rest my remains.
> I was born in New Orleans
> the 22nd of November, 1811,
> was brought up by good

friends: not taking their
advice was drowned
in this city
in the Ala. River
the 27th day of May, 1855.
Now I warn all young and old,
to beware of the dangers of
this river, see how I am fixed
in this watery grave. I have
got but two friends to mourn.

On a grave marker in Folsom, New Mexico, is this tribute:

In honored memory of
Sarah J. Rooke
Telephone Operator
Who perished in the flood waters
of the Dry Cimarron at Folsom
New Mexico, August 27, 1908
while at her switchboard warning
others of the danger. With heroic
devotion she glorified her calling
by sacrificing her own life that
others might live.

David Dean, died 1783, aged 27, whose epitaph is in Pine Hill Cemetery, East Taunton, Massachusetts, apparently fell from a superstructure during the building of a house:

Nine feet in height upon a stage
Active in health, in bloom of age
But suddenly the stage gave way
He falls and dies, here ends his day.

This inscription is found in Unitarian churchyard, Charleston, South Carolina:

Fatal

ACCIDENT

in the midst of life we are in

DEATH

13 yrs, 1 mo, and 19 days
Terminated the existence of Master
Charles Cleary
Hapless boy! on the 31st of May, 1813
accidentally fell from the lofty walls
of St. Paul's Church, when the immortal
part instantly ascended to the Church
triumphant on high, the abode of
unembodied Spirits, from whose
bourne no traveller returns
Bereaved Parents, Brothers and Sisters,
Also ye youthful COMPANIONS, Come
hither, Behold the narrow Lodging.
Read, go away, Reflect, return again,
and view the fate of your beloved
CHARLES.

A remarkable coincidence is related in an epitaph from Old Pleasant Street Cemetery, Athol, Massachusetts:

In Memory of
Luke Jones Garfield,
eldest son of
Mr. George & Mrs. Polly Garfield.
He was killed instantly
by the fall of a tree.
June 10, 1819,
aged 11 years, 9 mos. & 9 days.
Singular: Luke Jones
for whom he was named,
was instantly killed at the
same age & time in the year.

The gravestone of John Stockbridge, died 1768, aged 26, in Hanover Center, Massachusetts, records that he was

of fair and unblemished character, in deport-
ment and verulous . . . whose mortality has render-

ed the male issue of that branch of that respectable family extinct . . . His death was sudden,
premature, awfull and violent. Providentially
occasioned by the fall of a tree . . . No sums can
purchase such a grant that man shall never die.

This inscription in Old Farm Hill Cemetery, Middletown, Connecticut, tells of a victim of overpowering odds:

Joshua
Son of Mr Joshua
& Mrs Anna Miller
who was killed with a
Sawmill May 26th
AD 1781 in the 15th
year of his age.

A stone in Old Cemetery, Southwick, Massachusetts, records:

In memory of
Julius Lee
who was exploded
in a powder
mill
July 13, 1821
AE 21.

Elisha Woodruff, sawmill operator, died 1816, aged 70, is buried in
the Old Burial Ground, near Pittsford, Vermont, with an epitaph that
reads:

How shocking to the human mind
The log did him to powder grind.
God did command his soul away
His summings we must all obey.

These words commemorate the victims of a mine disaster who were
buried in a common grave in Bay View Cemetery, Bellingham, Washington:

In memory of the men who died at
Blue Canyon, April 8, 1895

"They were the tenements, the shells
of the souls of a company of Knights
Of Labor, which had received sudden
                                    orders
And crossed the river of death in a body."

A nineteenth-century explanation of lightning is given on a tomb-stone on Burial Hill, Plymouth, Massachusetts:

Bathsheba James, wife of Capt. William Holmes
Mariner and daughter to Capt. Joseph Doten Do.
She was kill'd instantaneously in a Thunder
storm by the Electrich fluid of lightning on
the 6th of July, 1830, aged 35 years and 26 days.

A stone in Bow Wow Cemetery, Sheffield, Massachusetts, marks the grave of Simon Willard, died 1766, aged 60:

Stop here, ye Gay
& ponder what ye doeth
Blue lightnings flew &
Swiftly seized my Breath
A more tremendous
flash will fill the skies
When I and all that sleep in death shall rise.

An epitaph on the left side of a double tombstone in Framingham Center, Massachusetts, reads:

In Memory of Mr
John Cloyes
who being struck with Light-
ning died June ye 3d. Anno Dom.
1777 in ye 42 year of his age.
O may you all both far and near,
Who of this dispensation hear,
Now hearken to the Call of Heaven
And take the Warning God has given.
Surprising Death to you soon may
Come in some unexpected way.

I pray that all make it their care
For sudden Death now to Prepare.

This is inscribed on the right side:

> In Memory of
> Abraham Rice
> who departed this Life in a
> sudden & Awful manner & as we
> trust enterd. a better June ye
> 3d. Anno Dom. 1777 in ye 81st
> Year of his Age.
> My trembling Heart with Grief overflows
> While I Record the death of those
> Who died by Thunder sent from Heaven,
> In Seventeen hundred and seventy seven.
> Let's all prepare for Judgment Day,
> As we may be Called out of Time,
> And in a sudden and awful way,
> While in our Youth and in our Prime.

Death by suffocation is described on a tombstone in the Old Village Cemetery, Claremont, New Hampshire:

> Chester and Elisha Putnam, sons of
> the late Capt. Solomon Putnam who,
> on the morning of the 29th of January,
> 1814, in the same bed were found suf-
> focated. A kettle of common coals hav-
> ing been placed in their room for com-
> fort proved the fatal instrument of
> their death; the former in the 27th,
> the latter in the 19th year of his age.
> How many roses perish in their bloom,
> How many suns alas go down at noon.

Mary Points was burned to death when her flowing skirts caught fire and her inscription in Aberdeen, Mississippi, is beneath the image of an attractive woman's face surrounded by sweeping flames:

To my
Mary
in Heaven
January 11, 1852
Wife of
Jacob C. Points

In an old family cemetery in Barnstead, New Hampshire, is a grave-stone to Joseph Salter, died 1802, aged 17, who "ascended in the flames of a Mansion house, on yonder Hill: Saturday morning . . . at 4 o'clock AM." At the bottom is a fitting verse from Isaiah 24:15: "Glorify ye the Lord in the Fires."

The whole tragedy of the great Chicago fire is abbreviated in a simple inscription in Rosehill Cemetery, Chicago:

Abbie Lomax,
Died Nov. 23 1871,
Aged 6 months.
Here lies a dear relic
Of the great Chicago fire.

Two men, apparently members of some kind of a bucket brigade, are honored in Meeting House Hill Cemetery, Ashburnham, Massachusetts:

In	In
memory of	memory of
Mr.	Mr.
Ebenezer Jones	Jonathan Wood
who fell in his well	who died in a well
from which the vital air	from which the vital
had been extracted by	air had been extracted
the burning of	by the burning of a
his house near it	house near it
Sept. 1, 1825	Sept. 1, 1825
Aet. 35	Erected by subscription
Erected by subscription	

A monument near the road three miles north of Goldsboro, North Carolina, indicates the site of a fatal automobile accident:

Burnette
In remembrance of Sister
Annie Cotton Burnette
Born May 25, 1873
Was burned to death at
This place in an
automobile wreck
Aug. 13 1924
Age 51 yrs. 2 mos. 19 days.
Prepare to meet thy God.

In Idlewild Cemetery, Hood River, Oregon, is this inscription to another victim of an automobile accident:

ASAD EXPERIENCE WILSON
1895   1946

His mother had given him the name when he was born out of wedlock.

Crime and Punishment

In 1789 Samuel Frost, after murdering his father, was acquitted on a plea of insanity, but four years later, after killing Elisha Allen, his guardian, with a hoe, he was sentenced to death and hanged. Allen's tombstone on Meeting House Hill, Princeton, Massachusetts, records:

In memory of
Capt. Elisha Allen,
who was inhumanly mur-
dered by Samuel Frost,
July 16th 1793
Aged 48 years.
Passengers behold! my friends and view
Breathless I lie; no more with you;
Hurried from life, sent to the grave;
Jesus my only hope to save;
No warning had of my sad fate
Till dire the stroke, alas! too late.

In Meeting House Hill Cemetery, New Boston, New Hampshire, is an inscription to a young woman murdered by a jealous suitor:

Sevilla
daughter of
George & Sarah
Jones
Murdered by
Henry N. Sargent
Jan. 13, 1854
Aet. 17 yrs. & 9 mos.
Thus fell this lovely blooming daughter,
By the revengeful hand a malicious Henry.
When on her way to school he met her
And with a six self cocked pistol shot her.

Henry, regretting his tragic act, asked that he might be buried in the same grave but was denied his request. He took his own life and is buried in the same graveyard with these lines:

Henry N.
Son of Daniel and
Charlotte Sargent
Died Jan. 13, 1854
Aet 23 Yrs & 5 Mos
Murderer of
Sevilla Jones

These words are carved into a common field stone in Pioneer Cemetery, Austinburg, Pennsylvania:

Samuel H. Ives
Son of Titus Ives was
murdered by
Rob Douglas
Aug. 25, 1824 A.D.
23 yrs. 2 mo. and 13 days.

The stone to the Reverend William Richardson, died 1771, aged 42, in Waxhaw Presbyterian churchyard, near Lancaster, South Carolina, does not mention his manner of death or of the subsequent effort

SEVILLA,
daughter of
George & Sarah
JONES.
Murdered by
HENRY N. SARGENT
Jan. 13. 1854.
Æt. 17 yrs. & 9 mos.

Thus fell this lovely blooming daughter
By the revengeful hand-a malicious Henry.
When on her way to school he met her.
And with a six self cocked pistol shot her.

Tombstone of Sevilla Jones, Meeting House Hill Cemetery, New Boston, New Hampshire. See p. 129.

to determine guilt by a curious custom of that time. He was found in
his room in a kneeling position with a bridle tightly drawn about his
neck. Whether he was a victim of someone's evil scheme or whether
he took his own life has never been learned, but when his beautiful
wife married George Dunlap within a year the parishioners began to
talk. They charged foul play, exhumed the body of Richardson, and
the widow was made to touch the corpse. Blood would flow, it was
believed, when a murderer's hand touched a victim. The ordeal was,
however, inconclusive and the people's minds were set at rest.

After Isaiah Wright "was shot and instantly killed near his own
house on the evening of Jan. 10, 1863, aged 41 yrs." his widow had this
epitaph put on his tombstone at West Barnstable, Massachusetts:

> Dear Husband, thou has left me
> Without one parting word
> But I hope in Heaven to meet you
> And there to dwell with God.
> I hope that God will spare me
> To hear thy murderer's doom,
> Then I hope to be prepared
> To leave this world and come.

These lines come from Old Cone Cemetery near Pittsfield, New
York:

> Reuben, Son of Hamblin & Tirza
> Gregory age 19 years who was
> shot 30th Sept. 1832, by George
> Denison who like a demon in
> human shape coolly took
> his life away.

A spectacular event in Worcester County, Massachusetts, during the
period of the Revolutionary War was the hanging of a woman and
the three men who killed her husband. The victim's epitaph in Brookfield says:

> Joshua Spooner
> Murdered Mar. 1, 1778,
> by three soldiers of the
> Revolution,

Ross, Brooks and Buchanan,
At the instigation of
his wife, Bathsheba.
They were all executed
at Worcester
July 2, 1778.

In Village Cemetery, Wethersfield, Connecticut, is this record of a domestic tragedy:

Here lie Interred Mrs. Lydia Beadle
Aged 32 years, Ansell Lothrop Elizabeth
Lydia & Mary Beadle her children; the
eldest aged 11 and the youngest 6 years,
who, on the morning of the 11th day of
Dec'r. 1782, Fell by the hands of William
Beadle, an infatuated Man, who closed the
horrid sacrifice of his Wife and Children
with his own destruction.
Pale, round their grassy tomb bedew'd with tears,
Flit the thin forms of sorrows, and of fears;
Soft sighs responsive swell to plaintive chords,
And Indignations half unsheath their swords.

In Hatfield Cemetery near Omar, West Virginia, stands a statue of "Devil Anse" Hatfield, died 1921, aged 82. This silent reminder of the famous Hatfield-McCoy family feud is a life-size figure of the bearded leader who is shown in frock coat and riding habit. On the granite pedestal are inscribed the names of his thirteen children.

A gravestone in Paris, Kentucky, comments:

George W. Watters
Born Oct. 20, 1827
Murdered in Cin. O. June 1st, 1862
Here lies an honest man, but an imprudent one.

The story of a poisoning is found on a tombstone in Knight's Corner Burying Ground, Pelham, Massachusetts:

> Warren Gibbs
> died by arsenic poison
> Mar. 23, 1860.
> AE. 36 yrs. 5 mos.
> 23 dys.
> Think my friends when this you see
> How my wife hath dealt by me
> She in some oysters did prepare
> Some poison for my lot and share
> Then of the same I did partake
> And nature yielded to its fate
> Before she my wife became
> Mary Felton was her name.
> Erected by his Brother
> Wm. Gibbs.

Town tradition fails to concur in William's explanation.

In Goshen Mill Village, New Hampshire, is this epitaph to Mary L. Rowell, died 1854, aged 17:

> Deeply beloved while on earth
> Deeply lamented in death
> Distracted and dead.
> Borne down by two cruel oppressors

Mary hung herself after gossips had linked her to the theft of a pair of black lace mitts.

For sixteen years, from 13 February 1866 to 3 April 1882, the thirty or more persons in the outlaw gang of Jesse James were the terror of railroads and banks from Minnesota to Texas and from the Rocky Mountains to West Virginia. Their exploits came to an end when James, living quietly under the name of Mr. Howard in St. Joseph, Missouri, was shot by twenty-year-old Robert Ford, a member of his gang who apparently wished to claim a $10,000 reward. The funeral of James, a son of a frontier minister, was held in the Baptist Church, Kearney, Missouri, and burial was at the family farm near Kearney. There his mother, who kept a long vigil near the grave, had a white marble slab inscribed:

In Loving Memory of My Beloved Son
Jesse W. James
Died April 3, 1882
Aged 34 Years, 6 Months, 28 Days
Murdered by a Traitor and Coward Whose
Name Is Not Worthy to Appear Here.

Twenty years later James' body was exhumed from the seven-foot grave and reinterred in Mount Olivet Cemetery, Kearney. The second burial was accompanied with military honors, for the outlaw had been engaged in guerrilla activities during the Civil War. All but the foundation of the marker has been taken by souvenir hunters.

When Frank James, Jesse's brother and companion, died in 1915, aged 72, his body was cremated and the ashes were deposited successively in the New England Safe Deposit Company, Kansas City, and the Kearney Trust Company. In 1944, the ashes were scattered, it is believed, over the Missouri River near Independence.

The tomb of Silas W. Sanderson, justice of the Supreme Court of California, died 1886, aged 62, in the recently cleared Laurel Hill Cemetery, San Francisco, was inscribed:

Final Decree.

The tribute on the monument to William Scott, justice of the Supreme Court of Missouri, died 1862, aged 58, in Woodlawn Cemetery, Jefferson City, Missouri, reads:

This monument is a supplement to the more enduring one which he builded for himself by his lucid
and just decisions.

The integrity of one member of the bar is described on the gravestone of Charles Elliot, died 1756, in Christ Episcopal churchyard, New Bern, North Carolina:

An Honest Lawyer Indeed.

Before his death, a Rockford, Illinois, lawyer specified that his headstone in Willwood Cemetery should comment:

Goembel
John E.
1867-1945
His Wives
Minnie Groskopf
1870-1936
Agnes V. Johnson
1886-1936
"The Defense Rests"

When Col. William L. Saunders, secretary of state in North Carolina, was called in 1871 to testify in a Congressional investigation of the Ku Klux Klan, he refused to answer the questions put to him. He died in 1891 and his tombstone in Calvary Episcopal churchyard, Tarboro, North Carolina, recalls this incident:

I decline to answer.

On the front pedestal of the monument to Eugene Talmadge, former governor of Georgia, died 1946, aged 62, on the State Capitol grounds, Atlanta, are the words:

A superb orator
A safe but progressive
Administrator
Of public trusts.

On the opposite side is a quotation:

"I may
Surprise you—
But I shall not
Deceive you."

E. T.

This noble tribute marks the grave of James Louis Petigru, jurist, orator, statesman and patriot, died 1863, aged 73, in St. Michael's churchyard, Charleston, South Carolina:

Future times will hardly know how great a life
This simple stone commemorates.
The tradition of his Eloquence, his
Wisdom and Wit may fade;

But he lived for ends more durable than fame,
His eloquence was the protection of the poor and wronged
  His learning illuminated the principles of Law.
   In the admiration of his Peers,
    In the respect of his People,
   In the affection of his Family,
    His was the highest place;
     The just meed
    Of his kindness and forbearance
    His dignity and simplicity
His brilliant Genius and his unwearied industry.
    Unawed by Opinion,
    Unseduced by Flattery,
    Undismayed by disaster,
  He confronted Life with antique Courage
   And Death with Christian Hope.
    In the great Civil War
  He withstood his People for his Country
  But his People did homage to the Man
Who held his conscience higher than their praise;
    And his Country
Heaped her honours on the grave of the Patriot,
    To whom, living,
   His own righteous self-respect sufficed,
    Alike for Motive and Reward.
"Nothing is here for tears, nothing to wait
Or Knock the breast, no weakness, no contempt,
Dispraise or blame, nothing but well and fair
And what may quiet us in a life so noble."

Each by His Own Trade

The occupations of persons are represented by a variety of inscriptional devices. The best-known American epitaph of this type is one Benjamin Franklin wrote for himself, which exists in several versions. The earliest known printed version appeared in an almanac for 1771 published by Nathaniel Ames in Boston the preceding year:

The Body of BENJAMIN FRANKLIN,
Printer,
Like the Covering of an old Book,
Its Contents torn out,
And stript of its Lettering and Gilding,
Lies here, Food for Worms;
But the Work shall not be lost,
It will (as he believed) appear once more,
In a new and more beautiful Edition,
Corrected and amended
By the Author.

Franklin's pride in his profession found expression, too, in his will, the opening words of which are "I, Benjamin Franklin, Printer, late Minister Plenipotentiary from the United States of America to the Court of France, now President of Pennsylvania . . ." When he died in 1790 he was buried in Christ churchyard, Philadelphia. His early epitaph was not used. Instead the wishes expressed in his will were respected: "I wish to be buried by the side of my wife, if it may be, and that a marble stone, to be made by Chambers, six feet long, four feet wide, plain, with only a small moulding round the upper edge, and this inscription:

$$\left.\begin{array}{c}\text{Benjamin}\\\text{and}\\\text{Deborah}\end{array}\right\} \begin{array}{l}\text{Franklin}\\\text{178-}\end{array}$$

A contemporary printer wrote an inscription using the symbols of printing:

> Benjamin Franklin, a * in his profession;
> the type of honesty; and ! of all; and
> although the ☞ of death put a . to his
> existence, each § of his life is without
> a ||.

An earlier example of the printing simile was written by Benjamin Woodbridge in an elegy on John Cotton, who died in 1652. Woodbridge's elegy, sixty-six lines in length, said in part:

> A Living Breathing *Bible;* Tables where
> Both *Covenants,* at Large, engraven were;
> *Gospel* and *Law* in's Heart, had each its Column;
> His Head an Index to the Sacred Volume;
> His very Name a *Title-Page;* and next,
> His Life a *Commentary* on the Text.
> Oh, What a Monument of Glorious Worth,
> When in a *New Edition,* he comes forth,
> Without *Errata's,* may we think he'l be
> In *Leaves* and *Covers of Eternity!*

Cotton was buried in the King's Chapel Burying Ground in Boston. His tomb no longer exists, and today little is known about it. Cotton's daughter Maria married Increase Mather and became the mother of Cotton Mather, who included Woodbridge's elegy in *Magnalia Christi Americana* (1702).

A diamond-shaped monument in Bennett's Cemetery near Canisteo, New York, is inscribed with words reminiscent of Franklin's words:

> In memory of Thial Clark, the Jeweler,
> who has quit running but is wound up
> in hopes of being taken in hand by the
> Supreme Master machinist for repairs
> and to be adjusted and set running for
> the world to come again.
> So mote it be.

A similar reading is found in Hanover Center, Massachusetts:

> This small stone points out the spot
> where the immortal part of Mrs Olive
> Josselyn, wife of Mr Stockbridge Josselyn,
> left its clay tenement, to smoulder
> into dust, till it shall again by its Master
> Builder be repaired and fitted up for
> immortality.
> Died Sept 10 1803
> Aged 35 yrs

A family of publishers are remembered by an unusual marker in Greenwood Cemetery, Bristol, Vermont. A white marble stone is set into the iron frame of an old-fashioned printing press. The frame and stone are supported by two arch-type legs. Inscribed on the front and back of the stone are the names of ten members of the Wilson family, printers of *The Bristol Herald*. The earliest date is that of Myron F. Wilson, died 1892, and the latest that of James S. Wilson, died 1941.

Lorenzo Ferguson, a journalist, is buried in Crown Hill Cemetery, Atlanta, Georgia, where his tombstone is identified by his pen name and an appropriate comment:

> Fuzzy
> Woodruff
> 1884-1929
> "Copy All In"

A pyramid constructed of more than 30,000 stones collected by newsboys in many parts of the world marks the grave of John E. Gunckel, founder of the National Newsboys' Association, died 1914, aged 68, in Woodlawn Cemetery, Toledo, Ohio. Inscribed is the following tribute:

The Newsboys' Friend

John Elstner Gunckel

"There was a man sent from God whose name was John."

Toledo Honors

a citizen without reproach

a friend without pretence

a philanthropist without display

a Christian without hypocrisy.

Surmounting a five-foot shaft in Evergreen Cemetery, New Haven, Vermont, is a marble anvil. The grave is that of a former village smithy, Clinton Tyler, died 1897, aged 46. The anvil is inscribed:

Master of the Art.

Below is the image of a horseshoe.

In a similar manner, an anvil and hammer, mounted on a stone pedestal, mark the grave of Alfred Hargrave, blacksmith, died 1898, aged 78, in Pine Forest Cemetery, Wilmington, North Carolina.

A log-shaped monument in Walnut Grove Cemetery, near Delphos, Ohio, marks the grave of Isaac Thurston, died 1914, aged 74, and is inscribed:

He sawed logs for forty years

But he won't saw this one.

Buried with his tools in Island Cemetery, Newport, Rhode Island, is a carpenter, George Whitehead, died 1870, aged 71. His tombstone reads:

My trowel and hammer lies decline

So does my rule and my line

My building is up my course is run

My scaffold struck my work is done.

The monument to Chester L. Graves, a carpenter, died 1923, aged 74, in Woodlawn Cemetery, Wellsville, New York, is inscribed with a picture of a house and the words:

Pyramid marking the grave of John E. Gunckel, Woodlawn Cemetery, Toledo, Ohio. See p. 140.

THOS. M. CAMPBELL
BORN
SEPT. 15, 1862.
DIED AUG. 22, 1884.

TRIP IS ENDED SEND MY SAMPLES HOME

Monument marking the grave of Thomas W. Campbell, Aspen Grove Cemetery, Burlington, Iowa. See p. 141.

When I've been dead ten
Thousand years
As dead as I can be
I'll have no joys I'll
Have no fears
Through all eternity.

In Sleepy Hollow Cemetery, Concord, Massachusetts, is a stone to a successful farmer who was a poor businessman, for other persons profited more than he from his labors:

Ephraim Wales Bull
The originator of the Concord Grape
Born in Boston March 4, 1806
Died in Concord September 26, 1895
He sowed, others reaped.

The epitaph to John Dana, died 1802, in Princeton, Massachusetts, warns:

Cut down at so early a period
In the midst of his commercial concerns
Let it teach thee reader to set
Thy affections on things above.

A monument in the shape of a drummer's sample case indicates the grave of Thomas W. Campbell of Chicago, a traveling salesman, died 1884, aged 21, in Aspen Grove Cemetery, Burlington, Iowa. On the stone are these words:

My Trip Is Ended.
Send My Samples Home.

Inscribed on the grave monument of Orie Elbridge Philbrick, died 1946, aged 78, in Waits River, Vermont, are the words:

And each tool is laid aside
Worn with the work that was done with pride.

Daniel Davenport, after preparing the graves of others, desired to prepare his own grave also. His headstone in North Burying Ground, Dorchester, Massachusetts, reads:

This grave was dug and finished
in the year 1833
by
Daniel Davenport, when he had been
Sexton in Dorchester 27 years.
Had attended 1135 Funerals and dug 734 graves.
As sexton, with my spade I learned
To delve beneath the sod
Where body to the earth returned
But spirit to its God.
Years 27 this toil I bore
And midst deaths oft was spared
Seven hundred graves and thirty-four
I dug, then mine I prepared.
And when at last I too must die
Some else the bell will toll
As here my mortal relics lie
May Heaven receive my soul.
He died December 24 1860
Age 87 years, 6 months, 19 days
He buried from March 3 1806
to May 12, 1852
1837 Persons.

The most colorful name in American railroad history is John Luther Jones, better known as "Casey" for Cayce, Kentucky, where he was born. He became an engineer in the service of the Illinois Central and was particularly honored among his fellows for his skill in handling his train and for his exceptional use of the train whistle. He was killed in a train wreck at Vaughan, Mississippi, in 1900. In death his hand clutched the whistle of the Cannonball Express. A Negro friend, Wallace Saunders of Canton, Mississippi, a cinder pit man, is credited with writing the first stanza of the ballad which within a few years gave the name of Casey Jones a national prominence. Jones is buried in Calvary Cemetery, Jackson, Tennessee, and his monument includes two lines from the ballad:

Tombstone of "Casey" Jones, Calvary Cemetery, Jackson, Tennessee.
See p. 142.

Headstone of Jess and Vivian Kinser, Southlawn Cemetery, Santa Cruz, California.

John Luther
Jones
1864-1900
To the memory of the locomo-
tive engineer, whose name as
'Casey Jones' became a part of
Folklore and the American
Language. 'For I'm going to run her
till she leaves the rail—or make it on
time with the southbound mail.'

Marking the grave of Willoby S. McMillan, "killed by his engine," died 1853, aged 21, in Greenridge Cemetery, Saratoga Springs, New York, are these lines:

My engine is now cold and still
No water does her boiler fill
The wood affords its flames no more
My days of usefulness are oer.

The grave of another railroad man, John Amos Barnes, died 1951, aged 77, in Bay View Cemetery, Bellingham, Washington, is inscribed:

A veteran Wabash Railroad engineer
Took his last orders and made his final trip to
a mansion in the sky.

John Snell, according to his ledger stone in Mount Hope Cemetery, Rochester, New York, was killed in 1857, aged 37, on

the New York Central Railroad
by means of an obstruction
willfully placed on the track, in the night.
But heroically keeping his post
on his engine, the Daniel Webster, to the last
he generously sacrificed his own life,
for the preservation
of the lives of those under his charge.

At the head of the stone is a carving of a wood-burning engine.

On the top of a granite monument to Charles B. Gunn, railroad conductor, died 1935, aged 88, in Evergreen Cemetery, Colorado Springs, Colorado, are the words:

Papa—Did you wind your watch.

Inscribed beneath a bas-relief sketch of a "horseless carriage" on the gravestone of George Baldwin Selden, died 1922, aged 75, in Mount Hope Cemetery, Rochester, New York, are the words:

Inventor of the
Gasoline Automobile.

A simple slab, bearing a replica of his skis, marks the grave of "Snowshoe Thomson," a mail deliverer, at Genoa, Nevada. Inscribed on the slab are the words:

In Memory of John A. Thomson
Departed this life May 15, 1876.
Aged 49 years 16 days.
Gone but not forgotten.

For nearly twenty years Thomson carried mail between Genoa and Hangtown, now Placerville. He is said to have averaged forty-five miles a day over snow thirty to forty feet deep. The people of Genoa, not then familiar with skis, mistook them for snowshoes. Thomson never received pay for this effort.

When *Clari, or, The Maid of Milan* closed after twelve performances at Covent Garden, London, in 1823, the American playwright John Howard Payne saw another in the series of failures that had become characteristic of his career. One lyric, "Home, Sweet Home," from the play, however, was to give his name a continuing fame. When he died in 1852, aged 61, he was buried in Tunis where he was serving as consul. Thirty-one years later his body was removed to Oak Hill Cemetery, Washington, D. C., and the marker to this man who never had a home of his own was inscribed:

Sure, when thy gentle spirit fled
To realms beyond the azure dome,
With arms outstretched God's angels said
Welcome to Heaven's home, sweet home.

The gravestone of Adam Allyn, a comedian, died 1768, in Trinity churchyard, New York City, comments:

> He Posesed
> Many good Qualitys
> But as he was a man
> He Had the Frailities
> Common to Mans Nature.

In Mount Hope Cemetery, Rochester, New York, the gravestone to Edward F. Hettig, died 1941, aged 65, is inscribed:

> He was eminent as an actor,
> Honored as a director;
> He played his part well
> Both in the mimic scene
> And on the stage of life.

The epitaph in Mount Pleasant Cemetery, Pleasantville, New York, of Al Shean, member of the vaudeville team of Gallagher and Shean, reads:

> Al Shean
> Beloved Father
> Born May 12, 1868
> I could have lived longer
> But now it's too late
> Absolutely Mr. Gallagher—Positively Mr. Shean
> August 12, 1949.

Inscribed on the white marble sarcophagus of Douglas Fairbanks, died 1939, aged 56, at the head of a 125-foot lagoon and spacious sunken garden in Hollywood Cemetery, Los Angeles, California, are the appropriate words from *Hamlet:*

> Good Night, Sweet Prince,
> And Flights of Angels Sing Thee to Thy Rest.

Four life-size baby elephants and a large full-grown elephant, all sculptured from Barre granite, mark the bounds of Showman's Rest in Woodlawn Cemetery, Chicago, Illinois. This is the burial place of members of the Showmen's League of America. In the center of the plot is a tablet inscribed:

> The Showmen's League of America
> maintains this plot and has erected
> this monument in memory of the
> departed showmen who lie here.

Each grave marker is uniform in size and bears only the name and date of a deceased member. The site was purchased in 1918 as a burial place for fifty-six circus personnel who were killed in an Indiana railroad wreck.

A large white marble elephant marks the grave of William F. Duggan, died 1950, aged 51, a circus owner, in Pleasant Grove Cemetery, Moultrie, Georgia, and atop a granite shaft in Somers, New York, is a wooden elephant which commemorates "Old Bet," who was brought to America by Hachaliah Bailey in 1815, and was one of the first elephants shown in this country.

"General Tom Thumb," P. T. Barnum's famous dwarf who, at maturity, reached a weight of seventy pounds and height of forty inches, died in 1883, aged 45, and is buried in Mountain Grove Cemetery, Bridgeport, Connecticut. His headstone gives his actual name, Charles S. Stratton. A few feet from the grave is a forty-foot shaft surmounted by a life-size statue. Next to the dwarf's grave in an infant's coffin lies Lavinia, died 1919, aged 78, also a dwarf. Her headstone is inscribed simply, "Wife."

An ordinary monument in Baptist Cemetery, White Plains, North Carolina, identifies the grave of another Barnum attraction, the Siamese Twins. Buried in a double-sized coffin, their double-sized marker reads:

Eng Bunker	Chang Bunker
May 11, 1811	May 11, 1811
Jan. 17, 1874	Jan. 17, 1874

Mystery long attended the visits of a veiled woman, dressed in black, to the tomb of the matinee idol, Rudolph Valentino, died 1926, aged 31, in Cathedral Mausoleum, Hollywood, California. Not only on the anniversary of Valentino's death, as newspapers have reported, but almost weekly the unidentified woman went to the crypt. In time all

manner of stories were invented. The visits, however, were not publicity stunts, as some journalists claimed, and when many other women,
all dressed in black, began their pilgrimages to the tomb, the original
visitor failed to appear again.

A weathered and nearly illegible inscription on a monument in
Greenwood Cemetery, Wellington, Ohio, describes the trials of an
ambitious young artist, Otis C. Pratt, who studied abroad until his
funds were exhausted and then returned disillusioned and bitter to
his home. Much of his subsequent life was spent as a semi-recluse. He
died in 1921, aged 76. The epitaph, which Pratt is said to have carved
himself, comments:

> Stranger: I lived in an age when
> Corruption was in our Government
> And the ballot box was beged for
> When martyred presidents and riots
> echoed over our land. When Law and
> Respect clung to the rich and shunned
> the poor. When money and fashion
> had the brains and talent went
> over the waters for want of Free
> Schools of Art supported by our
> Government. Such were the condit
> ions which caused my landscape
> discovery to decay with me as
> Nature shows.
>   Farewell.

An "inheritor of unfulfilled reknown" is described on a tombstone
in Colonial Cemetery, Savannah, Georgia:

> Sacred to the memory of
> Mr. Edward G. Malbone,
> The celebrated Painter
> Son of the late Gen. John Malbone of
> Newport, R. I.
> He was cut off in the meridian of his
> life and reputation

While traveling for the benefit of his Health.
Seldom do the records of mortality boast
The name of a victim
More pre-eminently excellent.
His death has deprived his country
Of an ornament, which
Ages may not replace, and left a blank
In the catalogue of
American genius which nothing has
A tendency to supply.
He closed his valuable life May 7, 1807
In the 29th year of his age.

A high-school principal, S. B. McCracken, erected his own monument in Elkhart, Indiana, before his death in 1933. On it are these words:

School is out
Teacher has gone home

Mrs. Joanna Winship, the first woman to teach in an American school, died 1707, aged 62, is buried in Harvard Square Cemetery, Cambridge, Massachusetts, with this epitaph:

This Good School Dame
No Longer School Must Keep
Which Gives Us Cause
For Childrens Sake To Weep.

Buried in Wrexham Church, Wales, is Elihu Yale, Boston-born philanthropist and one-time governor of Madras, died 1721, aged 73. The name of Yale University, New Haven, Connecticut, commemorates his generosity to that institution. His tomb is inscribed:

Born in America, in Europe Bred,
In Afric travelled, and in Asia wed,
Where long he lived and thrived, in London dead.
Much good, some ill, he did; so hope all's even,
And that his soul thro' mercy's gone to heaven.
You that survive and read this tale take care
For this most certain exit to prepare,

Where, blest in peace, the actions of the just
Smell sweet and blossom in the silent dust.

Dr. Frances Wyche Dunn, one-time Columbia University professor, died 1946, is buried in Ellsworth Burying Ground, Sharon, Connecticut, where her monument is inscribed:

She loved flowers, birds, and music.
Author of books and many articles.
Member of various honor societies.
She was a great friend and her friends
   are legion over the U. S.
After a full and busy life she now rests
   in the majesty of her Lord. Amen.

The gravestone of an astronomer in Elmwood Cemetery, East Otisfield, Maine, records:

Prof.
Joseph W. Holden
Born Otisfield Me.
Aug. 24, 1816,
Mar. 30, 1900.
Prof. Holden the
old Astronomer
discovered that the
Earth is flat and
stationary, and that
the sun and moon do
move.

The stone of Capt. James Maud Elford, died 1826, aged 44, in St. Michael's churchyard, Charleston, South Carolina, tells about a varied experience as sea captain and inventor of nautical devices, including "an admirable system of Marine Telegraphic Signals, which afford the Sea the same Facilities of language as the Land." The inscription concludes:

Skill'd in the Stars, in useful learning wise,
He serv'd the Earth, by studying the skies,

> To know them well his blest pursuits were given,
> He studied first, and then he entered Heaven.

Inscribed on the present monument of David Young, self-styled astronomer and founder of a farmer's almanac, died 1852, aged 71, in Presbyterian churchyard, Hanover, New Jersey, are the lines:

> He lived like Newton midst stars of light
> He died to see with unobstructed sight
> The works of God in nature and in grace
> And view his God and Saviour face to face.

His first tombstone contained this sentiment:

> Farewell, my wife, whose tender care
> Has long engaged my love
> Your fond embrace I now exchange
> For better friends above.

An inscription in the crypt of Allegheny Observatory, University of Pittsburgh, reads:

> Phoebe S. Brashear
> 1843-1910
> We have loved the stars too fondly
> to be fearful of the night.
> John A. Brashear
> 1840-1920.

An unusual monument in Lakeview Cemetery, Sarnia, Ontario, marks the grave of an athlete, John Thomas Bell, Jr., died 1950, aged 25. The front of the stone bears a carving of a football field. Near the goal post is a player identified with the numeral 19. At the bottom are the words: "It was his life." Inscribed within the replica of a football on the opposite side is this explanation:

> Died
> Oct. 17, 1950
> From injuries received
> in game with Balmy Beach
> Oct. 14, 1950.

Monument for "Babe" Ruth, Cemetery of the Gate of Heaven,
Hawthorne, New York. See p. 151.

Large letters on the marker of Julius Caesar, an enthusiastic baseball spectator, died 1906, aged 75, in Lone Fir Cemetery, Portland, Oregon, read:

PLAY BALL

A pedestal-type monument, inset with a sculptured portrait and surmounted by a large granite reproduction of a National League baseball, commemorates John J. ("Mugsy") McGraw, died 1934, aged 60, in Truxton, New York, and is inscribed:

A Great American
One of Baseball's Immortals
Dynamic Leader of the
New York Giants for
Thirty Years.

McGraw is buried in New Cathedral Cemetery, Baltimore, Maryland.

In the Cemetery of the Gate of Heaven, Hawthorne, New York, is a singularly handsome monument depicting the hand of Christ resting on the shoulder of a typical American boy and marking the grave of George Herman ("Babe") Ruth, died 1948, aged 53. On a side panel is this tribute:

"May
The Divine Spirit
That Animated
Babe Ruth
To Win the Crucial
Game of Life
Inspire the Youth
of America!"
Cardinal Spellman

A reproduction of "The Wrestlers" appears on the handsome monument of Carroll "Pink" Gardner, former holder of two wrestling titles and now a monument retailer, in Vale Cemetery, Schenectady, New York. Inscribed beneath is the following:

This statue is recognized as one of the
world's finest specimens of ancient sculpture.
Its origin is lost in antiquity but art authorities
agree that it must have been created some three

centuries before Christ, at least two centuries
before the days of Julius Caesar. The original
is in the Uffizi Gallery in Florence, Italy. In the
statue are expressed the strength and courage
of youth. Two able combatants are locked in
friendly battle. Each wrestles for the keen
pleasure of testing his muscles and skill with
a worthy opponent. The inborn urge for com-
petition governed by accepted rules of fair play
—that is their motivation—victory is their goal.
As in any match of brain or muscle only one
contestant can win, but the loser will learn
through losing and the knowledge will prepare
him for a return engagement. The world may
never know the name of the sculptor who created
this masterpiece, but his genius will live forever
for into the statue of "The Wrestlers" he has
molded the basic rule for success—the heart
to fight, the will to win, the ability to lose and
most of all the spirit to fight again.

The Course of True Love

Lysander in *A Midsummer Night's Dream* observed that "the course of true love never did run smooth." Many factors have interrupted the realization of true love. Grief-stricken James H. Caldwell, theater manager, chose these verses by Barry Cornwall for the grave of his clandestine love, Jane Placide, actress, died 1835, aged 31, in Girod Cemetery, New Orleans, Louisiana:

> There's not an hour
> Of day or dreaming night but I am with thee;
> There's not a breeze but whispers of thy name,
> And not a flower that sleeps beneath the moon
> But in its fragrance tells a tale of thee.

Jane died, it is said, of a broken heart when Caldwell's wife would not free him to marry her.

Legend relates that the curse of a father-in-law finally separated a married couple, buried in the old Jamestown graveyard in Colonial National Historical Park, Virginia. Col. Benjamin Harrison vowed that he would separate his daughter Sarah from her husband, the Reverend James Blair, died 1743, aged 88, founder and first president of William and Mary College. Many decades later, when a great sycamore uprooted and divided the couple's gravestones, the curse was fulfilled. Only fragments of the stones remain today.

A four-foot slab in Mount Memorial Cemetery, Liberty, Missouri, recalls a circus tragedy of a century ago. Two circuses visited Liberty at the same time. A performer in one group was thirty-eight-year-old James McFarland, a tightrope walker, and a performer in the other was a lady slack-rope artist, his estranged wife. Mrs. McFarland, asking for a room in Roberts House, told the proprietor about her domestic difficulties and insisted that her husband should not be admitted to her room. When McFarland requested to see his wife, the proprietor refused and McFarland drew a gun. The proprietor, however, was faster with his bowie knife. The epitaph reads:

Died in Liberty, Mo., May 27, 1858
For loving not wisely but too well.

The sentiment is from *Othello*.

This epitaph comes from Burial Hill, Plymouth, Massachusetts:

James Jordan. Drowned in Smelt Pond.
June 25, 1837, aged 27 y'rs.
Buried on the day he was to have been
Married.

A sunken grave in Presbyterian churchyard, Camden, South Carolina, is marked with a small headstone on which were inscribed, by a British bayonet, it is believed, the words:

Here Lies
The Body
of Agnes of
Glasgow, who
departed this life
Feb. 12, 1780. Aged 20.

An old story says that the girl came from Scotland to find her lover, a soldier under the command of Lord Cornwallis. When after much searching she found the soldier, he was dead and she, broken-hearted and fever stricken, soon died and was buried next to him. The fact that no British soldier had appeared in Camden by the date of Agnes' death has not lessened the ardor of the local storytellers.

Fate or circumstance has kept some persons single. One such individual is buried at a lone spot near Holmes Junior College, Goodman,
Mississippi. No dates commemorate his life, although he is known to
have been a pioneer and to have been shot and killed by an unknown
assailant. On his twelve-foot monument, erected, as he wished, within
sight of the railroad tracks, are words of his own choosing:

> Here lies buried
> John W. Shilcutt
> An old Bachelor.

The person who wrote the epitaph for Hermon Fife, died 1845, aged
45, in East Pembroke, New Hampshire, apparently considered Fife's
inventiveness to be compensation for the fact that he was unmarried:

> Here lies the man
> Never beat by a plan
> Straight was his aim
> And sure of his game
> Never had a lover
> But invented the revolver.

The gravestone of H. Amenzo Dygert, died 1924, aged 78, in Rural
Cemetery, Phoenix, New York, explains:

> An American by birth
> A German Dutchman by descent
> A Republican in Politics
> A Congregationalist in Religion
> A Druggist by Profession
> A Batchelor by fate.

From Foote Street Cemetery, Middlebury, Vermont, comes this sober
warning:

> F. Wytte
> Civil War veteran of 93 years.
> Died at Old Soldiers Home
> Lafayette, Ind.
> A bachelor lies beneath this sod,
> Who disobeyed the laws of God;

Advice to others here I give,
Don't live a bachelor, as I lived.

Inscribed on the Saltonstall table monument in Old Burying Ground, Woburn, Massachusetts, is an epitaph to a woman whose father forbade her to marry:

Here lyes the Remains of M'rs. Elizabeth
Cotton, Daughter of the Rev'd Cotton late of
Sandwich Dec'd Who Died a Virgin October 12th
1742
If a Virgin Marry She hath not Sinned
Nevertheless Such shall have trouble in the Flesh
But He that giveth her not in Marriage doth better
She is happier if She so Abide.

The tombstone to Elizabeth Peacock, died 1813, aged 56, in Middle Cemetery, Lancaster, Massachusetts, comments succinctly:

Her hand no wedlock ever bound.

The most frequent references to marriage on tombstones indicate married joy and felicity. The monument to Flossie Fay Gross, died 1923, aged 22, in Springhill Cemetery, Huntington, West Virginia, reads:

To	From
My only Honey	Her only Honey
My Wife	Her Husband
Flossie	Jimmy

Inscribed on the stone to Jennie E. Wilson, died 1882, aged 29, in College Hill Cemetery, Lebanon, Illinois, are these words:

She was more to me
Than I expected.

This epitaph, said to have been found in Saratoga, New York, and dated 1792, was printed in *Notes and Queries*, 4 December 1880:

Here lies the wife of Robert Ricular,
Who walked the way of God perpendicular.

In St. Michael's churchyard, Charleston, South Carolina, is this inscription to Dr. Joseph Chourler, died 1804, aged 42:

> Sleep on bless'd creature in thy urn
> Thy widow's tears cannot awake thee.
> I only wait until my turn
> And then, oh! then I shall overtake thee.

A six-foot monument to Mathies G. Braden, died 1882, aged 28, in Old Mandan Cemetery near Bismarck, North Dakota, bears these words:

> Stranger call this not a place
> Of Fear and Gloom.
> To me it is a pleasant Spot,
> It is my Husbands tomb.

Sarah Collins, wife of James Collins, died 1875, aged 36, is remembered by the following epitaph from Caribou, Colorado:

> Gone before us O our Sister
> To the spirit land
> Vainly look we for another
> in thy place to stand.

In the same graveyard a marker to the three small children of Samuel and Margaret Richards, died 5, 6, 8 July 1879, reads:

> Gone before us
> oh our children
> To the better land
> Vainly wait we
> for others in
> Your places to stand.

A tombstone in Pine Hill Cemetery, Dover, New Hampshire, is inscribed:

> Repository
> of
> Husband and Wife
> Joseph Hartwell, unanimated Apr. 1, 1867, Et 68
> Betsy Hartwell, unanimated Dec. 7, 1862, Et 68.

The following embraces a period of 41 years. In all of
our relations in life, toward each other, there has been
naught but continuation of fidelity and loving kindness. We
have never participated or countenanced in others, secretly
or otherwise, that which calculated to subjugate the masses
of the people to the dictation of the few. And now we will
return to our Common Mother with our individualities in life
unimpaired, to pass through together this ordeal of our earth
chemical Laboratory, preparatory to recuperation.

Her last acclamations,

"If you should be taken away, I would not survive you.
How happy we have lived together. Oh, how you will miss me.
Think not, Mr. Hartwell, I like you the less for being in the
situation you are in, No, it only strengthens my affections."

To those who have made professions of friendship and
have then falsified them by living act—

Pass On.

A Gothic tablet to Elizabeth Cothran, wife of Francis E. Harrison,
died 1925, aged 82, in a cemetery near Bradley, South Carolina, is
inscribed:

The Greatest Person
I Have Ever Known.

The epitaph to Rhoda Hopkins, died 1815, aged 68, in Burlington
Flats, New York, reads:

In our youth we joind for life
and i becom his lawful wife
Then we did rove the world in wide
Til deth has brought us side by side.

These lines from Bruton Parish churchyard, Williamsburg, Virginia,
are from the grave of Mrs. Ann Timson Jones, "consort of the Rev.
Scervant Jones." She was "Born 1 Sept 1787, Married 26 Dec 1805,
Baptized 3 Mar 1822, Died 6 June 1849," seventeen years having followed after her marriage to the reverend sire before she was baptized.

If woman ever yet did well
If woman ever did excel

If woman Husband ere adored
If woman ever loved the Lord:
If ever Faith and Hope and Love
In Human flesh did live and move
If all the graces ere did meet
In her, in her they were complete.
  My Ann, my all, my Angel Wife
  My dearest one, my love, my life
  I cannot sigh or say farewell
  But where thou dwellest I will dwell.

The disconsolate Mr. Jones was soon married again and a persistent tradition relates that the same coach which brought the tombstone for Ann from Richmond also carried Mr. Jones home from his second honeymoon.

On the gravestone to Agnes Howard, died 1857, aged 76, on Ocracoke Island, North Carolina, is written:

She was!
But words are wanting to say what
Think what a wife should be
She was that

Engraved on the tomb of the wife of George Mason, author of the Bill of Rights, at Gunston Hall, Lorton, Virginia, is this sentiment:

Ann Mason daughter of William Eilbeck of Charles
County Maryland, merchant, departed this life on
the 9th day of March 1773 in the 39th year of her
age after a long and painful illness which she bore
with uncommon Fortitude and Resignation.
  Once she was all that cheers and sweetens life,
  The Tender Mother, Daughter, Friend and Wife.
  Once she was all that makes mankind adore,
  Now view this marble and be vain no more.

Inscribed on the grave of Nathaniel Gibbs, died 1805, aged 53, in St. Peter's churchyard, Washington, North Carolina, are words addressed to his wife:

Weep not, my spouse, that I am gone
Twas Heaven's all wise decree
And soon our Judge will sentence pass
That you must follow me
Unto the realm of endless bliss
Where we shall part no more
And orphans there in praises join
The God whom we adore.

In the same graveyard is a husband's tribute to Sarah Bonner, died 1779, aged 23:

Where flies my wife oh lovely once and fair
Her face cast in the mould of beauty, where
Her eyes all radiance her cheeks like snow
Whose cheeks once tinctured with a purple glow
Where those ivory teeth and lips of celestial sound
Her lips like lilys set with roses round
Where's that soft marble breast white neck and where
That all of woman past description fair
Where's those active fingers that with artful ease
Which in her house once taught her family to please
Where's that sprightly wit even love's delight
All sunk alas in everlasting night
Earth take her bones chaste soul she smiles at rest
Whilst her image lives on immortal in my breast.

From the grave of Maria Michean, died 1793, aged 20, in First Presbyterian churchyard, Elizabeth, New Jersey, comes this:

Clos'd are those eyes in endless night
No more to beam with fond delight,
Or with affection roll.
Eternal silence seals that tongue
Where sence and soft persuasion hung
To captivate the soul.

On the sides of a memorial which L. H. Geer erected to his wife and daughter in Greenwood Cemetery, Orlando, Florida, are these inscriptions:

Erected by L. H. Geer
Husband and Father, in the memory of his loved ones.
Sleep, precious souls. No more sorrow or pain.
But the one that is left, will be there tomorrow.
Earth has no more pleasure, without you to remain.
Tomorrow has come, no one to mourn, all is lost in sorrow.
I am now in the bourne, I promised tomorrow.

Mrs. R. Geer
wife
of L. H. Geer, July 28, 1900
A good wife and mother. And only known to be loved.

In memory of Miss Lillie Geer
Daughter of
L. H. Geer,
died May 8, 1901
age 46 years
"I want to be laid next to Ma" Lillie said.
In life unassuming, In her death all is lost, Pa.

In memory of L. H. Geer,
died March 23, 1903,
age 75
No one to mourn, No one to caress, No one to own.
No life, Let me rest, Let me rest.

In the middle of the last century, Charles Durand, having buried his wife in the old Catholic Cemetery, St. Martinville, Louisiana, swore he would never marry again. For long hours each day he knelt to pray at his wife's tomb. In time he ordered an iron statue of himself in a kneeling position and had it placed at her grave. Within a year of his wife's death, however, he did marry and the statue, which became a source of derision, was removed.

This epitaph was recorded from Laurel Hill Cemetery, San Francisco, California, before the historic graveyard was cleared for modern construction:

Dearest Thomas thou art gone,
Thy kind heart I miss.

You did not say Good-bye, Tom,
Or give me the parting kiss.

A tombstone on Burial Hill, Plymouth, Massachusetts, shows an unusual relationship between a widow's grave and that of her husband Thomas:

Here lies Interrd.
the Body of Mrs
Sarah Spoon-
er, who dece-
ased January
ye 25th AD 1767
in ye 72d Year of
her age. ☞ She was
widow to

One of the most spectacular of all private memorials is the group of statues marking the graves of John Davis, died 1947, aged 92, and his wife Sarah, died 1930, in Mount Hope Cemetery, Hiawatha, Kansas. After his wife's death, Davis, a farmer, resolved to perpetuate her memory in an unusual fashion. He ordered from Italy two statues of Carrara marble which represented Sarah and himself as they appeared in early married life. Over these life-size statues and the grave slabs a granite canopy was erected. In time Davis ordered a total of eleven figures. Statues of an angel and John kneeling at Sarah's grave were carved. Suggestive of his loneliness after his wife's death is a statue of the sober-faced and heavily bearded husband sitting next to an empty chair appropriately labeled "The Vacant Chair." The statuary group is said to have cost more than a quarter of a million dollars, but Davis died in the county poorhouse.

A handsome horizontal tablet, supported by four marble pillars, in St. Paul's Cemetery, Alexandria, Virginia, tells of the death of an unidentified person and of her husband's grief:

To the memory of a
Female Stranger
whose mortal sufferings terminated
on the 14th of October 1816
Aged 23 years and 8 months

Monument marking the grave of John and Sarah Davis, Mount Hope Cemetery, Hiawatha, Kansas. See p. 162.

This stone is placed here by her disconsolate
Husband in whose arms she sighed out her
latest breath and who under God
did his utmost ever to sooth the cold
dead ear of death.
How loved how valued once avails thee not
To whom related or by whom begot
A heap of dust alone remains of thee
Tis all thou art and all the proud shall be.

Locally, the identity of "the Female Stranger" has long been the subject of romantic speculation.

After losing two wives within a year, a widower in Stowe, Vermont, considered a lecture to youth to be appropriate:

In Memory of	In Memory of
Betsey, consort of	Abigail, consort of
Capt. Elias Bingham	Capt. Elias Bingham
who died Sept. 10th	who died Sept. 14th
D. 1805	D. 1804
in the 20th year	in the 25th year
of her age	of her age

This double call is loud to all
Let none despise and wonder
But to the youth it speaks a truth
In accents loud as thunder.

A tombstone in Groton, Massachusetts, tells of a man who married sisters:

In Memory of
Mr. Joshua Davis
who died
July 5, 1827; aet. 79.
also Mrs. Sibel,
his wife
died Jan. 12, 1799, aet. 25.
and Mrs. Betsy
his wife

sister of his former wife
died Aug. 27, 1818; aet. 42.
Thrice happy shades now freed from cares
Our mortal frames at rest;
Secure from pain and grief and fears
With kindred souls we are blest.

In the old cemetery on the common, Little Compton, Rhode Island, are two slabs of identical size and shape. They record:

In Memory of	In Memory of
Elizabeth who	Lidia ye Wife of
should have been the	Mr. Simeon Palmer
wife of Mr.	who died Decembr
Simeon Palmer	ye 26th 1754 in ye 35
who died Augt 14th	Year of her Age.
1776 in the 64th Year	
of her Age.	

Through the years many tales have centered about this woman "who should have been the wife" of Simeon, one-time attorney and prominent in the life of the community. It has been said that Elizabeth never reconciled herself to Simeon's first marriage, although the town records reveal that Elizabeth's only child bore the name Lidia. Another legend says that on the evening of her wedding day, Elizabeth was asked by her frugal groom to partake of a supper of cat meat. Discovering too late the mistake she had made and yet realizing the obligations of her marriage vow, she continued for the next twenty-one years to perform wifely tasks but neglected to offer the love and attention he may have desired. An awkward expression has probably libeled a man who was undoubtedly a good husband to each wife.

One woman's accomplishments are chronicled concisely in her inscription at Mill River, Massachusetts:

Polly Rhoades
Died Sept. 7, 1855:
Aged 86 Yr's 5 Mo's
& 3 d's.

Being the widow of 5 husbands.
1st David Rockwell,
2nd Capt. Alpheus Underwood,
3rd Dea. Amos Langdon,
4th Hezekiah G. Butler,
5th James T. Rhoades.

Two small monuments in City Cemetery, Ithaca, New York, are lettered:

Ann	Olive Jane
Wife of	Wife of
Barnard Taber	Barnard Taber
Died	Died
March 4, 1843	Oct. 30, 1846
Aged 32 years	Aged 32 years
10 months 23 days	2 months 28 days

Next to these is a large monument reading:

Louisa A.
Wife of
Barnard Taber
Died
Sept. 9, 1871
Aged 49 years
4 m & 29 d
This monument ordered
by herself.

A man who seems to have had a partiality for a particular name built a monument to three wives in Maple Grove Cemetery, Russellville, Kentucky. The first side reads:

Sarah A.
Consort of Jas. M. Beall
Born Oct. 8, 1796
Married Sept. 17, 1822
Died Aug. 20, 1824

The second side reads:

Sarah Y.
Consort of Jas. M. Beall
Born Oct. 27, 1800
Married April 10, 1827
Died May 2, 1828

The third side reads:

Sarah Ann
Consort of Jas. M. Beall
Born April 25, 1809
Married Aug. 10, 1830
Died Oct. 24, 1854

And the fourth side summarizes:

As wives devoted
As mothers affectionate
As friends ever kind and true
In life they achieved all
the graces of the Christian
In death their radiant spirits
returned to God who gave them.
I loved them on earth
I will meet them in heaven.

A five-foot slab in River Burying Ground, East Lyme, Connecticut, tells of a man who outlived three wives but was himself outlived by his last wife:

William Keeney
died April 11, 1837
in his 87th year

Betsy, his wife, died
April 6, 1791, aged 40 years

Sally, his wife, died
July 21, 1810, aged 50 years

Naomi, his wife, died
Aug. 27, 1829, aged 64 years

Nancy, his *last* wife,
died July 9, 1839
aged 71 years

The monument of Theodore Marshall Manning, lawyer, died 1922, aged 86, in Warrenville, Illinois, is a tribute to his three wives:

Mary D. Jones
His Perfect Wife
Apr. 2, 1838-Feby. 3, 1868
Lucy Talbot
His 2d Sweet Wife
Dec. 29, 1839-Nov. 24, 1872
Mary E. Briggs
His Healthful 3d Wife
July 14, 1862-

The third wife outlived her husband and is buried elsewhere.

Buried in order from right to left in Oakland Cemetery, Sag Harbor, New York, are Captain David Hand and his five wives. Hand, a whaling captain and Revolutionary hero, was an actual prototype of Natty Bumpo, the character created by James Fenimore Cooper. The epitaph to Susannah, the first wife, died 1791, aged 27, reads:

Hark my fair Guardian chides my stay
And waves his golden rod.
Angel I come: Lead on the way
And waft me to my God.

Mary, the second wife, died 1794, aged 32, is eulogized with:

The Almighty spoke and she was gone,
Eternity now reigns alone;
If you would live with God on high,
Learn O ye living how to die.

This quatrain honors Hannah, the third wife, died 1798, aged 30:

Behold ye living mortals passing by,
How thick the partners of one husband lie;
Vast and unsearchable the ways of God,
Just but severe is his chastising rod.

He married and buried within the next two years his fourth wife, Charlotte, also aged 30, and wrote or chose for her stone an inscription in which he probably saw no incongruity:

> O death thou King of terrors where's thy sting
> What welcome tidings to my ears you bring;
> My faith discovers through thy dark abode,
> A seat prepar'd at the right hand of God.

Hand was more fortunate in his fifth marriage which continued for forty years and closed with the second Hannah's death in 1835, aged 69. No verse marks her grave. Hand lived five years more and died on 29 February 1840, aged 81, another woman having declined in the meantime, tradition says, to become his sixth wife. Near his grave, appropriately enough, stands the famous "Broken Shaft Whalers' Monument."

Another captain and a contemporary of Hand, Nathaniel Thurston, died 1811, aged 56, is buried in Bradford, Massachusetts, with six of his seven wives. The blue slate stones are decorated with quaintly carved figures. Betsey, the first wife, died 1790, aged 34, is remembered with the lines:

> Let mourning friends and kindred dear
> Lament the Dead, repent and fear,
> Let youths and children read this stone,
> Feel they must die and soon be gone.

These words were prophetic of Betsey's successors, for Martha, the second wife, died nine years later, aged 32. Her epitaph reads:

> See there all pale and dead she lies;
> Forever flow my streaming eyes.
> There dwells the fairest, loveliest mind,
> Faith sweetens it together joind
> Dwells faith and wit and sweetness there,
> O read the change and drop a tear.

Thurston's next four wives, Huldah, died 1801, aged 24, Clarissa, died 1803, aged 36, Martha, died 1804, aged 25, and Mary, died 1808, aged 27, are buried without poetic inscription. Before Thurston died he had married for a seventh time. When the captain died in Lansing-burgh, New York, his last wife returned with the body to Bradford and promptly, some say, married the undertaker who had accompanied her on the journey.

A large granite tomb in Harmony Cemetery, Boxford, Massachusetts, holds the remains of General Solomon Lowe, died 1861, aged 79, and his four wives. On the tomb is a medallion picture of the general. To the left are medallions of his first two wives, Huldah, died 1808, aged 28, and Dolly, died 1817, aged 31. In the pictures each is shown nursing a child. To the right of the general are pictures of his last wives, Martha, died 1855, aged 50, and Caroline, who survived her husband by sixteen years. Each one, having been childless, is repre-sented holding a Bible.

The survivor of a marriage has sometimes generously availed him-self of the advantage of having the last word. A striking instance is seen on the table tomb of John Custis IV, who died in 1749, on the Custis Plantation, Northampton County, Virginia. His marriage to Frances, daughter of Colonel Daniel Parke, was without domestic har-mony and Custis in revenge ordered positively that his inscription should read:

> Under this Marble Tomb lies ye Body
> of the Honorable John Custis Esq.
> of the City of Williamsburgh, and Parish of Bruton.
> Formerly of Hungars Parish on the Eastern Shore of
> Virginia and County of Northampton the
> Place of His Nativity.
> Aged 71 Years and Yet liv'd but Seven Years
> which was the space of time He kept
> a Batchelers house at Arlington
> on the Eastern Shore of Virginia.

The second husband of Custis' daughter-in-law was George Washing-ton.

An unintentional double meaning is found on the stone to Edward Oakes, died 1866, aged 24, in West Cemetery, Middlebury, Vermont:

> Faithful husband thou art
> At rest untill we meet again.

On the gravestone of Job Brooks, died 1788, aged 91, in Hill Burying Ground, Concord, Massachusetts, is this comment:

> He was considered by survivors as coming
> to the grave in a full age.

His aged wife, who had died two years previously, is remembered with
this epitaph:

> After having lived with her said husband up-
> wards of 65 years, she died in the
> belief of a resurection to a better Life.

Unintentional humor is suggested by this inscription in South
Plymouth, New York:

> Ruth S. Kibbe
> wife of
> Alvin J. Stanton
> May 5, 1861
> Apr. 5, 1904
> The Lord don't make any mistakes.

These words may have been selected by David Goodman Croly, died
1889, aged 59, for his monument in Evergreen Cemetery, Lakewood,
New Jersey, and not by his widow:

> He meant well,
> Tried a little,
> Failed much.

The words are from Robert Louis Stevenson's *Christmas Sermon*.

A white marble tombstone in Bethel Methodist churchyard, near
North East, Maryland, bears what seems to be a complimentary sentiment to Annie Cordes, died 1881, aged 32:

> Hard to beat.

A local story, however, alleges that Cordes's first wife died of abuse,
but that he did not have as much success in beating Annie, his second
wife.

An unusual log-shaped monument to Emily Spear, died 1901, aged

Tombstone of Elizabeth Brooks, Hill Burying Ground, Concord, Massachusetts. See p. 170.

64, in Glendale Cemetery, Cardington, Ohio, bears this curious comment:

> My husband
> promised me
> that my
> body should
> be cremated
> but other
> influences
> prevailed.

The epitaph to Thomas Gilbert, died 1868, aged 85, in Hadley Cemetery, East Hampstead, New Hampshire, indicates that he harbored bitter resentment to the end:

> Beneath this stone is grave for one
> Shamefully robbed in life
> By his wife's son and Squire Tom
> And Daniel Seavey's wife.

Equally vehement is the epitaph on the grave of Seth J. Miller, died 1848, aged 47, in Burial Hill Cemetery, Rehoboth, Massachusetts:

> My wife from me departed
> And robb'd me like a knave
> Which caused me broken hearted
> To descend into my grave.
> My children took an active part
> And to doom me did contrive
> Which stuck a dagger to my heart
> Which I could not survive.

As a final refutation to gossips who questioned the legality of her marriage, the wife of Sidney W. Saunders, died 1889, aged 41, erected an impressive granite tomb near the entrance to Old City Cemetery, Monroe, Louisiana. The tomb is surmounted by a life-size statue of Saunders which holds a scroll bearing these words:

> This is to certify that Sidney W. Saunders and
> Annie Livingston of Monroe, in the State of

Louisiana, were by me joined together in holy
matrimony, March 25, 1875.

Witnesses: John W. Young
John W. Rice   Justice of the Peace
Frank Gregory   City of St. Louis

This testimony of devotion appears on the pedestal:

It is in heaven
a crime to love too well
to bear too tender
or too firm a heart?

Saunders' chair and desk were placed in the tomb. There his wife sat
for many afternoons until one day she disappeared and was not seen
again. On file in the St. Louis County Court House, incidentally, is
the original marriage certificate.

Two monuments offer a vivid background to Longfellow's narrative
poem of tragic love, *Evangeline* (1847). A statue, thirteen feet in height,
at Grand Pré, Nova Scotia, depicts the Arcadian looking back wist-
fully on her native soil. A second statue, erected by Dolores del Rio
in 1929, when she played the title role in a movie adaptation of Longfellow's story, is located in Evangeline's reputed burial site, the churchyard of St. Martin Catholic Church, St. Martinville, Louisiana. Evangeline's old prototype is commemorated with this inscription:

Evangeline
Emmeline Labiche
Vieux Cimetière de St. Martin
Mémoire des Acadiens exilés de 1765.

Tomb of Sidney W. Saunders, Old City Cemetery, Monroe, Louisiana.
See p. 171.

In memory of
Mrs. Olive Watson,
wife of
Mr. Jacob Watson,
who died Aug.st 26th 1810.
Aged 32 Years.

While I lie mould ring in my grave,
No Mother will my children have,
They will go wand'ring after me,
O where is Ma'am, where can she be.

Tombstone of Olive Watson, Spencer, Massachusetts. See p. 174.

A Word or Two for Mother

Before the recent advances of medicine, many mothers lost their lives at childbirth. The epitaph to Florianna Forbes, died 1815, at Annapolis Royal, Nova Scotia, illustrates this:

> 18 years a maiden
> 1 year a wife
> 1 day a mother
> Then I lost my life.

The death of a mother and child is recorded on a headstone in Harvard, Massachusetts:

> In memory of Mrs. Nancy Worster . . .
> who Died in Childbirth Sept. ye 21.
> 1776, Aged 24 years 8 months & 21 days.
> Though she was fair while she had breath,
> And on her cheeks the Rose did bloom,
> Yet her Dear Babe became her Death,
> While she became the Infants Tomb.

These words on the stone to Nancy G. Hanford, died 1881, aged 36, in Willow Glen Cemetery, Dryden, New York, are addressed to her husband:

You must talk to the children
as I should have done had I
lived.

The tombstone of Olive Watson, died 1810, aged 32, in an old cemetery behind the Congregational Church, Spencer, Massachusetts, reads:

While I lie mouldr'ing in my grave,
No Mother will my children have,
They will go wandr'ing after me,
O where is Ma'am, where can she be.

Next to the gravestone of her mother in Post Mills, Vermont, is a stone of Ermina B. Hinckley, died 1833, aged 3, which comments:

Sleep sweet with Ma, Ermina B.
Soon Pa must come and rest with thee.

In Guilford, Indiana, is an epitaph to Ann, wife of I. H. B., died 1870, aged 44:

Dear angel wife
I gave thee parting kiss
Twenty one years we lived
In truth and bliss
    Always firm
    But ever mild
    I never saw
    Her strike a child.

This epitaph to Rachel Gorham, died 1808, aged 59, in West Parish Burying Ground, Barnstable, Massachusetts, makes apparent the loneliness of the widower:

Left behind a husband dear,
But not a child to shed a tear.

Some epitaphs tell of mothers of large families and include statistical evidence. In Buckminster Cemetery, Barre, Massachusetts, is this record:

In memory of
Mrs. Lydia Burnett, who
was first Consort of Mr.
Noah Ripley

by whom she had 8 sons & 11
daughters 17 of them lived to
have Families: her descendents
at her death were 97 grandchildren & 106 greatgrandchildren
she died June 17th 1816. Aged 91
Many daughters have done virtuously but
thou excelest.

Mrs. Mary Buell, however, excelled Mrs. Ripley, for her gravestone in Litchfield, Connecticut, reads:

She died Nov 4th
1768, aetat 90
Having had 13, Children
101 Grand Children
274 Great G. Children
22 Great G.G. Children
410 Total
336 survived her.

The grave of Ann Hutchinson, died 1801, aged 101, in Ely Burying Ground near Hightstown, New Jersey, says:

She was the mother of 13 children,
and grandmother, and great grandmother, and great great grandmother
of 375 persons.

If taken literally, the epitaph of Joanna Farley in Hollis, New Hampshire, would be a startling account:

This stone commemorates the memory of
Mrs. Joanna Farley. She was a woman
eminent for industry, usefulness, & piety.
Having lived 80 years and having been the
natural parent of 200 offspring, she died
20th of August 1797.

A remarkable progeny is recorded in a pair of inscriptions from the Old or Quarry Cemetery, Cromwell, Connecticut:

> Here lies interred the body of
> Mr. John Sage, who departed this
> life, January ye 22nd A. D. 1750-1,
> in the 83 year of his age. He left
> a virtuous and sorrowful widow with
> whom he had lived 57 years, and had
> 15 children; 12 of them married and
> increased ye family by repeated mar-
> riages to the number of 29, of whom
> there are now 15 alive; he had 120
> grandchildren, 105 of them now living;
> 40 great grandchildren, 37 of them
> are living, which makes the numerous
> offspring 189.

> Here lies interred the body of Mrs.
> Hannah Sage, once the virtuous con-
> sort of Mr. John Sage, who both are
> covered with this stone, and there has
> been added to the numerous offspring
> mentioned above forty-four by birth and
> marriages, which makes the whole 233.
> She fell asleep September the 28th, 1753,
> in the 80th year of her age.

Epitaphs to midwives are particularly interesting because of the statistics given. A tombstone in Phipps Street Cemetery, Charlestown, Massachusetts, records:

> Here lyes Interred ye Body of
> Mrs. Elizabeth Phillips who
> was Born in Westminster in Great
> Britain and commissioned by John,
> Lord Bishop of London, in ye year
> 1718 to ye office of a Midwife, came

Tombstone of Mary Harvey and infant, Old Deerfield, Massachusetts.

to this country in ye year 1719 & by
ye Blessing of God had brought into
this world above 3000 children.
Died May 6, 1761, Aged 76 years.

A grave memorial in Huntsville, Utah, reads:

In Memory
of
Mary Heathman Smith
Lovingly known as Granny Smith
Born in England January 21, 1818 where she
was trained in a maternity hospital. She
came to Utah in 1862. As doctor, surgeon,
midwife and nurse, for thirty years, in
storm or sunshine, during the bleakest
winter, or the darkest night, with little
or no remuneration, she attended the people
of Ogden Valley with a courage and faith-
fullness unexcelled. In addition to rearing
her own family of nine, under her skill and
attention she brought into the world more
than 1500 babies. She died at Huntsville,
Utah, December 15, 1895.

The grave of a stepmother, Mrs. Elizabeth Strong, died 1775, aged
55, in Old Burying Ground, New Marlborough, Massachusetts, reads:

The Stepchild of the deceased
remembering with gratitude
her kindness to them, in their
tender years, place this stone.
Ye Step-mothers!
Follow her example & ye
shall not lose your reward.

Mary Washington died in 1789, ten years before the death of her
famous son. Although her son provided adequately for her needs, she
complained that she "never lieved soe poore in all my life." The Vir-

ginia Assembly would have voted her a pension but her son insisted
that it would be both unnecessary and embarrassing. In May 1833,
Andrew Jackson laid the cornerstone for a grave monument near
Meditation Rock, Fredericksburg, Virginia. The donor was later unable to meet the financial obligations involved and it remained un-
finished. In 1893 a new shaft was erected which is inscribed with
simple dignity:

Mary

Mother of Washington

The prominence of her son brought a delayed monumental tribute
to the mother of Lincoln, whose grave in Lincoln State Park, Gentryville, Indiana, is inscribed:

Nancy Hanks

Lincoln

Mother of President

Lincoln

Died

Oct 5 AD 1818

Age 35 years

Erected by a friend of her martyred son

1879.

In the family graveyard on the Marshall property near Washington,
Kentucky, was formerly found this epitaph to the mother of Chief
Justice John Marshall:

Mary Randolph Keith Marshall

wife of Thomas Marshall, by whom she had

Fifteen Children,

was born in 1737 and died in 1807.

She was good but not brilliant

Useful but not great.

Inscribed on a twenty-one-foot obelisk of Quincy granite in Old
Granary Burial Ground, Boston, is this tribute to the parents of Benjamin Franklin:

Josiah Franklin

and

Abiah his wife,

Lie here interred,

They lived lovingly together in wedlock
Fifty-five years.
And without an estate or any gainful employment,
By constant labor and honest industry,
Maintained a large family comfortably,
And brought up thirteen children and seven
Grandchildren reputably.
From this instance, reader,
Be encouraged to diligence in thy calling,
And distrust not Providence.
He was a pious and prudent man;
She a discreet and virtuous woman.
Their youngest son,
In filial regard to their memory,
Places this stone.

J. F. Born 1655, Died 1744, AE. 89.
A. F. Born 1667, Died 1752, AE. 85.
The original inscription having been nearly
Obliterated
A number of citizens
Erected this monument, as a mark of respect
For the
Illustrious author,
MDCCCXXVII.

A distinguished grandfather is mentioned on a tomb in Yazoo City,
Mississippi:

Sacred to the memory of John H. Hancock
born in Fairfax Co. Va. Dec. 8th 1796
died Mch. 6th 1854.
   Here lie two grandsons of John
   Hancock the first signer of
   the Constitution.
Sacred to the memory of George Hancock
born in Frederick Co. Va. Sept. 30th 1806
died in Yazoo City, Oct. 28th 1853. Age 47 yrs.

The grave of America Pinckney Williams, died 1842, aged 38, in Forest Lawn Cemetery, Buffalo, New York, is inscribed:

Great Granddaughter of
Martha Washington.

When the monument at Wyuka, Nebraska City, Nebraska, to Caroline Morton, wife of J. Sterling Morton, Secretary of Agriculture under President Cleveland, was finished, the father took his four sons to the graveyard and told them that if they should ever do anything to disgrace their mother's name their own names would be removed from the inscription which reads:

Caroline
Wife of J. Sterling Morton
Died at Arbor Lodge
June 29, 1881, aged 47 years.
She was the Mother of
Joy, Paul, Mark and Carl Morton.

All of the names remain.

Brief Candles

Epitaphs to children are usually devoid of the conscious humor suggested on stones to older persons. More often the parents' grief is revealed in a curious explanation of or resignation to the Divine Will, or in an anguished appraisal of what the child might have become if he had lived.

The West Woods graveyard near Hamden, Connecticut, contains a tombstone to Milla Gaylord, died 1806, aged 5, which states:

> Soon ripe
> Soon rotten
> Soon gone
> But not forgotten.

Equally terse is the inscription marking the grave of Sidney Ellis, died 1836, aged 7 weeks, in Center Cemetery, Paxton, Massachusetts:

> He lived
> He wept
> He smiled
> He groaned
> And died.

A pitiful remembrance of an unnamed infant daughter of Elizur and Clarissa Abbott, died 1824, is found in the Old Colony Burying Ground, Granville, Ohio:

Joyless sojourner was I
Only born to gasp and die.

In Milford, Connecticut, is the epitaph to Jule Treat, died 1795, aged 8:

Christ called at Midnight as I lay
In thirty hours was turned to clay.

A small stone to Helen Christine Lehman, died 27 December 1908, in Greenwood Hills Cemetery, Portland, Oregon, records:

With us one day.

This query is on the tombstone of Ezra Thayer Jackson, died 1783, aged 25 days, on Burial Hill, Plymouth, Massachusetts:

What did the Little hasty Sojournr
find so forbidding & disgustful in
our upper World to occasion its
precipitant exit?

Found on the stone to Caroline Newcomb, died 1812, aged 4, in Crossroads Cemetery, Vineyard Haven, Massachusetts, are these words:

She tasted of life's bitter Cup
Refused to drink the Portion up
But turned her little head aside
Disgusted with the taste and died.

The parents of Agnes Crowell, died 1794, aged 10, inscribed her tombstone in First Presbyterian churchyard, Elizabeth, New Jersey, with this:

What in others is usually the effect of
Education and Habit seemed born with her
from a very Babe the utmost regularity
was observable in all her actions, what
ever she did was well done, and with an
apparent reflection far beyond her years.

"She was very Excellent for Reading & Soberness" reads the epitaph in Hill Burying Ground, Concord, Massachusetts, to Mary Brooks, died 1736, aged 11.

Shelter over the grave of a boy who was always afraid of the dark.
York Village, Maine.

In memory of
LYDIA G. AYER
daughter of
CAPT. WILLIAM and HANNAH AYER
Born 1813 — Died 1827
By tradition the school-mate
referred to by Whittier in the poem
In School Days
said by Holmes to be "the most beautiful
school-boy poem in the English language".

"I'm sorry that I spelt the word:
I hate to go above you,
Because;-the brown eyes lower fell,-
"Because you see, I love you"

Tombstone of Lydia G. Ayer, New Haverhill, Massachusetts.

Ardent religious zeal in tender years is described on the marble slab in Colonial Cemetery, Savannah, Georgia, to Mary Madeline Wilson, died 1837, aged 15:

> A Christian martyr, her Bible took fire on her
> Breast. A few painful hours & she slep in
> Jesus, to whom she devoted herself in her
> 9th year. Such timely, beautiful, the loviness
> Meekness to her God expressed; joing the
> Holy army above, her message was I die with
> A glorious hope of Heaven.

Inscribed to Thomas Cross, died 1824 of "the prevailing fever," aged 11, are these lines in St. Michael's churchyard, Charleston, South Carolina:

> The early developement of
> extraordinary mental powers
> seemed the bright dawn of great
> future eminence. His disposition
> was affectionate and confiding.
> His character was amiable, ingenuous,
> modest, manly and pious.
> Among his last words were:
> "Train up a child in the
> way he should go, and when he is old
> he will not depart therefrom."

William D. Jeffery, died 1822, aged 10, is remembered by his epitaph in Sweetman Cemetery, Galway, New York:

> Young as he was he regreted
> The fall of Adam but hopt
> He should be redy for the
> Resurrection.

Nathanael Mather, son of Increase Mather and brother of Cotton, died 1688, aged 19, after having published two almanacs and having graduated at 16 from Harvard where his father was president. His life was given wide publicity through a biographical sketch, entitled "Early Piety Exemplified," included in his brother's *Magnalia Christi*

Americana (1702). His epitaph in Charter Street Cemetery, Salem, Massachusetts, reads:

> An Aged person
> That had seen but
> Nineteen Winters
> in the World.

A comparable despair is found on the gravestone to F. W. Jackson, died 1799, aged 1, on Burial Hill, Plymouth, Massachusetts:

> Heav'n knows What man
> He might have been. But we
> He died a most rare boy.

Records the stone of a nameless child of 10 years, died 1885, in Block Island, Rhode Island:

> Oh he was a good
> If e'er a good boy lived.

Mark Twain selected these lines for the grave of his daughter, Olivia Susan Clemens, died 1896, aged 24, in Woodlawn Cemetery, Elmira, New York:

> Warm summer sun shine kindly here;
> Warm southern wind blow softly here;
> Green sod above lie light, lie light—
> Good night, dear heart, good night, good night.

The verse was widely copied and when authorship was generally credited to the father, Mark Twain had the name of Robert Richardson, Australian poet, added to the stone. To make the lines more meaningful Mark Twain had changed "northern wind" in the original to "southern wind."

In Hannibal, Missouri, is the gravestone to a childhood friend of Mark Twain who is best remembered for her literary role:

> Laura H. Frazer
> "Becky Thatcher"
> 1837-1928

The crushed hopes of a fond parent are revealed on a small stone in Barre, Massachusetts, to Elesabeth Caldwell, died 1777, aged 4:

> The Greaf of a Fond Mother & the Blasted
> Expectation of an Indigent Father.

These lines are from the tombstone to William F. Upham, died 1850, aged 10, in Old North Cemetery, Nantucket, Massachusetts:

> Mother oh Mother I am not sleeping
> Father look up to the soft blue sky
> Where beautiful stars bright watch are keeping
> Singing and shining there am I.

An old graveyard at Ft. Bridger, Wyoming, has a tombstone to Nannie F. Wilson, died 1865, aged 16, which reads:

> 'Tis but the casket that lies here,
> The gem that filled it sparkles yet.

Hyperbole is shown in this epitaph from the grave of Isabella Patton, died 1804, aged 5, in Old Masonic Burying Ground, Fredericksburg, Virginia:

> Like blossomed trees o'erturned by vernal storms
> Lovely in death the beauteous ruin lay.

Engraved on the tombstone to Timothy Hakins, died 1813, aged 4 months, in an old cemetery near Westmoreland, New Hampshire, is this:

> This rose was sweet a while
> But now is odour vile.

The name and date have been obliterated from a small child's stone in Van Duesen Cemetery, Great Barrington, Massachusetts, which bears this decipherable epitaph:

> Oh would that I could lift the lid and peer
> within the grave and watch the greedy worms
> that eat away the dead.

The persistent desire of parents to have a child with a particular name is suggested by a stone in First Presbyterian churchyard, Elizabeth, New Jersey:

In memory of
three children of
Jacob & Jennet Crane;
OBEDIAH, died Septr 28th
1805; aged 7 months
OBEDIAH, died July 10th
1811; aged 4 years & 7 months
OBEDIAH, died Augst 10th
1812, aged 28 days.

Perhaps no tombstone bears a name equal to that inscribed on an upright slab in Harrogate Cemetery near Wetumpka, Alabama:

Henry Ritter
Ema Ritter
Dema Ritter
Sweet Potatoe
Creamatarter
Carolinc Bostick
Daughter of
Bob & Suckey Catlen.
Born at Social Circle.
1843,
Died at Wetumka 1852.

It is presumed locally that the parents included on the stone all the names by which the child was known.

A tombstone in Elmwood Cemetery, Pike, New York, to Andrew Jackson Brown, died 1829, aged 1, who survived his twin by a few months, reads:

Andrew Jackson is a twin who died of late,
John Quinciemus is his mate,
Broke by sickness in a day,
The short lived beauties die away.

Quadruplets are buried in Staples Cemetery, Danby Four Corners, Vermont, and are remembered with this epitaph:

In memory of four infants
of Jacamiah & Mercy Palmer

was born alive at one birth
& died Nov. 25, 1795
Four twen infants thay are dead
And laid in one silant grave
Christ took small infants in his arms
Such infants he will save.

The tombstone to Sam. Wilson Smith, died 1801, in Shippensburg, Pennsylvania, comments:

This lovely Boy near 8 Years old
Lies Buried with his Brother
His Sister lies on the one Side
And his Nephew on the other.

One of the most memorable of all epitaphs to children is found in City Cemetery, Marion, Alabama:

OUR DARLING BILLY SUGAR
to the
Memory of
William King Modawell
son of
Wm. B. and Mary A. Modawell
born July 3, 1864
died November 28, 1870
aged 6 years 4 months and 25 days
TO OUR DARLING BILLY
In our thoughts love we seek thee ever
In our dreams thy bright form still we see
Nor can time nor thy absence e'er sever
That fond memory that binds us to thee
Papa
Mamma
Binion
Tattie
Sis
Lou

Papa Gentlemen
Bless Mama's Man
"Go 'Lijah and carry the news
another soul is gone home."
He beats his little drum, in harmony with the
Music of Heaven;
And runs his little Train, through the
Streets of the new Jerusalem.

Three identical stones in Mount Pleasant Cemetery, Newark, New Jersey, stand side by side and read:

And the streets	shall be full of	in the streets
of the City	boys and girls	thereof
	playing	
Alfred Alling	Emaline Alling 1816	[Name illegible]

In Charter Street Cemetery, Salem, Massachusetts, is this comment from the stone of Thomas Smith, died 1771, aged 4:

Now in my childhood I must die
And hasten to eternity
Leave all my playmates and my toys
Hoping to inherit eternal joys.

A large cement doll house is the unusual tomb of Mary Lucile Barcelona, died 1926, aged 3, in St. Joseph's Cemetery, Baton Rouge, Louisiana.

In Aspen Grove Cemetery, Burlington, Iowa, is a curious monument to Evelyn Price, a trained dancer, died 1922, aged 6. The marker consists of a glassed-in box in which newspaper clippings have been placed telling of the programs in which the child appeared, a brief penciled obituary, and photographs.

This consoling tribute marks the grave in Oak Grove Cemetery, Hyannis, Massachusetts, of 21-day-old Robert Crowell:

O, Robert, Robert, angel boy,
A father's pride, a mother's boy;
We will not mourn our darling mate
Sweet Robert, at the Golden Gate.

In Westernville, New York, is this inscription to William Reese, died 1872, aged 21:

> This is what I expected but
> not so soon.

A tombstone, dating back to about 1863, in Greenwood Cemetery, Canton, Illinois, reads:

> Stranger step lightly o'er this grave,
> Here lies the remains of
> Cary Cole
> Aged 18 years.
> An orphan whose spirit is now in heaven.
> The only friend she had on God's Earth
> was Amos B. Smith.

Fraternal Sod

Many gravestones indicate the name or symbols of fraternal lodges or orders. At Sater Church on Chestnut Ridge, near Baltimore, Maryland, is this unusual epitaph to Samuel S. Burnham, died 1812, aged 23:

> Stop Gentle friend and view this Sacred spot,
> Consider well, his fate will be thy lot.
> Cut off in manhood's prime a stranger here,
> Oh, drop the tribute of a brother's tear.
> Be this our prayer, a mark of Odd Fellow's love:
> Jesus admit him to thy Lodge above.

A tombstone in Jordan Station, Ontario, Canada, reads:

> Here lieth the remains of an unknown brother, whose body was washed ashore near the residence of Abram Martin, Esq., Louth, on 20th Apr., 1877. This tombstone is erected to show that while deceased had only on his person certain symbols to distinguish him as a Free Mason, yet were they sufficient to secure for the remains fraternal sympathy and Christian sepulture.

Dead, voiceless, battered, tempest-tossed,
A stranger, friendless and unknown,
The wave gave up its dead,
A brother came and saw
And raised above his lonely head
This sculptured stone.
The mystic points of Fellowship prevail—
Death's gavel cannot break that sacred tie—
'Gainst Light, the powers of Night can naught avail
To live in hearts we leave behind is not to die.

The grave of Rufus Sweet, died 1884, in Hope Cemetery, Perry, New York, records:

Here lies Rufus Sweet and wife
They fed the hungry and
clothed the naked
and fought secret societies
And here may they rest until
Gabriel blows his horn.

A tall and conspicuous monument in the old cemetery, Batavia, New York, was dedicated in 1882 by the Anti-Masonic National Christian Association Opposed to All Secret Societies, to William Morgan, a man who reportedly profited by the publication of Masonic secrets. At the top of the shaft is a life-size statue of Morgan and something of the bitterness of the anti-Mason factions of the time is found in the inscription:

Erected by Volunteer
Contributions from over
2000 Persons Residing in
Canada, Ontario
and Twenty-six of the
United States
and
Territories.

"The Bane of our Civil
Institutions is to be Found
in MASONRY, Already

Powerful and Daily Becoming
More so . . . I Owe to My
Country an Exposure of
Its Dangers"
Capt. Wm. Morgan

Sacred to the Memory of
Wm. Morgan,
a Native of Virginia,
a Capt. in the War of 1812,
a Respectable Citizen of
Batavia, and a Martyr
to the Freedom of Writing
Printing and Speaking the
Truth. He was Abducted
from Near this Spot in the
Year 1826, by Free Masons
and Murdered for Revealing
the Secrets of their Order.

In 1826, Morgan copyrighted a volume entitled *Illustrations of Masonry*, which had a substantial sale and was pirated by printers in many other countries. Morgan, whose war record is not indicated by War Department files, was not abducted by an official Masonic group, although he was held on various charges in Canandaigua, New York, and at Fort Niagara, and available evidence suggests that he died a natural death. The alleged body of Morgan was proved on a third inquest to be that of a Canadian and it is this body that the monument marks.

Written with an Iron Pen

The iron pen of the stonecutter commemorates the lives of those who have devoted themselves to writing. Occasionally a gravestone is inscribed with suitable sentiments from a person's own books. Few of these specimens are more appealing than those found on the handsome monument in Riverside Cemetery, Asheville, North Carolina:

Tom
Son of
W. O. and Julia E.
Wolfe
A Beloved American Author
Oct. 3, 1900–Sept. 15, 1938
The last voyage, the longest, the best.
Look Homeward, Angel.
Death bent to touch his chosen son with
mercy, love, and pity, and put the seal
of honor on him when he died.
The Web and the Rock.

Lines from the poetry of Paul Laurence Dunbar, died 1906, aged 34, are reproduced on his stone in Woodlawn Cemetery, Dayton, Ohio:

Lay me down beneaf de willers in de grass,
Where de branch'll go a-singin' as it pass.

> An' w'en I's a-layin' low
> I kin heah it as I go
> Sayin' 'Sleep, ma honey, tek yo' res' at las'.'

Three great American writers are buried in Sleepy Hollow Cemetery, Concord, Massachusetts. The gravestone of Henry David Thoreau, died 1862, aged 44, is marked with the single word:

> Henry

A square stone to Nathaniel Hawthorne, died 1864, aged 59, is inscribed:

> Hawthorne

The marker of Ralph Waldo Emerson, died 1882, aged 78, bears a quotation from his own pen:

> The passive master lent his hand
> To the vast Soul that o'er him planned.

The circumstances surrounding the death of Edgar Allan Poe are not known. He was found in a semi-conscious condition outside of a tavern in Baltimore, Maryland, which contained a polling place, on Wednesday, 3 October 1849, and was taken to a hospital. There he died on Sunday without ever recovering consciousness sufficiently to say what had happened to him. It was election time, and it has been suggested that he may have been drugged and "voted" several times. A single carriage held those who mourned at his burial in Westminster Presbyterian churchyard, Baltimore. In the rear of the churchyard is a marker reading:

> Original Burial Place of
> Edgar Allan Poe
> from
> Oct. 9, 1849
> until
> Nov. 17, 1875
> Mrs. Marie Clemm his mother in law
> Lies upon his right and Virginia Poe,
> his wife, upon his left, under the
> monument erected to him
> in this cemetery.

At the top of the marker is a stone relief of a raven with the super-scription: "Quoth the Raven nevermore."

In the front of the graveyard is a monument bearing a bronze cast of Poe's face, erected through gifts of school children.

When Poe was fifteen he met Jane Stith Stanard, the mother of a school friend, who died shortly afterward. He called her "the first pure ideal love of my life" and immortalized his idolatry in one of his poems, "To Helen." Her gravestone in Shockoe Cemetery, Richmond, Virginia, is inscribed:

> To the Memory of Jane Stith Stanard, Daughter
> of Adam Craig late of the city of Richmond and
> the beloved wife of Robert Stanard. This
> monument is dedicated by the conjugal affection
> which retaining fondly cherished recollection
> of the graces of mind and person by which it
> was inspired of the purity and tenderness of
> heart the gentleness, benignity of temper, the
> piety and virtue by which it was preserved,
> strengthened increased: mourns with deep
> but resigned sorrow the sad dispensation that
> has consigned it's beloved object to this
> early tomb. She departed this life on the
> 28th of April in the year 1824 in the thirty
> first year of her age.

At the foot of this stone is a brass plate reading:

> Poe's Helen
> Helen, like thy human eye
> There th' uneasy violets lie
> There the reedy grass doth wave
> Over the old forgotten grave
> One by one from the tree top
> There the eternal dews do drop.

Inscribed on the monument to Poe's mother, Elizabeth Arnold, died 1811, aged 24, in St. John's churchyard, Richmond, Virginia, is the following tribute which first appeared in *The Broadway Journal,* 19 July 1845:

> The actor of talent is poor at heart, indeed, if he do not
> look with contempt upon the mediocrity even of a king.
> The writer of this article is himself the son of an actress
> —has invariably made it his boast—and no earl was ever
> prouder of his earldom than he of the descent from a woman
> who, although well born, hesitated not to consecrate to the
> drama her brief career of genius and of beauty.

A bronze marker inset on an irregular boulder in Parish Burial Ground, Kittery Point, Maine, bears a verse that Robert Browning wrote for Levi Lincoln Thaxter, husband of the poet Celia Thaxter and an American interpreter of Browning's poetry, died 1884, aged 60:

> Thou, whom these eyes saw never! Say friends true
> Who say my soul, helped onward by my song,
> Though all unwittingly, has helped thee too?
> I gave of but the little that I knew:
> How were the gift requited, while along
> Life's path I pace, couldst thou make weakness strong!
> Help me with knowledge—for Life's Old—Death's New!
> R. B. to L. L. T., April 1885.

The last word in a long literary feud between Ella Wheeler Wilcox and John A. Joyce is inscribed on the monument Joyce erected for himself in Oak Hill Cemetery, Washington, D. C. On the monument are several quotations which Joyce, died 1915, aged 72, claimed as his own. One reads:

> Laugh and the world laughs with you
> Weep and you weep alone.

When the Wilcox poem "Solitude" was published in 1883, Joyce let it be known that twenty years earlier he had composed not only the two memorable lines but the entire poem. Mrs. Wilcox thereupon offered $5000 to anyone who could produce a printed copy of the poem which was dated earlier than her volume.

A few months before his death in 1944, Irvin S. Cobb, prolific writer and humorist, wrote and sealed directions for his own burial. The statement reads in part:

In death I desire that no one shall look upon my face and once more I charge my family as already and repeatedly I have done, that they shall put on none of the bogus habiliments of so-called mourning . . . I ask that my body be wrapped in a plain sheet or cloth and placed in an inexpensive container and immediately cremated—without any special formality or ceremony . . . When convenience suits, I ask that the plain canister—nothing fancy there, please—containing my ashes shall be taken to Paducah, and that at the proper planting season a hole shall be dug in our family lot or elsewhere at Oak Grove and a dogwood tree planted there and the ashes strewn in the hole to fertilize the tree roots. Should the tree live that will be monument enough for me. But should my surviving relatives desire to mark the spot further, I make so bold as to suggest that they use either a slab of plain Kentucky lime-stone set flat in the kindly earth, or a rugged natural boulder of Southern granite bearing a small bronze plate with my name on it . . . Also on the bronze tablet or the stone slab as the case may be, and provided it doesn't cost too much, I'd like to have inscribed certain lines from the epitaph which Robert Louis Stevenson wrote for himself . . . Or, if a simpler single line bearing the same imprint seems desirable, I offer this one as suitable: "I Have Come Back Home."

Sometime after Cobb's death on 10 March 1944, the ashes were deposited in a six-square-inch stone container, which in turn was buried in Oak Grove Cemetery, Paducah. The spot is marked by a dogwood tree and an eight-ton boulder upon which is inscribed:

Irvin Shrewsbury Cobb

1876-1944

"Back Home"

After his death, the ashes of Damon Runyon, journalist and story writer, died 1946, aged 62, were, according to a final request, dispersed by his friend Captain Eddie Rickenbacker over Manhattan from an airplane. "I desire," he asked, "that my body be cremated and my ashes scattered over the island of Manhattan, the place that I truly loved and that was good to me."

The poet Joaquin Miller, died 1913, aged 74, planned more than thirty years before his death for his exit in flames from this world. At The Hights, his estate above Oakland, California, he constructed the edifice upon which he planned that his body should be burned. "The funeral pile itself, a solid mass of masonry, ten feet square and eight feet high, he built with his own hands," writes Martin Severin Peterson in *Joaquin Miller, Literary Frontiersman* (1937). "He made it of six hundred and twenty granite boulders set in cement. He designed it for the centuries. It was to be approached from the west by three steps. These led up to the crematorium, a coffin-shaped hollow in the upper surface of the pile. Vents for securing a strong draft led into this hollow, and there was a place also for the funeral brands." Before his final illness he prepared the faggots that were to be used. His plans were interrupted somewhat, however, by authorities who required that his body be cremated at Oakland. A few weeks later friends deposited the ashes on the pyre and lit the faggots.

When John Gay died in 1732, aged 47, he was buried in Westminster Abbey and these lines were inscribed on his monument:

> Life is a jest, and all things show it;
> I thought so once, but now I know it.

The epitaph of the English poet and dramatist are reproduced—with a discreet variation—on the slab to Elizabeth Key, died 1813, aged 18, in Colonial Cemetery, Savannah, Georgia:

> Life is but a span
> And all things shew it,
> I thought so once
> But now I know it.

Inscribed on the grave of James E. Hill, died 1921, aged 69, in Evergreen Cemetery, Colorado Springs, Colorado, is an American's claim to distinguished ancestry:

> Direct descendant of Shakespeare.

Hill's background represents, perhaps, a collateral descendancy, for Shakespeare's last legitimate descendant died before 1700.

The Unlettered Muse

Epitaph writers often worked without the benefit of a copyreader, or so it would seem. For instance, the inscription to William B. Silvers, died 1848, aged 20, in Old Van Marten Cemetery, Lyons, New York, includes this confusion of metaphors:

> And thou art gone thy short life is fled
> And numbered with the early dead
> Like a flower blooming fresh and fair
> Sailing the great waters and taking the summer air
> Thou art gone, thy body sleeps
> In the new made grave while affection weeps.

A tombstone in Catholic Cemetery, La Pointe, Wisconsin, reads:

To the Memory
of
Abraham Beaulieu
Born 15 September
1822
Accidentaly shot
4th April 1844
As a mark of affection
from his brother.

Misspelling makes this inscription to Gertrude Walker, 1893, aged 4, in the Lt. John Walker Cemetery, near White Horn, Tennessee, unusually interesting:

Gone to be an angle.

Engraved on a common field stone in Old Settler's Burial Field, Lancaster, Massachusetts, are these words:

Sarah Prescott
Hur Blased Soul Asanded up to Heaven.
July 14 1709.

Copied from a monument to Marcy Hale, died 1719, aged 38, in Green Cemetery, Glastonbury, Connecticut, is this epitaph:

Here lies one wh
os life thrads
cut asunder she
was strcke dead
by a clap of thunder.

This strange epitaph to Esther Cathy, died 1825, aged 83, is found in Steele Creek Presbyterian churchyard near Charlotte, North Carolina:

Death like a mighty quonker roams
To call poor mortals to their tombs
Excusing none though e'er so young
Though e'er so virtuous, rich or strong.

In the now defunct Methodist Cemetery, St. Louis, Missouri, was once found a graveboard reading:

Here lize a stranger braiv,
Who died while fightin' the Suthern Confederacy to save
Piece to his dust.
Braive Suthern friend
From iland 10
You reach a Glory us end.

We plase these flowrs above the stranger's hed,
In honor of the shiverlus ded.
  Sweet spirit rest in Heven
  Ther'll be known Yankis there.

The mistake of a stonecutter—or the work of a practical joker—gives a strange variation to the frequently used gravestone sentiment, "My glass is run," on the tall marker to James Ewins, died 1781, aged 70, in Forest Hill Cemetery, East Derry, New Hampshire:

  My glass is Rum.

Long of interest was the inadvertent error in the inscription to Mrs. Susannah Ensign, died 1825, aged 54, in Presbyterian churchyard, Cooperstown, New York. The stonecutter, apparently crowded for space, omitted a final letter in a pious sentiment with this unusual result:
  Lord, she is Thin.

An "e" has recently been added to the line.

Some stonecutters were also good promotion men. One Ohio man was so proud of his work that he could not omit an advertising reference on the gravestone to his wife Jane who died in 1880. The inscription, now partly obliterated, from Springdale, Ohio, reads:

Here lies Jane Smith, wife of Thomas Smith, marble
cutter. This monument was erected by her husband
as a tribute to her memory and a specimen of his
work. Monuments of the same style 350 dollars.

Another stonecutter, who knew that tombstone inscriptions were read, put at the bottom of the stone to Mrs. Elizabeth Blake, died 1804, aged 83, in Old Washington Street Cemetery, Keene, New Hampshire:

  Made by Mose
  Wright of Rockingham
  Vt. Price 8 dollars.

A tombstone in Burlington Flats, New York, says:

  This in me
  Mory of Abig

al Chapin she was
Wife to Gad C.: She died: ifr
of Aug. 1806 in the 37th
year of her age.
These stons formd and
lettord by William Goff—
by the request of her kind
and frindly daughters.
Price 20s

In Old Hill Burying Ground, Concord, Massachusetts, is this inscription, carved on the first white marble tombstone erected in the vicinity and significant in suggesting the date when white marble superseded common slate:

This stone is designed
by its durability
to perpetuate the memory,
and by its colour,
to signify the moral character
of
Miss Abigail Dudley,
who died Jan. 4, 1812,
aged 73.

On the tombstone to James Lccson, died 1794, aged 38, in Trinity churchyard, New York City, is a curious inscription in the form of a cryptogram:

A Trinity Church guidebook offers this explanation:

By drawing two parallel lines across two other parallel lines at right angles, it will be found that a square is formed around which, by extension of the lines, eight uncompleted squares are made or suggested. Placing a dot in the center of each of the nine squares and beginning at the upper left corner, 'A' is found—see the 11th character of the legend; and going from left to right, the letters succeed

*naturally. 'I' and 'J' are identical. 'K' is the same as 'A' with one more
dot, and so on, until 'T,' when 'A's' corner is once more reached, and
now the dots are omitted. By the simple change of a starting point
and a different disposition of the dots an infinite variety of alphabets
may be constructed on this original scheme.*

R E M E M B E R   D E A T H

An example of the use of a punning epitaph is found in Oxford,
Massachusetts, on the gravestone of Capt. Hezekiah Stone, died 1771:

> Beneath this Stone
> Death's Prisner lies
> The Stone shall move
> The Prisner Rise.

A brief inscription is often more suggestive than a lengthy epitaph.
One such is in East Calais, Vermont:

P. S.
The Old Nuisance

A local legend says that Philip Sydney Bennett lived with a married
daughter during the last years of his life. When he overheard his son-
in-law asking how long the old nuisance would be around, he ordered
a tombstone carved to perpetuate the insult.

The laconic epitaph to Nicholas Eve, Parish Burial Ground, Kittery
Point, Maine, reads:

Old and Still

A slab, which omits family name and dates, in Burlington Flats,
New York, says simply:

Poor Elizabeth
Only 19

Even briefer is this from Norris Cemetery, Damariscotta, Maine:

Poor Betty

On a two-foot field boulder in the old cemetery at South Wheelock, Vermont, is carved:

T.H.
Exit N. 6 1811

A small stone in Pioneer Cemetery, Canandaigua, New York, reads:

Hic Jacit
Old Phillis

An inscription, dated 1784, in Steele Creek Presbyterian churchyard near Charlotte, North Carolina, wastes no words:

J	A	M	E	S
G	R	E	E	R
L	I	E	T	H
H	E	R	E	&c

The tribute to Mary Ann Andrews, died 1915, aged 93, in Christian churchyard near Conklingville, New York, records:

She hath done what she could.

In St. Andrew's churchyard, Staten Island, New York, is an epitaph to John Young, died 1836, reading:

Those that knew him best deplored him most.

These words mark a stone to Charles DuPlessis, died 1907, aged 53, in Rosehill Cemetery, Chicago, Illinois:

Now Aint
That Too Bad

This brusque sentiment is found on a stone in New Gray Cemetery, Knoxville, Tennessee:

Anything for a change.

More is suggested than is stated on the stone to Charles Bowker, died 1874, in Restland Cemetery, Wilmington, Vermont:

> It is all right.

On a marble shaft in Bradford, Vermont, is a two-line inscription to Mary Hoyt, died 1836, which states:

> She lived—what more can there be said
> She died—and all we know she's dead.

In Harvard, Massachusetts, is a tombstone to Deacon Lemuel Willard, died 1821, aged 69, which reads:

> When present usefull;
> Absent, wanted.
> Lived, respected:
> Died, Lamented.

A blunt sentiment concludes an inscription from a tombstone in Hill Burying Ground, Concord, Massachusetts:

> M. S.
> Lieut. Daniel Hoar
> Obt Feb. ye 8th 1773 AEt 93.
> By honest Industery &
> Prudent OEconemy he acquired
> a handsome fortune for a man
> in Privet Carrecter. He
> enjoyed a long life & uninter-
> rupted state of health Blessings
> that ever attend excersies &
> Temperance.
> S. V.
> Here's the last end of Mortal story He's Dead.

The inscription to Samuel McMillan, died 1815, aged 22, in Colonial Cemetery, Savannah, Georgia, concludes:

> Stranger here rests a body
> That was the tenement of a soul
> Of sterling value.

Mary Cross, died 1808, aged 27, is commemorated in St. Michael's churchyard, Charleston, South Carolina, in this manner:

> Her unrival'd virtues are embalm'd
> in the memory of her friends.

In Lewis Cemetery, Bemus Point, New York, is this epitaph to Levina Reed, died 1833, aged 45:

> Embalmed in Love
> She rests above.

An epitaph in Norway, Maine, relates:

> Asa Barton
> Aged 54 years.
> His faults are buried with him
> Beneath this stone. His virtues
> (if he had any) are remembered by
> his friends.
> This is his own epitaph.

An understatement is inscribed on the gravestone to Jonas Temple, died 1815, aged 80, in Old Cemetery, Boylston, Massachusetts:

> His private character was pure;
> allowing for human frailties,
> his Christian life was unblemished.

At a loss apparently to express their feelings in words the friends of Asenath Soule, died 1865, aged 87, prepared this epitaph for her tombstone in Mayflower Cemetery, Duxbury, Massachusetts:

> The chisel can't help
> her any.

Grave Figures

Length of life is commemorated in an epitaph in the Old Burying Ground, Shutesbury, Massachusetts:

> Erected by the Town of
> Shutesbury in memory of
> Ephriam Pratt
> Born in East Sudbury
> Nov. 1, 1686. Removed to
> Shutesbury soon after its
> first settlement where
> he resided until he
> Died May 22, 1804.
> In his 117 year.
> He was remarkably cheer-
> ful in his disposition and
> temperate in his habits.
> He swung a scythe 101 con-
> secutive years and mounted
> a horse without assistance
> at the age of 110.

Reliable records, however, indicate that the age of 117 is inaccurate; Mr. Pratt died at a mere 99.

According to his inscription in Union Church Cemetery, near Unionville, Missouri, Charles Golliher died in November 1888 at the age of 123.

Inscribed on the monument of John Hill, died 1832, aged 128, in Cedar Grove Cemetery, Chambersburg, Pennsylvania, is this biographical sketch:

> Born Herefordshire, England, Reign of Queen
> Ann—Enlisted under George I—Served Twenty-
> Eight Years in England, Ireland, Spain and
> America. At Close of French and Indian
> War, Settled in Franklin County. Buried
> in Unmarked Grave—Lutheran Graveyard,
> St. Thomas, Pa. Probably Oldest Man Ever
> Lived in Pennsylvania.

The tombstone of Triphena Shepard, died 1840, aged 99, in Village Cemetery, Plainfield, Vermont, suggests:

> I would not live always.

The unattractiveness of old age is suggested in an inscription in Milford, Connecticut:

> In memory of
> Sarah Prudden
> who with a happier
> world in view depar
> ted this mortal state
> July 27th 1788 in the
> 8oth year of her age.
> Our age to seventy years is set
> How short the term how frail the state
> And if to Eighty we arrive
> We rather sigh & groan than live.

The grave of another octogenarian, John Daby, died 1769, aged 80, buried in the Burial Grounds, Harvard, Massachusetts, is marked with these lines:

'Tis but a few whose Days amount
To three score and ten;
And all beyond that short Account,
Is Sorrow Toil and Pain.
Our Vitals with laborious strife,
Bear up the crazy Load,
And drag those poor Remains of Life,
Along the tiresome Road.

A particularly appealing epitaph emphasizes the length of life of Ebenezer Hawes, died 1812, aged 91, in Wrentham, Massachusetts:

Of no distemper, of no blast he dy'd,
But fell like autumn fruit, that mellow'd long;
E'en wondered at, why he no sooner dropt.
Fate seemed to wind him up for fourscore years,
Yet restless ran he on, ten winters more,
Till like a clock worn out with eating time,
The wheels of weary life at last stood still.

A remarkable coincidence is remembered in this epitaph in Old Burying Ground, Norwichtown, Connecticut:

Here Lyeth the Remains of
Doctor Theophilus Rogers
and of Mrs. Elizabeth his Wife
Daughter of Mr. William Hide
The Doctr died on the 29th of
Septemr 1753 in the 54th Year
of his age. And his Wife on the
24th of Novemr 1753 in the
54th Year of her age also.
Both continued to the same Year
of Life, Both died on the same
day of the Week, and both
deposited in this Grave.

The statistical record of Eunice Page, died 1888, aged 73, in Plainfield, Vermont, is stated on her stone:

> Five times five years I lived a virgin's life,
> Nine times five years I lived a virtuous wife,
> Wearied of this mortal life, I rest.

The three-year discrepancy is unexplained.

In Central Cemetery, Dunstable, Massachusetts, this unusual chronicle appears:

> In memory of Mrs. Easther Woodward
> w. of Mr. John Woodward
> who d. Jany 26, 1797, aged 32 yrs.
> On this day she was born,
> On this day, she was marred,
> On this day she deceast,
> Not many hours vared.

A coincidence in the dates of birth and death of a husband and wife is recorded on identical stones in Riverside Cemetery, Asheville, North Carolina:

Ida Mae Whiteside	Edw. W. Whiteside
June 23, 1877	April 12, 1864
June 23, 1908	April 12, 1930

Identical monuments to twins who died on the same day are found in Simsbury, Connecticut:

Eva Louisa Eno	Ada Letitia Eno Sanford
Born Feb. 14th. 1828	Born Feb. 14th. 1828
Died Nov. 16th. 1911	Died Nov. 16th. 1911
Not Separated in Death	Not Separated in Death

Twin brothers, both railroad engineers, who died in the same year, are remembered by this inscription in Bellevue Cemetery, Wilmington, North Carolina:

> Born 1875
>
> B. L. Grant   C. T. Grant
> Died Oct. 16, 1920   Died Jan. 30, 1920
> As twins to mortal life we came,
> As twins we rest together;

As twins we hope to rise again;
As twins with Christ forever.

An epitaph in St. Peter's Cemetery, Oxford, Mississippi, identifies the date of birth of a former president of the University of Mississippi in an unusual manner:

Sacred to the Memory of
Augustus Baldwin Longstreet
who was born in Augusta, Ga.
on the day the sun crossed the Line
A.D. 1790

Detailed figures sometimes give specific information concerning the hour of death. The tombstone to Joseph Oliver, founder of Milford, Delaware, in Christ Episcopal churchyard, Milford, says that he died in 1807 "aged about 80 years," at "twenty minutes to seven in the morning."

A similar detail is given on the grave in Old Burying Ground, Groton, Massachusetts, of Samuel Bowers, died 16 December 1768, at "half a hour after Three of the Clock in ye Afternoon and in the Fifty Eight year of his age."

This curious inscription is found in St. Michael's churchyard, Charleston, South Carolina, on the grave of John Singleton, died 1799, aged 40:

Sacred & Solemn
to
the Memory of 1 in 4 & 4 in 1.
A Husband, Father, Grandfather & Father in Law.

The Philosopher's Stone

These mute philosophies represent the layman's quest for truth and understanding. The parents of Sanford Holmes, died 1801, aged 10 months, wrote for his grave in Midway, Georgia:

> The cradle rocks us nearer to the tomb
> Our birth is nothing but our death begun.

In Congregational churchyard, Windsor, Connecticut, is the epitaph of Cynthia Gillet, died 1813, aged 15:

> How short!
> How precarious!
> How uncertain is Life,
> How soon the thread of life is spun.
> A breath, a gasp, a groan or two,
> And we are seen no more.
> Yet on this brittle thread hangs a
> Vast eternity (alarming thought).

The limitation of man's understanding is suggested on the tombstone of James Hill, died 1869, aged 5 months, in Scotland Graveyard, Bridgewater, Massachusetts:

> God knows why.

When Benjamin Butler, a loyal British subject who was imprisoned in 1776 on a charge of "defaming the Honourable Continental Congress," died in 1787 of "a Phthisis pulmonaris," aged 48, his grave in Old Burying Ground, Norwichtown, Connecticut, was inscribed:

> Alas, poor human nature!

The transitory nature of life is described on the stone to Thomas Jackson, died 1794, aged 67, on Burial Hill, Plymouth, Massachusetts:

> The spider's most attenuated thread
> Is cord, is cable, to man's slender tie.

The sonorous sounds of Ecclesiastes are suggested by the epitaph to Sally Simmons, died 1806, aged 23, in Mayflower Cemetery, Duxbury, Massachusetts:

> They that are born of a woman are of few days
> & full of trouble. They come forth like a
> flower & are cut down. They are altogether
> vanity.

From Meeting House Hill Burial Ground, Dunstable, Massachusetts, comes the following:

> Memento Mori. Here lies the body of Lieut. John
> Kendall who departed this life July the 27th, An.
> Dom., 1759, aged 63 years, 6 months, and 8 days.
> Few and Evil.
> Life is a Blessing can't be sold,
>   The Ransom is too high;
> Justice will ne'er be brib'd with gold,
>   That man may never die.
>
> You see the Foolish & the Wise,
>   The Timerous & the Brave,
> Quit their Possessions, close their eyes
>   And hasten to the Grave.

M. M. Secor, one-time mayor of Racine, Wisconsin, died 1911, aged 69, was apparently perplexed by a question that has puzzled theologians for centuries. His monument in Racine Cemetery reads:

The World is my Home
To do Good is my Religion
Why did the Good God
Create a bad Devil.

Before he died in 1873 at the age of 80, Dr. George W. Gale, eccentric physician in Exeter, New Hampshire, wrote this explanation of life which is inscribed on his stone in the local cemetery:

God
Who Is
Omnipotent, Omniscient, Omnipresent
Electric fluid in his life principal
of man, which ceased to act through
the organization of
Dr. George W. Gale
The breath of life is the breath of life, after
it ceased to act, in the formation of dust, which
is returned to earth from which it was taken.
Man has no power independent of any other power.

Another Yankee physician, Dr. George W. Packard, was buried ten years later, aged 53, in Pine Hill Cemetery, Westfield, Massachusetts, with these words on his gravestone:

Anchored for want of breath. The same power
which carried me through the revolving cycles
of earth will carry me farther if called upon
to go. I die thoroughly convinced of a wise
disposition of all events and scepticle of all
ancient and modern mythological humbug myths,
as taught for position and power. Meet me,
dear friends, when the chemistry of the uni-
verse will permit.   G.W.P.

On the grave of Albert B. Sheldon, died 1935, aged 93, in Sherman, New York, is this epitaph:

He gave banquets when defeated.
He never run up the flag of truce.

No king was more generously blessed in death than James Richey, died 1806, aged 51, whose tombstone in East Hill Cemetery, Peterborough, New Hampshire, relates:

> A coffin, sheat & grave's
> My earthly store;
> Tis all I want; & kings
> Can have no more.

This epitaph is reported in *Notes and Queries* for 19 July 1884, as having been transcribed from a tombstone in Ohio:

> Earls and monarchs of the dead,
> Who so long the worms have fed,
> I am coming to your chilly bed;
> Edge close, and give me room.

Every tombstone offers mute evidence that the Grim Reaper, sooner or later, visits every son of Adam. Some epitaphs, however, emphasize this truth. The inevitable visit is described on the headstone to Bennett Williamson, died 1836, aged 21, in Old Colonial Cemetery, Savannah, Georgia:

> Neither poverty nor influence can sway
> Youth, health nor strength can stay
> All submit to the scrutinizing search
> Of the pale monster in his onward march.

The inscription to John H. Brown, died 1778, in the same cemetery says:

> Long at his couch, Death took his patient stand
> And menaced oft oft & oft with held the blow
> Say, are you sure his mercy shall extend
> To you so long a span, alas ye sigh!
> Make then while yet ye may your God your friend
> And learn with equal ease to sleep or die.

An unusual epitaph to George Hicks, Jr., died 1848, aged 20, in Deerfield, New York, offers poor consolation to the survivors:

> Farewell my friends to all below
> The monster death has laid me low
> Deeply would your hearts rejoice
> To hear again my living voice.

A soldier of the Revolution, Jacob Parmenter, died 1836, aged 74, fought for freedom but at last was out-fought by death. His tombstone in Eastman Cemetery, Attica, New York, records:

> In early life in freedom's cause
> He fought to set his country free.
> But now a slave to nature's laws
> The tyrant death has conquered thee.

An epitaph, dating back to about 1800, in the burial grounds of the Estelle family, near Lakewood, New Jersey, laments:

> Death did to me
> Short warning give,
> Therefore, be careful
> How you live.
> My weeping friends
> I leave behind—
> I had not time
> To speak my mind.

Short notice was given to John Burdick, died 1823, aged 18, whose gravestone at Brookfield, New York, reads:

> I died in a moment.

Polly Youngs, died 1809, aged 33, is buried in Congregational churchyard, Windsor, Connecticut, with this curious epitaph:

> No warning given, unceremonious fate
> A sudden rush from life's meridian joys
> A wrench from all we love, from all we are
> A restless bed of pain, a plunge opaque.

The inscription to Lizzie Angell, died 1932, aged 83, in Forest Hill Cemetery, East Derry, New Hampshire, complains:

> I don't know how to die.

Death was faced courageously by James Seward, died 1792, aged 6 months, and buried in Copp's Hill Burying Ground, Boston, Massachusetts:

> He bore a lingering sickness with patience,
> And met the King of Terrors with a smile.

The epitaph to an inventor, Jonathan Kilborn, died 1785, in Old Cemetery, Colchester, Connecticut, reads:

> He was a man of invention great
> Above all that lived nigh
> But he could not invent to live
> When God called him to die.

Not infrequently did the older inscriptions beg that passers-by pause and shed tears. This request appears on the tombstone to Eunice Davison, died 1776, aged 23, in Milford, Connecticut:

> See there, all plae and dead she lies
> Forever flowing from my streaming eyes
> Eunice is fled, the lovliest mind
> Faith, sweetness, witt, together joined
> Dwell faith & wit & sweetness there
> O view the change and drip a tear.

A macabre invitation is on the gravestone to the Reverend Jedediah Dewey, died 1778, aged 65, in Old Cemetery, Bennington, Vermont:

> Of comfort no man speak! Let's talk of
> graves and worms and epitaphs. Make
> dust our paper, and with rainy eyes, write
> sorrow on the bosom of the earth!

The words are from Shakespeare's *Richard II.*

An unusual display of grief was shown by friends of Rebecca Corey, seamstress, died 1810, who was buried in Middle Cemetery, Lancaster, Massachusetts:

> Her neighbors and friends stood weeping
> and showing the coats and garments which
> she made while she was with them.

Tradition says that a young Charleston, South Carolina, merchant, having gone to Salem College to visit his sweetheart, died before he returned to his home. The story cannot be verified, but an inscription on a slab in the Moravian graveyard, Winston-Salem, North Carolina, indicates that three years later the young woman had not forgotten him:

> To the memory of Samuel Clary, a native of South
> Carolina, formerly a respectable merchant of
> Charleston. He was born in the District of
> Williams-Burgh in the year 1792 and died at this
> place on the 6th of September, 1828.
>> Ah, friends at home and kindred dear!
>> If chance should bring you here,
>> Remember that his Leonora dear
>> Bedewed this grave with many a tear.
>>> Sept. 10, 1831.

Inscribed in the McKinstry burying place, Ellington, Connecticut, is the following:

> Here Rests ye Last Rema-
> ins of Mr Alexander McKin-
> stry ye Kind husband ten-
> der Parent Dutiful Son
> Affectionate Brother Faith-
> ful Frind Generous Master
> Compasionate & obliging
> Neighbour ye unhappy
> hous look Diselate &
> Mourns & Every Door
> Groans doalful as it turns
> ye Pillers Languish and each
> Silent wall in Greaf lament
> ye Masters fall who Departed
> this life Novemr ye 9th, 1759
> in ye 30th Year of his Age.

The futility of tears is implied by the epitaph to Fitch Welch, died 1787, aged 52, in Milford, Connecticut:

> In vain we mourn & drop these friendly tears
> Death & the grave have neither Eyes nor Ears.

On Burial Hill, Plymouth, Massachusetts, the gravestone to Sally C. Robbins, killed "by a fall from a chaise" in 1828, aged 25, solemnly declares:

> Our home is in the grave;
> Here dwells the multitude; we gaze around,
> We read their monuments, we sigh and
> while we sigh, we sink.

A variation of the familiar lines by Edna St. Vincent Millay are on the monument of N. Hardy Payne, died 1936, aged 48, in Memorial Gardens, Lubbock, Texas:

> He burnt his candle at both ends
> It did not last the night,
> But oh, my dears, and oh, my friends,
> It made a lovely light.

Memento Mori

Memento Mori is the solemn motto on many old tombstones warning the living: "Remember you must die." Some persons have anticipated death with elaborate preparations, mindful, perhaps, of the words of Benedick in *Much Ado about Nothing:* "If a man do not erect in this age his own tomb ere he dies, he shall live no longer in monument than the bell rings and the widow weeps."

Fearful of a curse placed on his life, Wylly Barron of Augusta, Georgia, constructed a costly granite tomb for himself in Magnolia Cemetery twenty-four years before his death. Barron, a picturesque gentleman gambler, ruled that no one should patronize his tables who was financially unable to meet his losses. This rule and his tomb were the result of the suicide of a youthful customer who had lost heavily and died with the bitter prophecy that Barron would die penniless and without a burial place.

The immense square vault assured Barron that he would not be buried in a pauper's field. He provided a metal casket and specified that after his burial the key should be put in a pipe in the center of the vault. In front of the vault Barron later placed a small iron dog in memory of a little black terrier which had been his constant companion for years. One day in New York City, the dog jumped to his death from a hotel window in a frantic effort to get to the side of his master on the street below.

The inscription of Barron's tomb records:

Farewell, vain world, I have enough of thee
And now am careless what thou sayest of me;
Thy smiles I court not nor thy frowns I fear;
My cares are past, my head lies quiet here.
What faults you know in me take care to shun
And look at home, enough there's to be done.

W. W. Barron.   Born in Elbert Co., Oct. 8, 1807.
Died Dec. 19, 1884.   Aged 88 years.

Barron died penniless.

The fear of being buried alive haunted the mind of Timothy Clark Smith, appointed American consul in Odessa, Russia, in 1861, and consul in Galatz, Romania, in 1878. A native of Monkton, Vermont, Smith died in Middlebury, Vermont, while he was a guest at the Middlebury Inn. Aware of his fear of being buried alive, his family kept his body in the hotel room until town authorities ordered him interred. His body was then removed to a vault in Evergreen Cemetery, New Haven, Vermont, where it was kept until his grave preparations were completed. Guards were placed at the vault in case Smith should come to life. When the grave was finished, a piece of plate glass, about fourteen-inches square, was set into the top of a cement tube that led into the underground tomb. In his hand was placed a bell which was to be rung in the event that his burial was in error.

The inscriptions on some graves notify later generations that certain plots are already in use. The epitaph to John Mather, died 1775, aged 38, in St. James' churchyard, My Lady's Manor, Monkton, Maryland, says:

My Pilgrimage I run apace,
My resting place is here.
This stone is got to keep the spot,
Lest man should dig too near.

A similar plea marks the grave of Betsy Darling, died 1809, aged 43, in Copp's Hill Burying Ground, Boston, Massachusetts:

She was the mother of 17 children, and around
her lies 12 of them, and 2 were lost at sea.
Brother Sextons,
please leave a clear birth for me
near by this Stone.

In the First Presbyterian churchyard, Elizabeth, New Jersey, the tombstone of General Matthias Ogden, died 1791, aged 34, recounts Ogden's accomplishments and concludes:

> Then reader Weep, for Ogden's dust lies here.
> Weed his grave clean ye men of genius
> for he was your kinsman
> Tread lightly on his ashes ye men of feeling
> for he was your brother.

The inscription to Sarah A. Ring, died 1822, aged 51, in Siloam Cemetery, Vineland, New Jersey, asks that the flowers on the grave be spared:

> Disturb me not, nor my repose
> Nor from my grave to take one rose,
> But let them bloom and fade away,
> Like me, to bloom another day.

Respect for a grave site is tactfully suggested on the tomb of William C. Byrne, died 1834, aged 21, in St. James' graveyard, Wilmington, North Carolina:

> Oh silent grave to thee I trust
> This precious part of mortal dust.
> Keep it safe in sacred tomb
> Until a brother seeks for room.

Friends of John Christie, died 1830, affirmed his good name and their honesty when they provided his tombstone in Agawam Cemetery, Wareham, Massachusetts:

> Hibernia's son himself exiled,
> Without an inmate, wife or child.
> He lived alone.
> And when he died, his purse, tho' small,
> Contained enough to pay us all,
> And buy this stone.

Among those who planned carefully for their own funeral and burial was Brigham Young, pioneer Mormon leader, who died in 1877, aged 76, and is buried in Salt Lake City. Four years before his death he specified:

I want my coffin made of plain one-and-a-quarter redwood boards, not scrimped in length, but two inches longer than I would measure, and from two to three inches wider than is commonly made for a person of my breadth and size, and deep enough to place me on a little comfortable cotton bed, with a good suitable pillow in size and quality. My body dressed in my Temple clothing, and laid nicely into my coffin, and the coffin to have the appearance that if I wanted to turn a little to the right or left I should have plenty of room to do so; the lid can be made crowning.

The purpose of the epitaph on the gravestone of Stephen Hopkins, died 1813, aged 69, in Burlington Flats, New York, is evident:

> I leave this hear
> as will appear
> When I am dead and rotten
> That my friends may see
> and remember me
> and i be not forgotten.

A similar suggestion comes from the stone to Joseph Fairbank, Jr., died 1784, aged 40, in Harvard, Massachusetts:

> Tho' I am dead & in my grave
> & all my bones are rotten!
> When this you see remember me,
> If not yet quite forgotten.

Society's expectation that the husband of Abigail Wanton, died 1726, aged 28, perpetuate her memory is found in an inscription in Island Cemetery, Newport, Rhode Island:

> If tears alas could speak a husband's woe
> My verse would streight in plaintiff numbers flow
> Or if so great a loss deplor'd in vain
> Could solace so my throbbing heart from pain
> Then would I oh sad consolation chuse
> To sooth my cureless grief a private muse

But since thy well-known piety demands
A publick monument at thy George's hands
O Abigail I dedicate this tomb to thee
Thou dearest half of poor forsaken me.

The stone to John Warham, died 1644, in Congregational churchyard, Windsor, Connecticut, says that although the vogue of generous
lapidary sentiment was strong in other communities, local disposition
minimized its use:

Who when hee lived wee drew our vitall breath,
Who when hee dyed his dying was our death.
Who was ye stay of church, of state, of churches staff,
Alas, the times forbid an epitaph.

A strange pink granite monument in Old North Cemetery, Hartford, Connecticut, is almost bitter in stating:

Those who cared for him while living will
know whose body lies resting here. To
others, it does not matter.

This inscription which is dated September 1882 has no further identification and cemetery records list the buried person as "unknown."

The tombstone to Mrs. Sarah Pomeroy, died 1783, aged 48, in Milford, Connecticut, says:

Thou dear departed with no laboured bust
Nor panegyric I insult thy dust
Yet let a child with duty in arrear
Say while he heaves a sigh & drops a tear
The tenderest of all parents Slumbers here.

The name of Captain Thomas Prentice, died 1709, is remembered
because of his inscription in Centre Street Cemetery, Newton Center,
Massachusetts, although the need of an epitaph is questioned:

He that's here interr'd needs no versifying,
a vertuos life will keep ye name from dying,
he'll live, though poets cease the'r scrib'ling rime,
when y't this stone shall mouldred be by time.

The epitaph to Mary Fowler, died 1792, aged 24, in Milford, Connecticut, reads:

> Molly tho pleasant in her day
> Was suddenly seized and sent away
> How soon she's ripe, How soon she's rotten
> Sent to her grave & soon forgotten.

Several years before he died in 1891, Francis Magranis, a shoemaker, wrote these lines which appear on his gravestone in Evergreen Cemetery, South Hadley, Massachusetts:

> My shoes are made
> My work is done
> Yes, dear friends, I'm going home
> And where I've gone
> And how I fare
> There's nobody knows
> And there's nobody cares.

Isaac Sirine of Cherry Valley, Ohio, selected an epitaph before his death in 1867 and had an Ashtabula craftsman put it on a tombstone. Sirine carried the stone home on his back and it was later erected over his grave in the local cemetery. The last two lines were added by members of his family at a later date:

> Here the old man lies
> Nobody laughs, nobody cries
> Where he has gone and how he fares
> Nobody knows, nobody cares.
> But his brother James and his wife Emeline
> They were his friends all the time.

Requiescat in Pace

This Latin phrase from the Mass means "May he rest in peace" and is found frequently inscribed on graves, particularly those of Roman Catholics. A similar idea is expressed in numerous epitaphs. The gravestone to Elizabeth Fernald, died 1816, in Parish Burial Ground, Kittery Point, Maine, for example, says:

> By my request
> Let this dust rest.

The desire for eternal rest is expressed in the inscription to Susannah T. George, died 1872, aged 65, in Groton, Massachusetts:

> My feet are wearied and my hands are tired—
> My soul oppressed;
> And with desire have I long desired
> Rest—only Rest.

In Old Walloomsac Cemetery, Hoosick, New York, is a stone dated 1845 to Peleg Sweet and his wife Desier, both buried in the same grave, which bears these words:

> There is a calm for those who
> Weep,
> A rest for weary pilgrims found.

They softly lie and sweetly
Sleep,
Low in the ground.

A gravestone in Pritchett Cemetery near Boulder, Illinois, comments:

Kiss me and I will go to sleep.
Alice
First and Last
Wife of
Thos. Phillip
Talked to Death by Friends.

Memorial lines to Mrs. Lucretia Crocker, died 1799, aged 22, in West Parish Burying Ground, Barnstable, Massachusetts, suggests:

Here no unwelcome visitors intrude
To interrupt thy happy solitude.

Inscribed on the marker of Louisa Adler, died 1933, aged 60, in Palm Springs, California, is the comment:

Died of Grief
Caused By A Neighbor
Now Rests in Peace

A stone in Chilmark, Massachusetts, reads:

In memory of
Jonathan Tilton
who was born
June 10, 1770
and died May . . . 1837
Here lies the body of Jonathan Tilton,
Whose friends reduced him to a skeleton,
They wronged him out of all he had
And now rejoice that he is dead.

The quatrain is largely obliterated by what appear to be chisel strokes. A volume of local history, Hime's *Story of Martha's Vineyard* (1908), gives these details: "[Tilton] had agreed to transfer his property to a

relative in consideration of being cared for for the remainder of his
days, and the relative faithfully carried out his part of the agreement,
but Tilton appears to have . . . [had] the last word, for he had his
gravestone cut and stored under his bed along with his coffin." Part
of the agreement, the story continues, "was that this stone should be
put over his grave and it was; but the weather must have been extraor-
dinarily violent, for the inscription wore out in a single night so 'tis
said." Another chronicle, Norton's *Martha's Vineyard: History, Leg-
ends, Stories* (1923), says that Tilton's relatives, having befuddled him
with strong drink one night, got from him the deeds to all of his
property. The epitaph represented his final judgment of these relatives.

Death brought release from a world of trouble to Simon Parrett,
died 1718, aged 84, whose inscription at Newport, Rhode Island, records:

> Here doth Simon Parrett Lye
> Whose wrong Did for Justice cry
> But none Could have
> And now the Grave
> Keeps him from Injurie.

A monument, dated 1850, in a private plot in Stonington, Connecticut, marks the grave of a man who could not rest in peace in another
state:

When Rhode Island by her legislation from 1844 to 1850,
Repudiated her Revolutionary Debt Dr. Richmond removed
from that State to this Borough and selected this as his
Family Burial Place: unwilling that the remains of himself
and family should be disgraced by being a part of the common
earth of a Repudiating State.

This epitaph to Mrs. Ammey Hunt, died 1769, aged 40, is from
Copp's Hill Burying Ground, Boston, Massachusetts:

> A sister of Sarah Lucas lieth here,
> Whom I did love most dear;
> And now her soul hath took its flight,
> And bid her spiteful foes good night.

In Oakwood Cemetery, Niagara Falls, New York, are inscriptions
to two persons whose lives contained unusual adventures:

Tombstone of Amun-Her-Khepesh-Ef, West Cemetery, Middlebury, Vermont. See p. 229.

Persecuted for wearing the beard.

Tombstone of Joseph Palmer, Evergreen Cemetery, Leominster, Massachusetts. See p. 229.

Annie Edson Taylor
First to go over
the Horseshoe Fall
in a barrel
and live
Oct. 24, 1901

Carlisle D. Graham
First to go
through the Whirl-
pool Rapids in a
barrel and live
July 11, 1886

Laid to rest in West Cemetery, Middlebury, Vermont, is a royal personage whose inscription reads:

Ashes of Amun-Her-Khepesh-Ef
Aged 2 Years
Son of Sen Woset 3rd
King of Egypt and His Wife
Hathor-Hotpe
1883 B.C.

A century ago the mummy of this child was taken from an Egyptian tomb and in time was secured by the Sheldon Museum of Middlebury. With the passing years the mummy began to disintegrate and its disposal became necessary. The mummy was then cremated and the ashes were buried in the family lot of George W. Mead, a museum associate, who erected the stone in 1945 to the Egyptian who died more than 3700 years before.

Beneath the image of a heavily bearded man on a monument in Evergreen Cemetery, Leominster, Massachusetts, are these words:

Joseph Palmer
Died
Oct. 30, 1873,
AE. 84 yrs. 5 ms.
Persecuted for
wearing the beard.

At a time when most men were clean-shaven, Palmer decided to let his whiskers grow. The idea became in time a fixed principle with Palmer who resisted the coaxing of the clergy and the wheedling of the laity, some of whom looked with suspicion upon bearded persons. At one time some of his townsmen attempted to shave him and because of the resulting skirmish Palmer was jailed. He lived, however, to see the popularity of the beard return.

An earlier persecution in Massachusetts centered at Salem in 1692, when scores of persons were accused of witchcraft and more than 77 were hanged. All manner of unusual experience or coincidence led neighbors to place the hand of guilt frequently on the most unassuming of persons. One such person was Rebecca Nurse, 71 years old, a great-grandmother, and nearly deaf. Her husband was a prosperous farmer and she had not always sympathized with the opinions of the Rev. Samuel Parris, a local clergyman. A tribunal which included John Hathorne, ancestor of the novelist Nathaniel Hawthorne, convicted her. Although forty persons affirmed her innocence by petition, she was hanged on 19 July 1692, on the summit of Gallows Hill, Salem. That night members of her family took her body to the Nurse farm at Danvers for burial. Eighteen years afterward she was exonerated by the General Court and two years later by the Salem church. In 1885 a monument was raised over her grave and a set of verses by John Greenleaf Whittier was included in the inscription:

Rebecca Nurse

Yarmouth, England

1621

Salem, Mass.

1692

O Christian martyr, who for Truth could die

When all about thee owned the hideous lie,

The world redeemed from Superstition's sway

Is breathing freer for thy sake today.

Accused of witchcraft

She declared,

'I am innocent and God will

clear my innocency.'

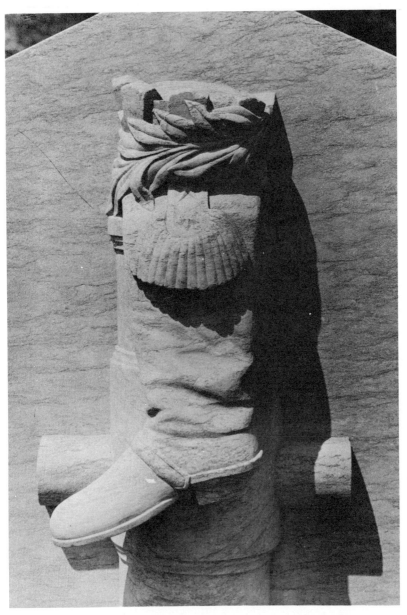

Monument in memory of Benedict Arnold, Saratoga National Historical
Park, New York. See p. 231.

Memorial monument for Jonathan Buck, Buck Cemetery, Bucksport, Maine. See p. 231.

Once acquitted yet falsely
condemned, she suffered
death, July 19, 1692.
In loving memory of her Christian character
Even then truly attested by forty of her neighbors.

Tradition associates a witch's curse with the granite obelisk in Buck
Cemetery, Bucksport, Maine, honoring Colonel Jonathan Buck, "a
worthy citizen & first settler in Buckstown," died 1795, aged 77. De-
spite all efforts to remove it, the outline of a leg and foot is seen on
his monument. The story is that Colonel Buck presided at the execu-
tion of a witch at Haverhill, Massachusetts, and that before her death
she placed a curse on him. To this day the strange defect in the stone
is pointed to as evidence that she would not let people forget her.

"Rest in pieces" might be a fitting comment on the following inscriptions. When an accident made it necessary to amputate a leg of
27-year-old Samuel Jones, the leg was buried with due ceremony in
Washington, New Hampshire, with these words carved on a small
stone:

Capt. Samuel
Jones' Leg which
was amputated
July 7 1804.

On a double headstone in Old Burying Ground, Newport, Rhode
Island, is carved the image of a woman's arm and these inscriptions:

Wait daughtr   also William
William and   their son
Desire Tripp   Died March
died April 24   7th 1784 aged
1780 aged 10   22 mo
mo 10 days   Also his wife's
          arm amputated Feby 20th 1786.

A monument in Saratoga National Historical Park, New York, commemorates the left leg of Benedict Arnold. Carved in bas-relief on
one side of the marble marker are the images of a boot, a cannon,
and a wreath. Arnold's leg was hit by a musket ball as he led an

attack against the forces of General John Burgoyne. Inscribed on the opposite side of the stone is this record, which omits Arnold's name:

In Memory of
the "most brilliant soldier" of the
Continental Army,
who was desperately wounded
on this spot, the sally port of
Burgoynes "Great (Western) Redoubt"
7th October 1777,
winning for his countrymen
the Decisive Battle of the
American Revolution
and for himself the rank of
Major General.

When Arnold died in 1801, aged 59, his body was interred in the vault of St. Mary Parish Church, Battersea, London. It is uncommemorated.

Here Lies

Although *Hic Jacet* is an adequate identification for a grave, some persons have expressed this sentiment in unusual ways.

A monument in Chadbourne Cemetery, Lyman, Maine, is constructed in the shape of a house. The large structure has a door at the front on either side of which is a window. Two chimneys rise above the slanting roof. On the front are the names of William G. and Caroline W. Chadbourne, whose homestead was next to the cemetery. Next to the large house is a smaller one which has a single chimney. On the door is engraved the name "Sally P. Chadbourne." She died in 1900, aged 76.

August Hefner, died 1856, aged 70, lies buried in the community in which he chose to live. His epitaph, however, indicates that he doubted whether the citizens of Waverly, Ohio, appreciated his contributions to the village life. On the slab erected in Evergreen Cemetery is pictured a four-wheeled wagon and a large bell and a dog. Hefner was a scissors and knife grinder who was usually seen in the company of his pet dog. The inscription reads:

> The deceased being asked on the evening of
> his arrival in Waverly where he was going
> answered here and no farther.
>> When your razor is dull
>> and you want to shave
>> think of the man
>> that lays in this grave.

> For there was a time
> It might have been whet
> you was afeared of a dime
> And now its to late.

Lieutenant Noah Jones, died 1781, aged 70, wrote his own grave-stone inscription:

> Beneath this ston's inter'd the bons,
> Ah! frail Remains—Lieut. Noah Jones.
> (His epitaph)

Jones is buried in the "hidden graveyard" on the common, Worcester, Massachusetts. In 1853, the city council voted that the stones in this ancient burying place should be laid flat, their inscriptions carefully copied, and then covered with earth. The grave markers of more than 300 early settlers are now lost from sight.

A curious grave marker in St. Michael's churchyard, Charleston, South Carolina, is a bedstead inscribed with the name "Mary Ann Luyten" and dated September 9, 1770.

A meteor particle marks the grave of George Heady, died 1937, aged 87, in Greenwood Cemetery, Wayne, Nebraska. Heady found the rock one day in his youth when he was digging a well near Wayne. He claimed it was a meteorite and geologists affirmed his belief. Before he died he asked that the oval-shaped stone, which is sixteen inches long and weighs about 250 pounds, be used on his grave. A small granite tablet, cemented to the meteorite, bears his name and dates.

The grave of Louis Agassiz, geologist and naturalist, died 1873, aged 66, in Mt. Auburn Cemetery, Cambridge, Massachusetts, is identified by a medium-sized glacial boulder which was brought from the glacier of the Aar, Switzerland, where Agassiz made extensive studies.

A two-ton glacial boulder of jasper conglomerate, obtained in Canada by Henry A. Ward, one-time associate of Agassiz, died 1906, aged 72, identifies his grave in Mount Hope Cemetery, Rochester, New York.

Indicating the grave of Philo Upson in Mt. Everett Cemetery, South Egremont, Massachusetts, is a large monument cut from the last block taken from his quarry. The inscription says:

This monument covers the
remains of
Philo Upson, aged 37.
The quarry which gave
him so many while he
lived gives this last block
to perpetuate his memory.

On the left side is this further explanation:

Energetic upright
benevolent in all the
relations of life exempl-
ary in business imbued
with the spirit of the age.
While preparing to exe-
cute large & honorable
plans. He was suddenly
removed leaving the record
of his virtues more indilebly
engraved upon the minds
of numerus friends than
this inscription upon the
marble.

An epitaph from New Milford, Connecticut, looks beyond the grave:

Rest here my body till th' Arch Angel's voice,
More son'rous far than nine fold thunder, wakes
The sleeping dead: then rise to thy just sphere,
And be my house immortal!
Composed by the deceased,
Patridge Thacher, Esq.

In 1699 a 700-acre tract in Maryland was patented to John Coats. Later this property, called "Clear Drinking," was taken over by Walter C. Jones who attempted unsuccessfully to establish a mill. When he realized that his venture would not succeed he prepared an epitaph on an old millstone to memorialize the experience:

Here lies the body and bones
Of old Walter C. Jones.
By his not thinking,
He lost "Clear Drinking"
And by his shallow pate
He lost his vast estate.

The millstone was later placed on Jones' grave on his own property in Rockville, Maryland. The section has now been industrialized and the graveyard is gone.

The will of Sarah E. Griffiths, died 1887, aged 66, instructed her executor to provide "a suitable monument and fit up the lot" in the private Griffiths Cemetery near Newmarket, New Hampshire. The executor thought this meant that all of Sarah's fortune should be spent on a monument and so he provided a large one. The sole heir, incensed by this interpretation of the will, erected a small stone to mark his own grave near by. On it was carved a hand which pointed to the towering memorial. Beneath are the words:

A Suitable Monument
and fit up the lot. S.E.G.

The only unusual feature about the vault of Colonel Henry G. Wooldridge, died 1899, aged 77, in Maplewood Cemetery, Mayfield, Kentucky, is that the top bears a carving of a double-barreled shotgun. Standing guard at the vault, however, is one of the most spectacular group of statues to be found anywhere. In 1883 Wooldridge ordered from Italy a life-size standing figure of himself. Between that year and the time of his death, other statues were placed on the lot. From tintypes and meager descriptions, stonecutters carved life-size images of his mother, three sisters, and four brothers, and two grandnieces. Also included in the group are statues of Old Towhead, a hound; Bob, a hunting dog; and a deer and a fox. A second statue of Wooldridge shows him riding his favorite saddle horse, Old Fop.

In 1932, S. P. Dinsmoor of Lucas, Kansas, died at the age of 89. He had given many years to the making of a concrete Garden of Eden in which he had built his own tomb and prescribed the manner of his own burial. Using 2273 bags of cement, Dinsmoor constructed a two-story cement house, a cement tree of life guarded by a cement angel, a cement devil high in another cement tree, cement images of Adam and Eve, and, of course, a cement serpent. In the mausoleum, which rises to a height of forty feet, are cement coffins for himself and his wife. On the top of his coffin is a plate-glass lid which serves two purposes. As Dinsmoor wrote:

I have a will that none except my wife, my descendants, their husbands and wives, shall go in to see me for less than a $1. That will pay some one to look after the place, and I promise everyone that comes in to see me (they can look through the plate glass and . . . see my face) that if I see them dropping a dollar in the hands of the flunky, and I see the dollar, I will give them a smile.

There was an added purpose:

It seems to me that people buried in iron and wooden boxes will be frying and burning up in the resurrection morn. How will they get out when this world is on fire? Cement will not stand fire, the glass will break. This cement lid will fly open and I will sail out like a locust.

At the foot of his coffin Dinsmoor placed a cement jug large enough to hold two gallons of water. He wrote:

In the resurrection morn, if I have to go below, I'll grab my jug and fill it with water on the road down. They say they need water down below.

Several years ago, Robert Quillen, a journalist, erected in the garden of his property at Fountain Inn, South Carolina, a monument inscribed:

In Memory of Eve
The First Woman

When asked the reason for this cenotaph to Eve, Quillen answered enigmatically: "She was a relative of mine on my mother's side."

A memorial stone in Center Cemetery, East Granby, Connecticut, tells of a person buried elsewhere:

Mary H. Kilborn
wife of Byron of Milwaukee
and daughter of Whitfield Cowles

died at Huron, June 24, 1837, aged 36 years
In a coffin of ice conveyed to Worthington, Ohio
and there entombed.

Hic jacet would be an inadequate designation for the grave site of
Bezaleel Beckwith, whose body was taken from Old Cemetery, Acworth, New Hampshire, and whose tombstone was destroyed. A new
slate marker which was afterward erected records:

This stone tells the death
of Bezaleel Beckwith
not where his Body lies.
He died Oct. 21, 1824, ae. 43
The 13th night after his
body was stolen from the grave.
Now twice buried the mourner cries
My friend is dead his body gone
God's act is just my heart replies
Forgive O God what man has done.
Erected by friends of the deceased
in Acworth in place of one destroyed
by some ruthless hand
in Apr. 1853.

Alexander T. Stewart, successful New York merchant and founder
of Garden City, died in 1876, aged 73, and was buried in St. Mark's
Church in-the-Bouwerie, New York City. Two years later, on the
night of 6 November 1878, the coffin, which had been buried at a
depth of twelve feet, was removed and the body held for a ransom
of $200,000. The body which was returned to his family three years
later when a small portion of the ransom was paid, was then reinterred
in the Cathedral of the Incarnation, Garden City, which Mrs. Stewart
had built in her husband's memory.

"Here waits" would be an appropriate epitaph for Ferrenzo Concepio, who died in 1909 but is yet to be buried. When Concepio, a
musician in a traveling carnival, was hit over the head with a tent
stake at McColl, South Carolina, he was taken to Laurinburg, North
Carolina, where he died in a hospital. His body was embalmed at the
McDougald Funeral Home at the request of his father, who promised

to send the burial expenses. Before burial arrangements were completed, however, the father died. Forty years later the body of Ferrenzo was still at the funeral home awaiting instructions from the next of kin.

Many years ago, John Kiernan erected an impressive monument for himself in Atlantic, Iowa. The great shaft, rising to a height of forty feet and surmounted by a cross, became known as "the corpseless grave," for Kiernan died in Florida and for unexplained reasons was buried there. The lot in time became the property of the cemetery and the monument now marks what the community calls "The Field of Glory," a memorial to those killed in World Wars I and II.

"Here sits" or "here stands" might properly indicate several unconventional burials. A pre-Revolutionary English army officer, buried in Old Burying Ground, Beaufort, North Carolina, requested that he be interred in his uniform with all accouterments and that his coffin be placed in an upright position. Evidence for the validity of this tradition is seen in the square of brick masonry instead of the ordinary rectangular vault. This burial is consistent with that of successful warriors of ancient times who were frequently buried upright with lance or pike in hand.

Britt Bailey, died 1832, wanted no man to say, "Here lies Britt Bailey." In his life he refused to look up to any man and he wanted this principle to be maintained after death. He was buried, therefore, on his lonely property, Bailey's Prairie, Brazoria County, Texas, in a standing posture. Having always journeyed westward, his face in death is turned toward the setting sun. A local story relates that at stated intervals a weird light arises from the grave and after meandering about the countryside returns finally to the grave. This spectacle, known as Bailey's Light, is said to be Bailey's ghost rising occasionally to look for the fellow who stole a jug of whiskey from the grave.

Before his death in 1884, aged 34, Alonza Lyman Credle, asked to be buried upright in St. George's Episcopal Cemetery, Hyde County, North Carolina. For many years he had suffered from asthma and had found it impossible to rest comfortably when in a reclining position. Friends fulfilled his wish.

A persistent tradition at Aberdeen, Mississippi, says that when Mrs. Alice Whitfield died in 1854, aged 61, she was interred, as she desired, in a mausoleum in Old Cemetery. She was placed in a sitting position in her favorite rocking chair.

Within a stone tomb in Mt. Prospect Cemetery, Amesbury, Massachusetts, sits Reuben Smith, died 1899, aged 71. He asked in death to be seated in a chair before a table on which would rest his pipe, a newspaper and a checkerboard. It is reported that he offered to pay a substantial sum to any woman who would spend a night with his corpse in the tomb. Concerning Smith's strange burial, *The Amesbury Daily News* commented on 25 January 1899:

Arrangements for the funeral of the late Reuben Smith have been perfected. The body will be laid out in the reclining chair as directed by Mr. Smith and will be taken to the Mt. Prospect cemetery in that condition by Undertaker Austin. Agreeable to Mr. Smith's desire the tomb, a costly one of his own design, will be left open an hour for public inspection after the body is placed there, when the door will be bricked up. Mr. Smith made arrangements with Mr. Austin about two weeks before his death and told him where the key to the tomb was.

A number of stories tell of the embalming of persons in beverage alcohol. This kind of embalming is said to have been used when a young woman, Nancy Martin, died at sea in 1857, aged 27. Her father did not wish her body to be given to the sharks, so he had her placed in a cask of alcohol and returned to the States. Cask and all were buried in Oakdale Cemetery, Wilmington, North Carolina, where a small granite cross indicates the grave. On the marker is a single name:

Nance

Admiral Nelson, according to some of his biographers, was returned to England from Trafalgar in a barrel of rum or wine. Benjamin Franklin speculated on the possibility of embalming in wine in a letter to Barbeu Dubourg in 1773:

I wish it were possible, from this instance, to invent a method of embalming drowned persons, in such a manner that they may be recalled to life at any period, however distant; for having a very ardent desire to see and observe the state of America hundred years hence, I should prefer to any ordinary death, the being immersed in a cask of Madeira wine, with a few friends, till that time, to be then recalled to life by the solar warmth of my dear country! But since in all probability we live in an age too early and too near the infancy of science, to hope to see such an art brought in our time to its perfection, I must for the present content myself with the treat, which you are so kind as to promise me, of the resurrection of a fowl or a turkey cock.

Franklin's speculations were aroused when he revived two flies that had been drowned in a bottle of Virginia wine that had been shipped to London.

Man's Best Friend

Immediately adjacent to the Infantry School, Fort Benning, Georgia, is a bronze tablet to Calculator, a crippled dog mascot of the infantry students:

Calculator

Born ?

Died Aug. 29, 1923

He made better dogs

of us all.

On a marker in the Aspin Hill Cemetery for Pets, Aspen, near Rockville, Maryland, is the following:

Major

Born a dog

Died a gentleman.

In Oakdale Cemetery, Wilmington, North Carolina, the body of a faithful dog is buried within the arms of his master. Above their common grave is a monument that honors both. On one side are these words:

The citizens of Wilmington, the several fire
companies and the Christian Assoc. of St.
Paul's Evangelical Lutheran Church, have erected this monument to the memory of

Capt. William A. Ellerbrooke
A native of
Hamburg, Germany, who lost his life in doing
service at a fire, corner of Front and Dock St.
April 11, 1880.
Age 24 years and 24 days.

On the reverse side is a carving of a sleeping dog and the words:

Faithful unto death.

When Ellerbrook had been trapped in the burning building, the dog had plunged into the flames and had died at the side of his master whose body was pinned by a fallen rafter.

In Island Cemetery, Newport, Rhode Island, is a tombstone bearing this epitaph:

Faithful Unto Death
My Friend
Jack Hammett
The Best of Dogs
Aged 11 Years
In life ever by my side, always
ready to comfort and protect me,
Dying at my feet in his old age,
he now rests beside the one he
loved.
Cease carping fools your gibes and sneers,
A true and faithful friend rests here.
He loved his master, to him was true
Can the recording Angel say this of you?

These words are found on a monument in Central Park, New York City:

Dedicated to the indomitable spirit of
the sled dogs that relayed anti toxin
six hundred miles over rough ice across
treacherous waters through Arctic blizzards
from Nenana to the relief of stricken
Nome in the winter of 1925.
Endurance   Fidelity   Intelligence

A statue of a small dog surmounts a marble monument in Pine Forest Cemetery, Wilmington, North Carolina. Inscribed are these words:

"Jip" Jones
Born Sept. 23 1894
Died May 18, 1904
This was the only dog we ever knew that
attended church every Sunday. He was be-
loved by everyone who knew him.

A monument to a dog in Pine Ridge Animal Cemetery, near Dedham, Massachusetts, is inscribed:

Print
?—1951
I helped Don
Deliver his mail.

In the same cemetery is a granite monument, cut to resemble the fea-
tures of an iceberg, which commemorates a pet dog of Rear Admiral
Richard E. Byrd. It is inscribed:

Igloo
He was more than a friend.

Near by is a marker with this epitaph:

Baby
June 29, 1925   15 yrs.

Not a common doggie
Human as could be
Surely there in Heaven
You are waiting Babe for me.

A statue of a great hunting dog stands over his master's grave in
Aspen Grove Cemetery, Burlington, Iowa. Around the dog are carved
images of the rifle, flask, and powder horn of Jacob Bonn, died 1885,
aged 31.

Formerly inscribed on the tomb of Marther Fitzpatrick, died 1917,
in Oakland Cemetery, Rome, Georgia, are the words:

A True Wife Is Man's Best Friend
His Dog Next.

A costly monument to Sarah J. Wood in Mt. Vernon Cemetery, West Boxford, Massachusetts, is inscribed in part:

> Here at my feet lies my dear pet cat,
> Tommy, Aug. 24, 1875, aged 17 yrs.

Among the fascinating tributes to pets in the Canine Cemetery, Hartsdale, New York, are these epitaphs from markers on the Irene Castle plot:

> Rastas
> The smartest
> most lovable
> Monkey
> that ever lived.

> My blessed
> Joy
> A Belgian Griffon
> Died
> May 8, 1924
> A piece of my Heart
> is buried here.

Most distinguished of animals and sometimes most honored in burial are horses. Daniel Webster, who was especially fond of his horses, buried them on his property at Marshfield, Massachusetts, in the stately manner reserved traditionally for the horses of kings and potentates. This means that the horses were buried in a standing position and wearing their halters, saddles, and other trappings. He wrote for the grave of one of his horses this Latin sentiment:

> Siste Viator! Viator te major hic sistit.

This translates: "Pause, traveler! A greater traveler than you lies here."

The epitaph President John Tyler wrote for the grave of his favorite horse says:

> Here lies the body of my good horse,
> The General. For twenty years he bore
> me around the circuit of my practice,
> and in all that time he never made a

blunder. Would that his master could say
the same.

Carved on plaques at Spiegel Grove, home of President Rutherford
B. Hayes at Fremont, Ohio, are inscriptions to family horses. Two
horses are remembered with these epitaphs:

Old Whitey
A Hero
of Nineteen Battles
1861-65

Old Whitey
The last surviving war horse
of General R. B. Hayes
During the War for the Union.
Died in Spiegel Grove in 1880
Aged 30 years.

Interesting inscriptions to two other horses read:

Piddig
A Filipino pony
Ridden by Colonel W. C. Hayes
when awarded
The Congressional Medal of Honor
For Gallantry at Vigan, P. I.
4 December 1899
Died at Spiegel Grove
in 1901.

Black Yauco
The last surviving war horse
of Colonel W. C. Hayes.
A veteran of his campaigns
In Cuba, Porto Rico and the Philippines;
The fastest runner, the highest jumper
And the fastest swimmer in the military carnival
At Manila, P. I. during Christmas week, 1899;
Ridden at the 2nd McKinley Inauguration

> And the funeral parade in 1901;
> Ridden by Midshipman Hayes
> At the Taft Inauguration in 1909.
> Died at Spiegel Grove in 1922.
> Aged 30 years.

Many of the great horses of the American turf are buried in grave-yards in the vicinity of Lexington, Kentucky. Occasionally the complete body of a gallant race horse is interred, although more frequently only the heart is buried. Life-size statues of a number of the famous winners have been erected on the farms where they were trained. On a monument at Mt. Brilliant Farm near Lexington are these words:

> Here lies the fleetest runner
> the American turf has ever
> known, and one of the gamest
> and most generous of horses.
> Domino

Domino was foaled in 1891 and died in 1897.

In Cory Grove Cemetery, near Sac City, Iowa, is the monument of Earl Dew, leading jockey of America in 1940 and veteran of 2576 races, who died in a racing accident at the Santa Anita race track on 2 February 1941, aged 20. The inscription reads:

> A real friend and a great rider.
> "He will ride the favorite up there, find the track wide,
> The turns well banked, and clear sailing along the rail."

The grave of T. D. Jones, died 1906, aged 89, in Maplewood Cemetery, Henrietta, New York, reads:

> A friend of horses.
> My monument sugar maple trees
> The golden rule is my creed
> My religeon is obedience to the
> Angelic environments around us.

On the monument a horse and two trees are engraved.

Visitors still add rocks to the stone cairn marking the grave of a cow pony on Warren Ranch near Cheyenne, Wyoming. Surmounting the cairn is a headboard on which appears this epitaph:

> Erected to the
> Memory of
> Old Blue
> The Best Cowpony
> That Ever Pulled
> A Rope
> by the Cowpunchers
> of the
> 7XL
> Outfit
> Rest in Peace.

An old landmark near K Ranch, Maybell, Colorado, was a sandstone slab which bore these words:

> Here lies Bill
> He done his damndest
> Angels could do no more.

Years ago the mound attracted considerable attention for near the stone a hat brim protruded from the earth and a few feet away the toes of an old pair of shoes stuck out. Actually a government mule which died in 1908 was buried at this site by a party of soldiers who had camped at the spot.

In Fairplay, Colorado, is a monument to a faithful, shaggy burro named Prunes which lived to the age of 63 years. The burro was owned by Rupe Sherwood, a prospector, whose ashes were buried, as he had requested, next to the body of the animal, his partner on many a pioneering trail for gold. Inscribed on the simply constructed monument is this information:

> Prunes
> A Burro
> 1867-1930
> Fairplay
> Alma

All Mines
in this
District.

In an old graveyard near Winchendon, Massachusetts, is the tombstone of an ingenious Yankee, Stephen F. Fassett, died 1856, aged 54, which says:

I began the preserving
of cow's milk with white
sugar for the use of steamers
crossing the Atlantic Ocean.

A marble slab marks the grave of a champion cow on Highfield Farm, Lee, Massachusetts:

Here Lies
Highfield Colantha Mooie
A
Holstein-Friesian
Cow
Who Held the
World Record
For Lifetime
Milk Production
Born, Lived and Died
On This Farm
1919-1937

Her total production was more than 200,000 pounds.

Inscribed on a stone pyramid marking the grave of a world-famous Hereford sire at the Wyoming Hereford Ranch, Cheyenne, Wyoming, are the words:

Erected to the memory of
Prince Domino
499611
Calved Sept. 13, 1914
Died April 4, 1930
He lived and died
and won a lasting name.

Another cow's record is inscribed on an unusual monument in Evergreen Cemetery, Central Village, Connecticut:

Rosa
My first Jersey Cow
Record 2 lbs. 15 ozs. Butter
From 18 qts. 1 day milk.

Rosa, whose image is depicted on the monument, belonged to a man who did not disdain to share a monument with her. He was Gurdon Cady, who died in 1897, aged 74, a farmer and leader of a local dance orchestra. His musical interests are indicated by the carving of a violin crossed by a bow on a second side of the shaft. Above the bow is inscribed:

All ready, Mr. Cady.

When the floor manager at a dance had paired couples for a square dance, he would turn to Cady and call these words. On a third side is the name of Mary Lee, Cady's housekeeper, and this tribute to her:

Kind to Dumb Animals.

On the tombstone to Mary Brackett, died 1679, in Old Granary Burial Ground, Boston, Massachusetts, is this suggestion of kindness to animals:

Under these clods a pretious gemmly hear
Beloved of God & of her husband dear
Pius and prudent helpful to neighbors all
By night and day whenever they did call
Pelican like she freely spilt her blood
To feed her chickens & to do them good.

The death of a horned toad, known as "Old Rip," was reported by leading newspapers in the United States on 28 January 1929. The toad had been exhibited in many parts of the nation and was granted an audience in the White House by President Coolidge. Old Rip's story began in 1897, when during the dedication of the County Courthouse, Eastland, Texas, Ernest Wood playfully placed the horned toad in the cornerstone. Thirty-one years later, on 28 February 1928, the cornerstone was opened. The idea that a horned toad might actually live for that period of time in such circumstances brought several

EARL DEW
1921 — 1941
LEADING RIDER OF AMERICA
1940

A REAL FRIEND AND A GREAT RIDER.
"HE WILL RIDE THE FAVORITE UP THERE, FIND THE TRACK WIDE,
THE TURNS WELL BANKED, AND CLEAR SAILING ALONG THE RAIL"

Monument for Earl Dew, Cory Grove Cemetery, near Sac City, Iowa.
See p. 247.

Monument for Rosa the cow, Evergreen Cemetery, Central Village,
Connecticut. See p. 250.

thousand persons to the ceremony. After the removal of a Bible and other items, the flat, dust-covered toad was lifted out and held high that all might see. The body swelled with the first breath of fresh air. The toad, whose achievement surpassed that of the original Rip Van Winkle by eleven years, lived for eleven months. When it died of what was diagnosed as pneumonia it was embalmed and at the present time is on exhibition in a conspicuous spot in the courthouse lobby.

A monument in Enterprise, Alabama, honors a pest, the Mexican boll weevil. In 1915, when the pest made its first appearance in Coffee County, the annual yield of 35,000 bales of cotton was cut by 40 per cent. The ravages of the pest spread throughout the entire cotton belt from Texas to Georgia. Threatened by bankruptcy, the farmers turned to diversified farming and began the successful growing of corn, potatoes, and peanuts. In 1919, when the county's peanut crop was yielding more than a million bushels annually, a monumental fountain with this inscription was constructed:

> In profound appreciation
> of the Boll Weevil
> and what it has done
> as the herald of prosperity
> this monument was erected
> by the citizens of
> Enterprise, Coffee County, Alabama.

Sources

Listed here are only the volumes of a general nature which have been examined. Space prohibits the inclusion of numerous periodical, newspaper, manuscript, and other references that have been used.

Alden, Timothy, *A Collection of American Epitaphs*, 5 vols., New York, 1814.

Andrews, William, *Curious Epitaphs*, London, 1899.

Beable, W. H., *Epitaphs*, New York, 1925.

Bowden, John, *The Epitaph-Writer*, Chester, England, 1791.

Box, Charles, *Elegies and Epitaphs*, Gloucester, England, 1892.

Boyd, Hugh Stuart, *Tributes to the Dead; in a Series of Ancient Epitaphs translated from the Greek (of Gregory of Nazianzum)*, London, 1826.

Briscoe, John Potter, *Gleanings from God's Acre*, Edinburgh, 1883.

Burt, D. A., *Epitaphs Original and Selected*, Taunton, Mass., 1863.

Caldwell, Thomas, *A Select Collection of Ancient and Modern Epitaphs and Inscriptions*, London, 1796.

Cary, Alpheus, *A Collection of Epitaphs Suitable for Monumental Inscriptions from Approved Authors*, Boston, 1865.

Croy, Henry, *The Last Word*, Hollywood, Calif., 1932.

Dodd, Henry Philip, *The Epigrammatists*, London, 1876.

Eaton, Arthur Wentworth, *Funny Epitaphs*, Boston, 1902.

Fairley, William, *Epitaphiana*, London, 1873.

Forbes, Harriette Merrifield, *Gravestones of Early New England and the Men Who Made Them*, 1653-1800, Boston, 1927.

Frobisher's New Select Collection of Epitaphs, York, England, 179?.

Hackett, John, *Select and Remarkable Epitaphs*, 2 vols., London, 1757.

Howe, Walter Henry, *Here Lies*, New York, 1901.

Hunt, Cecil, *Here I Lie*, London, 1932.

Kelke, William Hastings, *Notices of Sepulchral Monuments*, London, 1850.

Kippax, J. R., *Churchyard Literature,* Chicago, 1877.

Loaring, Henry James, *Epitaphs: Quaint, Curious and Elegant,* London, 1873.

MacGregor, Robert Guthrie (tr.), *Epitaphs from the Greek Anthology,* London, 1857.

Mogridge, George, *The Churchyard Lyrist,* London, 1832.

Moore, Earl Austin, *The Epitaph as a Literary Form in England and America,* Bloomington, Ind., unpublished thesis.

Munby, Arthur J., *Faithful Servants,* London, 1891.

Norfolk, Horatio Edward, *Gleanings in Graveyards,* London, 1866.

Palliser, F. and M. A., *Mottoes for Monuments or Epitaphs Selected for Study or Application,* London, 1872.

Pettigrew, Thomas Joseph, *Chronicles of the Tombs,* London, 1888.

Pike, Robert E., *Granite Laughter and Marble Tears, Epitaphs of Old New England,* New York, 1938.

Pulleyn, William, *Church-yard Gleanings and Epigrammatic Scraps,* London, [1836?].

Ravenshaw, Thomas F., *Antiente Epitaphs,* London, 1878.

Richings, Benjamin, *A General Volume of Epitaphs, Original and Selected,* London, 1840.

Richings, Benjamin, *Voices from the Tombs,* London, 1858.

Robinson, Joseph B., *Epitaphs,* London, 1859.

Safford, Susan Darling, *Quaint Epitaphs,* Boston, 1898.

Simpson, Joseph, *A Collection of Curious, Interesting & Facetious Epitaphs,* London, 1854.

Tegg, William, *Epitaphs,* London, 1875.

Tissington, Silvester, *A Collection of Epitaphs and Monumental Inscriptions,* London, 1857.

Tolderoy, William, *Select Epitaphs,* 2 vols., London, 1755.

Valsey, H. B., *Writing of Epitaphs,* London, 1924.

Webb, T., *A New Select Collection of Epitaphs,* London, 1775.

Weever, John, *Ancient Funerall Monuments,* London, 1631.

The woodcuts in this volume are reproductions of the work of Alexander Anderson (1775-1870) from the print collection in the New York Public Library.

Consultants

It is impossible to list here the names of all librarians, genealogists, clergymen, morticians, monument dealers, cemetery caretakers, and others who have through correspondence and conversation contributed to this book. Listed here are those whose assistance has been especially helpful.

The editor is particularly appreciative of extensive and generous co-operation offered by staff members of these libraries: *Keuka College Library,* Keuka Park, N. Y.; *Library of Congress,* Washington, D. C.; *New York State Library,* Albany, N. Y.; *Cornell University Library,* Ithaca, N. Y.; *University of Rochester Libraries, Rochester Public Library,* and *Colgate-Rochester Divinity School Library,* Rochester, N. Y.; *New York Public Library,* New York, N. Y.; *Boston Public Library,* Boston, Mass.; and *Wyoming State Library* and *State Historical Department,* Cheyenne, Wyo.

Many contributions and suggestions have been made by these fellow collectors of epitaphs: *Mrs. Homer D. Abbott,* Grand Forks, N. D.; *Mr. and Mrs. Morris W. Abbott,* Milford, Conn.; *Jeanne Bailey,* Fort Atkinson, Wis.; *Esther Willard Bates,* Hampton, Conn.; *Roy W. Black,* Bolivar, Tenn.; *Peter A. Brannon, Department of Archives and History,* Montgomery, Ala.; *Harriet E. Brownell,* Saratoga Springs, N. Y.; *Mignonne F. Crofut,* Bridgeport, Conn.; *Grace Douglas,* Auburn, N. Y.; *Marie B. Dower,* Holyoke, Mass.; *Shirlie S. Fenn,* Kooskia, Idaho; *Joseph B. Fennell,* Brookfield, Conn.; *Irma Mae Griffin,* Roxbury, N. Y.; *Clara J. Hallett,* Hyannis, Mass.; *Edward J. Hamel,* Cranston, R. I.; *Sidney H. Herrick,* Cincinnati, Ohio; *Reid Kellogg,* Woonsocket, R. I.; *L. A. Kingsbury,* New Franklin, Mo.; *Lloyd W. Maffitt,* Burlington, Iowa; *Grace H. Mathewson,* Lyndon Center, Vt.; *Percy Chase Miller,* Oak Bluffs, Mass.; *Earl A. Moore,* Bowling Green, Ky.; *Louis T. Moore, New Hanover Historical Commission,* Wilmington, N. C.; *C. L. McDill,* Charleston, S. C.; *E. M. Oswald,* Chicago, Ill.;

Mrs. R. P. Paterson, Detroit, Mich.; *Mary Agnes Perry,* Bellingham, Wash.; *Prentiss Price,* Rogersville, Tenn.; *Charles E. von Rhein,* Portland, Ore.; *Clayburne B. Sampson,* Jamestown, N. Y.; *Raymond Spinney,* West Somerville, Mass.; *Mrs. Vernon Spurr,* Surry, N. H.; *J. Howard Stegner,* Spokane, Wash.; *Hayward Sturtevant,* Webster Groves, Mo.; *Mayo Tolman,* Picayune, Miss.; *Mrs. Daniel H. Wetzel,* Utica, N. Y.; *Ruth R. Wheeler,* Concord, Mass.; *Elizabeth Whitaker,* Rome, N. Y.; *George F. Whitcomb,* Bristol, Vt.; *Mrs. H. S. Whitsel,* Huntington, W. Va.; and *Dana M. Wood,* Knoxville, Tenn.

These persons, too, have aided in significant and generous ways: *Mrs. F. E. Anderson, Wethersfield Public Library,* Conn.; *Katherine Anderson, Library Association of Portland,* Ore.; *Anna E. Avery,* Lyons, N. Y.; *Dorothy C. Barck, New-York Historical Society,* New York, N. Y.; *Sarah R. Bartlett, Concord Free Public Library,* Mass.; *Albert N. Beard,* Milford, Conn.; *Helen Bloom,* Rochester, N. Y.; *Susan Borden, Goldsboro Public Library,* N. C.; *Eleanor G. Brackett, Providence Public Library,* R. I.; *Jean Bradley,* Cassville, N. Y.; *Ann M. Bresnahan, Cambridge Public Library,* Mass.; *Carrie L. Broughton, State Library,* Raleigh, N. C.; *Alice C. Bullock,* Little Compton, R. I.; *I. R. Bundy,* St. Joseph, Mo.; *Mrs. Roger H. Burrill,* West Bridgewater, Mass.; *Burton H. Butterworth,* Cromwell, Conn.; *Ruth Campbell, State University Library,* Baton Rouge, La.; *Jean D. Cochran, Augusta Library,* Ga.; *Henry T. Coe,* Forestdale, Mass.; *Mrs. Arthur Cotter,* Marianna, Ark.; *Richard A. Curtis,* Deadwood, S. D.; *Howard E. DeCamp,* Corning, N. Y.; *Harry S. Douglass,* Arcade, N. Y.; *E. E. Dove,* Baltimore, Md.; *Elizabeth Faries, Dayton Public Library,* Ohio; *Frances Flanders,* Monroe, La.; *Pearl F. Devens,* Ryegate, Vt.; *Mattie B. Frazier,* Vienna, La.; *C. V. Froman,* Kearney, Mo.; *Mary W. Fullam,* Westminster, Vt.; *Lucille Cummings Gamble,* Hempstead, N. Y.; *Grace Gaylord,* Ft. Bridger, Wyo.; *Mabel R. Gillis, State Library,* Sacramento, Calif.; *Warner F. Gookin,* Oak Bluffs, Mass.; *Eleanor Gow, Thomas Crane Public Library,* Quincy, Mass.; *Axel Gravander,* Grass Valley, Calif.; *Lilla M. Hawes, Georgia Historical Society,* Savannah, Ga.; *Adah S. Hawkins,* Harmony, R. I.; *Russella F. Hazard, John Jermain Memorial Library,* Sag Harbor, N. Y.; *Edwin E. Huebner,* Groveland, Mass.; *Ethel L. Hutchins, Cincinnati Public Library,* Ohio; *O. F. Johnson, Jr.,* Moultrie, Ga.; *Louis C. Jones, State Historical Association,* Cooperstown, N. Y.; *Robert L. Jones,* Philadelphia, Pa.; *Barbara Kell, Missouri Historical Society,* St. Louis, Mo.; *Donald*

H. Kotz, Kenosha, Wis.; *Ruth Kronmiller*, Utica, N. Y.; *Mrs. William H. Mansfield*, Putnam, Conn.; *O. L. Martin*, Plainfield, Vt.; *Lucille W. Maslyn*, Webster, N. Y.; *J. C. Mathewson*, Harrisville, R. I.; *Marie McGrath*, Auburn, N. Y.; *E. W. Miller, Free Public Library*, Jersey City, N. J.; *Clarence W. Moody*, Burlington, Iowa; *Nell Murbarger*, Costa Mesa, Calif.; *Gertrude McDevitt, Idaho Historical Society*, Boise; *Fred G. Neuman*, Paducah, Ky.; *Lela B. Nunnelley*, Tombstone, Ariz.; *Mary T. O'Keefe, Free Public Library*, Worcester, Mass.; *James C. Olson, State Historical Society*, Lincoln, Nebr.; *Robert Olson*, Attica, Kan.; *Alice Bright Parker*, Fort Atkinson, Wis.; *Walter O. Pennell*, Exeter, N. H.; *DeWolf Perry*, Charleston, S. C.; *Mrs. Leslie Phillips*, Vernon, Vt.; *George Raffalovich*, New Orleans, La.; *Thomas S. Ramsdell*, Great Barrington, Mass.; *Stephen T. Riley, Massachusetts Historical Society*, Boston; *Charles A. Ross*, Elizabeth, N. J.; *Edith W. Rounds*, Kittery, Me.; *Marian B. Rowe, Maine Historical Society*, Portland; *Virginia Rugheimer, Charleston Library Society*, S. C.; *Ruth Beers Ruskin*, Stratford, Conn.; *A. M., William J., and Robert F. Schnacky*, Rochester, N. Y.; *Floyd C. Shoemaker, State Historical Society*, Columbia, Mo.; *Clark Skadden*, Stockton, Calif.; *Eugenia M. Southard, Portland Public Library*, Me.; *Archie J. Stark*, Newport, R. I.; *L. G. Stemple*, Wellington, Ohio; *David H. Stratton, University of Colorado Libraries*, Boulder, Colo.; *Curtis Thacker*, Charlottesville, Va.; *Ella May Thornton, State Library*, Atlanta, Ga.; *Mary L. Thornton, University of North Carolina Library*, Chapel Hill; *Marie Taveau, Sturgis Library*, Barnstable, Mass.; *William H. Tripp, Old Dartmouth Historical Society*, New Bedford, Mass.; *Martha Walker*, Angleton, Texas; *Charles C. Wall*, Mount Vernon, Va.; *Sarah L. Wallace, Minneapolis Public Library*, Minn.; *William H. Webb*, Newark, N. J.; *Helen A. West*, Hamilton Square, N. J.; *Wayne Westman*, Paterson, N. J.; *Hazel M. White, Plymouth Public Library*, Mass.; *Malcolm M. Willey*, Minneapolis, Minn.; *Carrie L. Williams, Clift Rodgers Library*, Marshfield Hills, Mass.; *R. J. Williamson, Arlington National Cemetery*, Va.; *Mary Overslaw Wood*, Wichita, Kan.; *James R. Wray*, Mogollon, N. M.; *Willard O. Youngs, Seattle Public Library*, Wash.; and *Camille Yuill*, Deadwood, S. D.

Index of Names

Abbott child, 181-2
Agassiz, Louis, 234
Adams, John (President), 11-12
Adams, John, 80
Agnes of Glasgow, 154
Akers, John R. and Ralph A., 112
Allen, A. J., 68
Allen, Elisha, 129
Alling, Alfred and Emaline, 188
Allyn, Adam, 145
Amun-Her-Khepesh-Ef, 229
Andrews, James J., 31-2
Andrews, Mary Ann, 204
Angell, Lizzie, 216
Annis, Belvera, 82
Anthony, James, 37
Arnold, Benedict, 231-2
Arnold, Elizabeth, 195-6
Atchison, David Rice, 21-2

Bacon, Henry, 17
Bailey, Britt, 239
Bailey, Thomas, 93
Bailey, Timothy, 79
Baker, Abner, 30
Baker, Peter, 119
Barcelona, Mary Lucile, 188
Bardwell, Elijah, 116-17
Barnerd, James, 36
Barnes, John Amos, 143
Barron, Wylly, 220-21
Barry, John Decatur, 31
Bartholomew, Isaac, 87
Barton, Asa, 206
Barton, Clara, 115
Beadle, Lydia and children, 132

Beall, Sarah A., Sarah Ann, and Sarah Y., 165-6
Beardsley, Ransom, 30
Beattie, Aaron J., Sr., 90
Beaulieu, Abraham, 199
Beckwith, Bezaleel, 238
"Becky Thatcher," 184
Bee, Barnard Elliott, 31
Bell, John Thomas, Jr., 150
Ben, Fannie, 107
Bennett, Charles, 65
Bennett, Philip Sydney, 203
Bent, Charles, 56
Bethune, Colin, 45
Bingham, Abigail and Betsey, 163
Blair, James and Sarah, 153-4
Blair, John, 110
Blake, Elizabeth, 201
Blue, Mary, 117-18
Bonn, Jacob, 244
Bonner, Sarah, 160
Booth, John Wilkes, 16-17
Bowers, Samuel, 211
Bowker, Charles, 205
Bowman, Elisha, 19
Boyer, Lewis, 26-7
Brackett, Mary, 250
Braddock, Edward, 23-4
Braden, Mathies G., 157
Bradford, Governor William, 4
Bradford, Major William, 4
Brann, William Cowper, 102
Brashear, John A. and Phoebe S., 150
Breese, Samuel Livingston, 37
Brennan, Michael and family, 67
Bronco Charlie, 61

Brooks, Job and wife, 170
Brooks, Mary, 182
Brown, Andrew Jackson, 186
Brown, Elisha, 24-5
Brown, John H., 215
Brush, Tomkins, 86
Buchanan, Moses, 20
Buck, Jonathan, 231
Buckingham, Anne, 80
Buell, Mary, 175
Bull, Ephraim Wales, 141
Bullock, Seth, 64
Bunker, Chang and Eng, 146
Burdick, John, 216
Burke, Martha Jane, 64
Burnette, Annie Cotton, 128
Burnham, Benjamin M., 90
Burnham, Samuel S., 190
Burns, Daniel, 39
Burr, Aaron, 11
Butler, Benjamin, 213
Byrne, William C., 222

Cady, Gurdon, 250
Caesar the Ethiopian, 72
Caesar, Julius, 151
"Calamity Jane," 64
Caldwell, Elesabeth, 185
Caldwell, Hannah, 26
Campbell, Thomas W., 141
Carrington, Edward, 13
Carter, Malelecl W., 78
Cary, Edward, 84
Casey, James P., 68
Cash, Samuel, 9
Cathy, Esther, 200
Catlen, Caroline Bostick, 186
Cerny, Frances, 112
Chadbourne, Caroline W. and
    William G., 233
Chadbourne, Sally P., 233
Chapin, Abigal, 201-2
Chappell, Daniel, 38
Choate, Potie, 76
Chourler, Joseph, 157
Christie, John, 222
Claghorn, Lydia, 38

Clanton, Billie, 61
Clark, Thial, 139
Clary, Samuel, 218
Clay, Henry, 20-21
Claypool, Sarah B., 84
Cleary, Charles, 123
Clemens, Olivia Susan, 184
Clough, George Augustus, 109-10
Cloyes, John, 125-6
Cobb, Irvin Shrewsbury, 197
Coil, John, 59-60
Colby, Maria Otis, 106-7
Cole, Cary, 189
Cole, Daniel E., 75
Collins, Sarah, 157
Columbus, Christopher, 42-3
Concepio, Ferrenzo, 238-9
Cooke, Henry, 120-21
Cooke, John, 4-5
Coolidge, Calvin, 17-18
Cooper, Ruth, 79
Corbin, David, 116
Cordes, Annie, 170
Corey, Rebecca, 217
Cothran, Elizabeth, 158
Cotton, Elizabeth, 156
Cotton, John, 138
Coveney, Joseph, 100-101
Cox, Hatter, 110
Crane, Hannah, 86-7
Crane, Obediah, 186
Credle, Alonza Lyman, 239
Crocker, Lucretia, 227
Croly, David Goodman, 170
Cross, Mary, 206
Cross, Thomas, 183
Crowell, Agnes, 182
Crowell, Robert, 188
Cubberly child, 119
Curry, Louis, 68
Curtiss, Jotham W., 118
Cushman, Mary, 3
Custis, John, 169
Cutter, Caroline H., 98

Daby, John, 208-9
Dana, John, 141

Darling, Betsy, 221
Davenport, Daniel, 141-2
Davis, Betsy, Joshua, and Sibel, 163-4
Davis, John and Sarah, 162
Davison, Eunice, 217
Dayton, James, 66
Dean, David, 122
Deeter, Hattie, 102-3
DeLaney, Bill, 62
Devine, Henry, 20
Dew, Earl, 247
Dewey, Jedediah, 217
DeWitt, Margaret, 106
Dinsmoor, S. P., 236-7
Dodge, Henry Chee, 53
Dow, Peggy, 95
Dowd, Dan, 62
Dudley, Abigail, 202
Duggan, William F., 146
Duggan, William H., 90-91
Dunbar, Paul Laurence, 193-4
Dunn, Frances Wyche, 149
DuPlessis, Charles, 204
Durand, Charles, 161
Dygert, H. Amenzo, 155

Eaton, Lucy, 5
Edward, the Black Prince, 85
Elford, James Maud, 149-50
Elginbrodde, Martin, 54
Ellerbrooke, William A., 243
Elliott, Charles, 134
Ellis, Sidney, 181
Ellison, Matthew, 95
Emerson, Daniel, 44
Emerson, Ralph Waldo, 194
Eno, Eva Louisa, 210
Ensign, Susannah, 201
"Evangeline," 172
Eve, 237
Eve, Nicholas, 203
Ewins, James, 201

Fairbank, Joseph, Jr., 223
Fairbanks, Douglas, 145
Farley, Joanna, 175

Fassett, Stephen F., 249
Ferguson, Lorenzo, 139
Fernald, Elizabeth, 226
Fife, Hermon, 155
Fitzpatrick, Marther, 244
Forbes, Florianna, 173
Fortune, Amos, 71
Fortune, Violate, 71
Fossett, Emily, 113
Fossett, Thomas, 112-13
Fowler, Elihu, 118-19
Fowler, Mary, 225
Frame, Lem S., 58
Franklin, Àbiah and Josiah, 178-9
Franklin, Benjamin, 137-8
Frazer, Laura H., 184
French, William, 24
Frush, W. H., 91

Gale, George W., 214
Gardiner, David, 108
Gardner, Carroll (Pink), 151-2
Garfield, Luke Jones, 123
Gay, John, 198
Gaylord, Milla, 181
Geer, L. H., Lillie, and R., 160-61
George, Susannah T., 226
Gibbs, Nathaniel, 159-60
Gibbs, Warren, 133
Gilbert, Thomas, 171
Gillet, Cynthia, 212
Glazier, Silence, 78
Godfrey, Henry Hudson, 78
Goembel, John and wives, 135
Golliher, Charles, 208
Gorham, Rachel, 174
Graham, Carlisle D., 229
Grant, B. L. and C. T., 210-11
Graves, Chester L., 140-41
Gray, John, 9
Greer, James, 204
Gregory, Reuben, 131
Griffiths, Sarah E., 236
Grigsby, N., 19
Grosclose, Jake, 56-7
Gross, Flossie Fay, 156

Gunckel, John Elstner, 140
Gunn, Charles B., 144

Hacker, Jeremiah, 102
Haine, Arthur, 100
Hakins, Timothy, 185
Hale, Marcy, 200
Hale, Martha, 45
Hall, James, 68
Hallenbeck, Robert R., 20
Hambleton, Erastus B., 78
Hamilton, Alexander, 10-11
Hammett, Jack, 243
Hancock, George and John H., 179
Hand, Andrew C., 119
Hand, David and wives, 167-8
Hanford, Nancy G., 173-4
Hansell, Leslie, 105
Hargrave, Alfred, 140
Harlow, Hannah, 106
Harris, Frank (Shorty), 66
Harris, Henry, 116
Harris, Martin, 96
Harrison, John Scott, 111-12
Hartwell, Betsy and Joseph, 157-8
Hatch, Freeman, 40
Hatfield, William A. (Devil Anse), 132
Hawes, Ebenezer, 209
Hawthorne, Nathaniel, 194
Heady, George, 234
Healy, John, 56-7
Heath, John, 62
Hefner, August, 233-4
Henry, Patrick, 12-13
Hettig, Edward F., 145
Hickok, James Butler (Wild Bill), 63-4
Hicks, George, Jr., 215-16
Hidden, Samuel, 44
Hill, James, 212
Hill, James E., 198
Hill, John, 208
Hills, Margaret, 121
Hinckley, Ermina B., 174
Hoar, Daniel, 205

Hodges, Jacob, 72-3
Holden, Joseph W., 149
Holmes, Bathsheba James, 125
Holmes, Elezer, 77
Holmes, Sanford, 212
Hopkins, Rhoda, 158
Hopkins, Stephen, 223
Hornbeck, Solomon, 89
Howard, Agnes, 159
Howard, Tex, 62
Howe, Artemas, 105
Howe, Zadock, 8-9
Hoyt, Mary, 205
Humbrick, Jeems, 58-9
Humphrey, Mary, 81
Hunt, Ammey, 228
Hurst, Allen, 34-5
Hutchinson, Ann, 175

Ives, Samuel H., 130
Iyanough, 49-50

Jack, John, 70-71
Jackson, Andrew, 13-14
Jackson, Ezra Thayer, 182
Jackson, F. W., 184
Jackson, Rachel, 13-14
Jackson, Thomas, 213
James, Frank, 134
James, Jesse W., 133-4
Jefferson, Thomas, 11-12
Jeffery, William D., 183
Jenner, Nathan, 80-81
Johnson, George, 62
Johnston, Douglas H., 52-3
Jones, Ann Timson, 158-9
Jones, Ebenezer, 127
Jones, John L., 104
Jones, John Luther (Casey), 142-3
Jones, John Paul, 35
Jones, Noah, 234
Jones, Rebecca, 31
Jones, Samuel, 231
Jones, Sevilla, 130
Jones, T. D., 247
Jones, Walter C., 235-6

Jordan, James, 154
Josselyn, Olive, 139
Joyce, John A., 196

Keeney, William and wives, 166-7
Kellogg, M. E., 62
Kelly, Dan, 62
Kendall, John, 213
Kerr, John, 89-90
Key, Elizabeth, 198
Kiernan, John, 239
Kilborn, Jonathan, 217
Kilborn, Mary H., 237-8
Kirkwood, William C. J., 38
Kittredge, William, 82
Knapp, Clarrisa, 108
Knapp, Lewis, 99
Knapp, Susan, 99
Konkapot, John, 54

Labiche, Emmeline, 172
Lacey, James, 36
Lafitte, Jean, 35
Lake, Thomas, 54
Lebec, Peter, 67
Ledyard, Nathaniel, 120
Lee, Julius, 124
Lee, Mary, 250
Lees, John, 109
Leeson, James, 202-3
Lehman, Helen Christine, 182
L'Enfant, Pierre Charles, 8
Lincoln, Abraham, 15
Lincoln, Nancy Hanks, 178
Little, David, 93
Littlefield, Augustus N., 37
Logan, 51
Lomax, Abbie, 127
Longstreet, Augustus Baldwin, 211
Lord, Benjamin, 94
Love, Alonzo P., 91
Lowe, Solomon and wives, 169
Luciani, Pasqual, 35
Lusk, Alvin, 103-4
Luther, Emma, 76
Luyten, Mary Ann, 234

Magee, James, 39-40
Magranis, Francis, 225
Malbone, Edward G., 147-8
Malcom, Daniel, 6
Mann, Herbert, 39-40
Manning, Theodore Marshall and wives, 167
Margarita, 61
Marshall, Mary Randolph Keith, 178
Martin, Nancy, 240
Mason, Ann, 159
Mather, John, 221
Mather, Nathanael, 183-4
Maurer, Gordon Bostwick, 113-15
Mays, James H., 76
McCracken, S. B., 148
McFarland, James, 154
McGraw, John J. (Mugsy), 151
McKinstry, Alexander, 218
McLowery, Frank and Tom, 61
McMahon, Abel, 121
McMillan, Samuel, 205
McMillan, Willoby S., 143
Merritt, Emily, 87
Michean, Maria, 160
Miller, Charles A., 75
Miller, James, 30
Miller, Joaquin, 198
Miller, Joshua, 124
Miller, Seth J., 171
Miner, Hazel, 117
Mitchel, William, 19
Mitchell, Joseph D., 30
Mitchell, Robert, 109
Modawell, William King, 187-8
Monday, William, 56-7
Monk, Henry James (Hank), 60
More, Richard, 3
Morgan, William, 191-2
Morrow, John Allen, 61
Morton, Caroline, 180
Mullen, W. T., 91
Munroe, Ebenezer, 25

Napoleon Bonaparte, 35
Nation, Carrie A., 91
Newcomb, Caroline, 182

Newcomb, Seth, 77
Newman, Robert, 25
Norris, B. H., 19
Noyes, Timothy, 87
Nurse, Rebecca, 230-31

Oakes, Edward, 169
Oakhurst, John, 59
Ockanickon, 50
Ogden, Matthias, 222
Oliver, Joseph, 211

Pabodie, Elisabeth, 5
Packard, George W., 214
Paddy, William, 86
Page, Eunice, 209-10
Paine, Thomas, 9-10
Palmer, Elizabeth, 164
Palmer, Joseph, 229-30
Palmer, Lidia, 164
Palmer, Margaret, 108-9
Palmer quadruplets, 186-7
Park, James, 97-8
Parker, Pink, 17
Parks, Nath., 118
Parmenter, Jacob, 216
Parrett, Simon, 228
Partridge, Albert V., 37
Patterson, John, 45
Patton, Isabella, 185
Payne, John Howard, 144
Payne, N. Hardy, 219
Peacock, Elizabeth, 156
Peary, Robert E., 37
Pease, Jonathan, 79
Perkins, Abial, 121
Petigru, James Louis, 135-6
Petty, Charles H., 39
Philbrick, Orie Elbridge, 141
Phillip, Alice, 227
Phillips, Elizabeth, 176-7
Pike, George W., 60
Pinckney, Charles Cotesworth, 27
Pinneo, Bezaleel, 95
Pitcairn, John, 25
Placide, Jane, 153
Pocahontas, 49

Poe, Edgar Allan, 194-6
Points, Mary, 126-7
Polk, Ezekiel, 14-15
Pomeroy, Sarah, 224
Pond, Richard C. S., 89
Pope, George, 96-7
Pratt, Ephriam, 207
Pratt, Otis C., 147
Prentice, Thomas, 224
Prescott, Sarah, 200
Price, Evelyn, 188
Prudden, Sarah, 208
Putnam, Chester and Elisha, 126

Randolph, John, 20-21
Red Jacket, 50-51
Red River Tom, 61
Reed, Levina, 206
Reese, William, 189
Remick, James W., 92
Rhoades, Polly, 164-5
Rice, Abraham, 126
Richards children, 157
Richardson, Jonathan, 102
Richardson, William, 130-31
Richey, James, 215
Richmond, Doctor, 228
Ring, Sarah A., 222
Ripley, Lydia Burnett, 174-5
Ritz, Frederick, 44
Robbins, Sally C., 219
Roberts, Fred, 115
Rockwell, Harry, 36-7
Rogers, Theophilus, 209
Rolfe, Rebecca, 49
Rooke, Sarah J., 122
Roosevelt, Kermit, 34
Roosevelt, Quentin, 34
Roosevelt, Theodore, Jr., 34
Rothwell, William P., 115
Rowe, Benjamin, 105-6
Rowell, Mary L., 133
Runyon, Damon, 197
Ruth, George Herman (Babe), 151
Rutledge, Ann, 15-16
Ryan, Timothy, 118

Sabine, Lorenzo, 78
Sage, Hannah, 176
Sage, John, 176
Sailor, Moses, 46
Salter, Joseph, 127
Sample, Red, 62
Sanderson, Silas W., 134
Sandridge, Benjamin, 71-2
Sandridge, Catherine, 72
Sanford, Ada Letitia Eno, 210
Sarasen, 51
Sargent, Henry N., 130
Saunders, Sidney W., 171-2
Saunders, William L., 135
Savage, Adelaide, 76
Schockler, John, 121-2
Scott, William, 134
Sealth (Seattle), 52
Secor, M. M., 213-14
Selden, George Baldwin, 144
Seward, James, 217
Shakespeare, William, xi
Shannon, Ellen, 120
Sharpe, Abner Columbus, 19
Shattuck, Prudence, 88
Shean, Al, 145
Sheldon, Albert B., 214
Sheldon, Elizabeth, 81-2
Shepard, Triphena, 208
Sherwood, Rupe, 248
Shilcutt, John W., 155
Silvers, William B., 199
Simmons, Sally, 213
Simons, Abraham, 82-3
Singleton, John, 211
Sirine, Isaac, 225
Six-Shooter Jim, 62
Smith, Henry Weston (Preacher), 64-5
Smith, Jane, 201
Smith, John, 43-4
Smith, Mary Heathman, 177
Smith, Reuben, 240
Smith, Sam. Wilson, 187
Smith, Thomas, 188
Smith, Timothy Clark, 221
Smith, Venture, 71

Snell, John, 143
Soule, Asenath, 206
Spear, Emily, 170-71
Spencer, George F., 101-2
Spooner, Joshua, 131-2
Spooner, Sarah, 162
Sprague, Ruth, 111
Stanard, Jane Stith, 195
Stanton, Ruth, 170
Starman, John, 44
Stern, Charlotte, 48
Stetson, Thomas, 41
Stevens, Thaddeus, 73-4
Stewart, Alexander T., 238
Stockbridge, John, 123-4
Stone, Hezekiah, 203
Story, Benjamin Saxon, 90
Strange, William, 45
Stratton, Charles S., 146
Stratton, Lavinia, 146
Strong, Elizabeth, 177
Subers, J. J., 115
Sullivan, James, 69
Surratt, Mary E., 16
Sutter, John A., 65
Swain, William, 39
Swarbreck, Lucy, 80
Sweet, Desier and Peleg, 226
Sweet, Rufus, 191

Taber, Ann, 165
Taber, Louisa A., 165
Taber, Olive Jane, 165
Tabor, Horace A. W., 65-6
Tachoop, 50
Tahlihina (Tiana Rogers), 52
Talcott, Joseph, 120
Talmadge, Eugene, 135
Taylor, Annie Edson, 229
Temple, Abigail, 88
Temple, Anna, 88
Temple, Isaac, 86
Temple, James, 88
Temple, John, 88
Temple, Jonas, 206
Temple, Mrs. Louis, 88
Temple, Peter, 88

Thacher, Patridge, 235
Thaxter, Levi Lincoln, 196
Thomas, Joseph, 96
Thomas, Richard, 6
Thomson, John A. (Snowshoe), 144
Thoreau, Henry David, 194
Thurston, Isaac, 140
Thurston, Nathaniel and wives, 168-9
Tilton, George Fred, 39
Tilton, Jonathan, 227-8
Tindall, Lockhart, 119
Tomlinson, Richard, 82
"Tom Thumb," 146
Trahlyta, 53-4
Treat, Jule, 182
Tripp, Desire, 231
Truett, George W., 97
Turpin, Francis, 86
Tute, Jemima, 55
Tute, Jonathan, 110-11
Two Bits, 52
Tyler, Clinton, 140

Upham, William F., 185
Upson, Philo, 234-5

Valentino, Rudolph, 146-7
Velton, Christian, 56
Vivia, 34

Walker, Gertrude, 200
Walker, Jonathan, 73
Walker, Joseph R., 47
Wallace, James and Melissa, 46
Wanton, Abigail, 223-4
Ward, Henry A., 234
Warham, John, 224
Washington, George, 7
Washington, Mary, 177-8
Watson, Olive, 174
Watters, George W., 132
Weare, Meschech, 5-6
Webber, Rodney, 78
Welch, Fitch, 218-19

Whitehead, George, 140
Whiteside, Edw. W. and Ida Mae, 210
Whitfield, Alice, 239
Whittell, Hugh, 47-8
Wilcox, Eunice, 85
Willard, Lemuel, 205
Willard, Simon, 125
Willcox, Lucina, 85
Willett, Alletta, 81
Willett, Joannah, 81
Williams, America Pinckney, 180
Williams, Joseph, 57
Williams, William G., 29
Williamson, Bennett, 215
Willkie, Wendell L., 22
Wilson, Asad Experience, 128
Wilson, James S. and Myron F., 139
Wilson, Jennie E., 156
Wilson, John, 94-5
Wilson, Mary Madeline, 183
Wilson, Nannie F., 185
Wilson, Samuel, 18
Wine, Maggie Cate, 107-8
Winship, Joanna, 148
Winters, Rebecca, 47
Wolfe, Thomas, 193
Wood, Jonathan, 127
Wood, Sarah J., 245
Woodruff, Elisha, 124
Woodruff, Fuzzy, 139
Woodward, Easther, 210
Wooldridge, Henry G., 236
Worster, Nancy, 173
Wright, Isaiah, 131
Wright, Phineas Gardner, 75
Wytte, F., 155-6

Yale, Elihu, 148-9
York, Jenny, 91-2
You, Dominique, 35
Young, Brigham, 222-3
Young, David, 150
Young, John, 204
Youngs, Polly, 216

Index of Places

Alabama
 Clayton, 91
 Enterprise, 251
 Marion, 187
 Montgomery, 35, 121
 Troy, 17
 Wetumpka, 186
Arizona
 Fort Defiance, 53
 Phoenix, 59
 Tombstone, 61, 110
Arkansas
 Brookland, 115
 Marianna, 45
 Pine Bluff, 51
California
 Colma, 47
 Death Valley National Monument,
 66
 Grass Valley, 67
 Lebec, 67
 Los Angeles, 145, 146
 Martinez, 47
 Oakland, 198
 San Francisco, 47, 52, 68, 69, 134,
 161
Colorado
 Caribou, 157
 Colorado Springs, 144, 198
 Cripple Creek, 60
 Denver, 65
 Fairplay, 248
 Maybell, 248
Connecticut
 Bridgeport, 146
 Brookfield, 86
 Central Village, 250
 Cheshire, 87
 Chesterfield, 38

Connecticut (Cont.)
 Colchester, 217
 Coventry, 120
 Cromwell, 176
 East Granby, 237
 East Haddam, 71
 East Hampton, 36
 East Lyme, 166
 East Thompson, 102
 Easton, 78
 Ellington, 218
 Glastonbury, 200
 Hamden, 181
 Hartford, 108, 120, 224
 Hebron, 95
 Litchfield, 175
 Middletown, 124
 Milford, 80, 89, 95, 106, 118, 182,
 208, 217, 218, 224, 225
 New Milford, 121, 235
 Norwichtown, 94, 209, 213
 Oneco, 91
 Putnam, 75
 Ridgefield, 28
 Sharon, 149
 Simsbury, 210
 Stonington, 228
 Wethersfield, 132
 Windsor, 212, 216, 224
Delaware
 Milford, 211
Florida
 Orlando, 160
Georgia
 Atlanta, 135, 139
 Augusta, 109, 220
 Fort Benning, 242
 Lumpkin County, 53
 Macon, 115

Georgia (Cont.)
Midway, 212
Moultrie, 146
Rome, 244   [215
Savannah, 80, 147, 183, 198, 205,
Washington, 82
Idaho
Cascade, 56
Emmett, 46
Illinois
Boulder, 227
Canton, 189
Chicago, 127, 204
Lebanon, 156
Petersburg, 16
Rockford, 134
Springfield, 15
Warrenville, 167
Indiana
Elkhart, 148
Gentryville, 178
Guilford, 174
Merriam, 18
Pekin, 19
Rushville, 22
Iowa
Atlantic, 239
Burlington, 71, 141, 188, 244
Sac City, 247
West Branch, 112
Kansas
Attica, 19
Colby, 46
Greensburg, 30
Hiawatha, 162
Lucas, 236
Kentucky
Lexington, 21, 247
Mayfield, 236
Paducah, 197
Paris, 132
Russellville, 165
Washington, 178
Louisiana
Baton Rouge, 188
Jefferson Parish, 35
Monroe, 171
New Orleans, 35, 90, 153

Louisiana (Cont.)
St. Martinville, 161, 172
Vienna, 76
Maine
Bridgton, 76
Bucksport, 231
Damariscotta, 203
East Otisfield, 149
Eastport, 78
Kennebunk, 93
Kittery Point, 92, 121, 196, 203,
226
Knowles' Corner, 79
Lyman, 233
Norway, 206
Sandy Point, 37
Waldoboro, 44
West Ripley, 104
Winslow, 6
Maryland
Aspen, 242
Baltimore, 17, 151, 190, 194
Cambridge, 86
Monkton, 221
North East, 170
Rockville, 236
Smallwood, 119
Massachusetts
Amesbury, 240
Ashburnham, 25, 127
Athol, 81, 123
Barnstable, 76, 112, 174, 227
Barre, 174, 185
Barre Plains, 78
Boston, 6, 24, 25, 54, 86, 110, 138,
217, 221, 228, 250
Boxford, 169
Boylston, 86, 206
Bradford, 168
Bridgewater, 212
Brookfield, 131
Cambridge, 148, 234
Charlestown, 176
Chilmark, 227
Concord, 28, 70, 88, 141, 170, 182,
194, 202, 205
Cummaquid, 49
Danvers, 230

Massachusetts (Cont.)
Dedham, 244
Dorchester, 141
Dunstable, 210, 213
Duxbury, 206, 213
East Taunton, 122
Eastham, 40
Edgartown, 120
Fairhaven, 4
Foxboro, 8
Framingham Center, 125
Great Barrington, 185
Groton, 88, 97, 163, 211, 226
Groveland, 45
Hanover Center, 123, 139
Harvard, 40, 173, 205, 208, 223
Harwick, 9
Holyoke, 118
Hyannis, 188
Lancaster, 5, 156, 200, 217
Lee, 249
Leominster, 229
Marshfield, 245
Mill River, 164
Montague, 116
Nantucket, 79, 84, 185
New Bedford, 38
New Marlborough, 81, 177
Newbury, 80, 87
Newton Center, 224
North Attleboro, 39, 72
North Oxford, 115
Oxford, 203
Paxton, 181
Pelham, 132
Plymouth, 3, 4, 40, 49, 77, 106,
    125, 154, 162, 182, 184, 213, 219
Princeton, 105, 129, 141
Quincy, 11
Rehoboth, 171
Salem, 3, 184, 188
Sheffield, 125
Shutesbury, 207
South Egremont, 234
South Hadley, 225
Southwick, 124
Spencer, 174
Stockbridge Center, 54

Massachusetts (Cont.)
Tewksbury, 82
Wareham, 222
Watertown, 93
West Barnstable, 106, 131
West Boxford, 245
Westfield, 214
Winchendon, 249
Woburn, 156
Worcester, 234
Wrentham, 209
Michigan
Bay City, 90
Buchanan, 100
Mottville, 30
Muskegon, 73
Minnesota
Blue Earth, 46
Elgin, 20
Winona, 112
Mississippi
Aberdeen, 126, 239
Goodman, 155
Oxford, 211
Port Gibson, 20
Yazoo City, 179
Missouri
Belton, 91
Hannibal, 184
Jefferson City, 134
Kearney, 133
Liberty, 154
Montgomery City, 19
Plattsburg, 21
St. Charles, 90
St. Louis, 200
Unionville, 208
Montana
Billings, 62
Nebraska
Gering, 47
Nebraska City, 180
Wayne, 234
Nevada
Carson City, 60
Genoa, 144
New Hampshire
Acworth, 238

New Hampshire (Cont.)
Barnstead, 127
Chester, 94
Claremont, 126
Dover, 157
East Derry, 201, 216
East Hampstead, 171
East Pembroke, 155
Exeter, 214
Goshen Mill Village, 133
Hampton Falls, 5
Hollis, 175
Jaffery, 71
Keene, 77, 201
Kensington, 105
Marlboro, 44
Milford, 98
New Boston, 129
Newmarket, 236
Peterborough, 215
Portsmouth, 90
Surry, 85
Tamworth, 44
Washington, 231
Westmoreland, 185
New Jersey
Burlington, 50
Elizabeth, 26, 86, 160, 182, 185, 222
Emerson, 48
Hamilton Square, 119
Hanover, 150
Hightstown, 175
Johnsonburg, 96
Lakewood, 170, 216
Newark, 119, 188
Princeton, 11
Vineland, 75, 102, 222
New Mexico
Folsom, 122
Santa Fe, 56
New York
Albion, 79
Attica, 216
Auburn, 51
Batavia, 191
Bemus Point, 82, 206
Brookfield, 216
Buffalo, 29, 51, 180

New York (Cont.)
Burlington Flats, 158, 201, 203, 223
Canandaigua, 72, 204
Canisteo, 139
Conklingville, 204
Cooperstown, 53, 92, 201
Deerfield, 215
Dryden, 173
Elmira, 184
Galway, 183
Garden City, 238
Gravesville, 117
Hartsdale, 245
Hawthorne, 151
Henrietta, 247
Hoosick, 226
Hoosick Falls, 111
Ithaca, 80, 165
Jamaica, 81
Ludingtonville, 87
Lyons, 199
Manchester, 118
Margaretville, 113
New Rochelle, 10
New York, 10, 36, 145, 202, 243
Niagara Falls, 228
Orchard Park, 78
Perry, 191
Phoenix, 155
Pike, 186
Pittsfield, 131
Pleasantville, 145
Rochester, 143, 144, 145, 234
Roxbury, 116
Sag Harbor, 167
Saratoga National Historical Park, 231
Saratoga Springs, 143
Schenectady, 151
Sherman, 214
Somers, 146
South Plymouth, 170
Staten Island, 204
Tarrytown, 36
Troy, 18
Truxton, 151

New York (Cont.)
Utica, 37
Virgil, 78
Warsaw, 108
Wellsville, 140
Westernville, 189
North Carolina
Aberdeen, 45
Asheville, 193, 210
Bath, 108
Beaufort, 239
Charlotte, 109, 200, 204
Dobson, 19
Goldsboro, 127
Hendersonville, 105
Hyde County, 239
Laurinburg, 238
New Bern, 134
Ocracoke Island, 159
Raleigh, 31
Statesville, 19
Tarboro, 135
Washington, 159, 160
White Plains, 146
Wilmington, 17, 31, 140, 210, 222,
    240, 242, 244
Winston-Salem, 218
North Dakota
Bismarck, 157
Center, 117
Ohio
Ava, 9
Cardington, 171
Cherry Valley, 225
Dayton, 193
Delphos, 140
Fitchville, 118
Fremont, 246
Granville, 181
Greenville, 103
Liberty, 84
North Bend, 112
Piqua, 26
Springdale, 201
Toledo, 140
Waverly, 233
Wellington, 147

Oklahoma
Fort Gibson, 34, 52
Tishomingo, 52
Oregon
Canyon City, 61
Hood River, 128
Portland, 91, 151, 182
Salem, 65
Pennsylvania
Austinburg, 130
Bethlehem, 50
Chambersburg, 208
Farmington, 23
Fort Necessity National Battlefield
    Site, 23
Girard, 120
Lancaster, 73
Lititz, 65
Milford, 89
Philadelphia, 138
Pittsburgh, 150
Shippensburg, 187
Wellsboro, 75
Williamsport, 116
Rhode Island
Block Island, 184
Harmony, 76
Little Compton, 5, 164
Newport, 37, 140, 223, 228, 231,
    243
Pawtucket, 115
Providence, 57, 89
South Carolina
Bradley, 158
Camden, 154
Charleston, 27, 109, 122, 135, 149,
    157, 183, 206, 211, 234
Columbia, 32
Fountain Inn, 237
Jefferson, 30, 96
Lancaster, 130
Pendleton, 31
South Dakota
Deadwood, 63
Tennessee
Blountville, 82, 107
Bolivar, 14
Chattanooga, 32

Tennessee (Cont.)
  Jackson, 142
  Knoxville, 30, 204
  Maynardville, 34
  Nashville, 13
  White Horn, 200
Texas
  Brazoria County, 239
  Dallas, 97
  Eastland, 250
  Lubbock, 219
  San Antonio, 29
  Waco, 102
Utah
  Clarkston, 96
  Huntsville, 177
  Salt Lake City, 223
Vermont
  Bennington, 217
  Bradford, 205
  Bristol, 139
  Danby Four Corners, 186
  East Calais, 203
  Felchville, 55
  Lyndon Center, 101
  Middlebury, 155, 169, 229
  New Haven, 140, 221
  Pittsford, 80, 124
  Plainfield, 121, 208, 209
  Plymouth, 17
  Post Mills, 174
  Ryegate, 20
  South Wheelock, 204
  Stowe, 163
  Vernon, 55, 110
  Waits River, 141
  West Berkshire, 103
  Westminster, 24
  Wilmington, 205
Virginia
  Alexandria, 28, 162
  Arlington National Cemetery, 3, 33, 37
  Colonial National Historical Park, 153
  Fredericksburg, 78, 178, 185
  Manassas National Battlefield Park, 31
  Monticello, 12

Virginia (Cont.)
  Mount Vernon, 7
  Northampton County, 169
  Lorton, 159
  Red Hill, 12
  Richmond, 13, 21, 195
  Williamsburg, 158
Washington
  Bellingham, 124, 143
  Vancouver, 100
West Virginia
  Alderson, 95
  Huntington, 156
  Omar, 132
  Strange Creek, 45
Wisconsin
  Kenosha, 98
  La Pointe, 199
  Racine, 213
Wyoming
  Cheyenne, 248, 249
  Douglas, 60
  Ft. Bridger, 185
  Guernsey, 46
District of Columbia
  Washington, 16, 144, 196
Alaska
  Fort Richardson, 34
Canada
  Annapolis Royal, Nova Scotia, 173
  Grand Pré, Nova Scotia, 172
  Jordan Station, Ontario, 190
  Sarnia, Ontario, 150
Dominican Republic
  Ciudad Trujillo, 42
England
  Canterbury, 85
  Gravesend, Kent, 49
  London, 43, 198, 232
  Stratford-on-Avon, xi
France
  Chaméry, 34
  St. Laurent, 34
Scotland
  Elgin, 54
Spain
  Seville, 42
Wales
  Wrexham, 148